LIVING WITHOUT LAW

LIVING WITHOUT LAW

BX7748.D43 BRA

Living Without Law
An ethnography of Quaker decision-making, dispute avoidance and dispute resolution

ANTHONY BRADNEY and FIONA COWNIE

Ashgate

DARTMOUTH

© Anthony Bradney and Fiona Cownie 2000

Published by
Dartmouth Publishing Company Limited
Ashgate Publishing Ltd
Gower House
Croft Road
Aldershot
Hants GU11 3HR
England

Ashgate Publishing Company
131 Main Street
Burlington
Vermont 05401
USA

Ashgate website: http://www.ashgate.com

British Library Cataloguing in Publication Data
Bradney, Anthony
Living without law : an ethnography of Quaker
decision-making, dispute avoidance and dispute resolution.
- (Socio-legal studies series)
1. Society of Friends 2. Quakers - Legal status, laws, etc.
3. Decision making - Great Britain 4. Conflict management -
Great Britain 5. Dispute resolution (Law) - Great Britain
I. Title II. Cownie, Fiona
347.4'1'09'088286

Library of Congress Cataloging-in-Publication Data
Bradney, Anthony.
Living without law : an ethnography of Quaker decision-making, dispute avoidance, and dispute resolution / Anthony Bradney and Fiona Cownie.
p.cm.
"Socio-legal series."
Includes bibliographical references.
ISBN 1-85521-555-1
1. Decision-making--Religious aspects--Society of Friends. 2. Conflict management--Religious aspects--Society of Friends. 3. Society of Friends--Government.
4. Dispute resolution (Law) I. Cownie, Fiona. II. Title.

BX7748.D43 B73 2000
262'.096--dc21   00-034841

ISBN 1 85521 555 1

Reprinted 2002

Printed in Great Britain by Biddles Limited, Guildford and King's Lynn

Contents

Introduction

This book is a study of Quaker decision-taking, seen as a form of dispute avoidance, and Quaker dispute resolution. At its core is an ethnography of one Quaker Meeting, a faith group which meets for worship at a Quaker Meeting House. In Part III of the book we set out the method that we used to acquire the information which forms the basis for our analysis, the findings that came from the use of that method and the conclusions that we have derived from it. Thus the focus of this book is on one particular community. We are concerned not with Quakers as a whole but with one individual Meeting. However, the Meeting that is the subject of this ethnography does not exist in isolation. It is part of a wider Quaker world and, as a community, derives its sense of its self in part both from that world and from Quaker history. Some members of our Meeting are very conscious of the wider Quaker world and very knowledgeable about Quaker history. They participate in its affairs and contribute to its development. Other members know little about either. Nevertheless, whether members of our Meeting are conscious of its impact or not, Quaker history and the wider Quaker world are important in having been part of that which shaped and continues to shape our Meeting. For this reason Part II of this book sets out the essential elements of this history and gives some information about the contemporary British Quakers. Because of its special significance to our work Chapter 4 in Part II sets out the theory of Quaker decision-taking, the Quaker business method. Finally, in Part I of the book, we set out those arguments within the academic legal community that we believe the book relates to and at which its conclusions are aimed.

We would like to thank all the individual Friends who so willingly gave of their time to answer our questions, and the Quaker meeting which permitted one of us to carry out participant observation in its midst over such a long period.

PART I

THE ISSUES

1 Alternative Dispute Resolution and Legal Pluralism

Introduction

This chapter sets out the intellectual debates to which we think this book can contribute.

This book is a study of the ways in which Quakers take decisions, the impact which that process of decision-taking has on the likelihood of disputes arising within individual local Quaker Meetings and the way in which such disputes as do occur are resolved. Quakers in general and Quaker dispute avoidance and resolution procedures in particular have been the subject of relatively little research. Pioneering studies such as those by Dandelion in the United Kingdom and Sheeran in the United States have told us something but not enough (Dandelion, 1996; Sheeran, 1983). This lack of previous research into Quakers and their way of life would, in itself, justify this book. As Aristotle observes, as human beings we are motivated first and foremost by curiosity (Housman, 1961, p. 16). The fact of ignorance is the best and the only necessary reason for research. If this book does no more than tell us a little more about the experience of the life of a Quaker Meeting, and thus contributes to the development of Quaker studies, it will still have served a valuable purpose. If it does contribute to the development of Quaker studies it may, thus, also be of some small use to the Quaker community and, once again, will thus have served a valuable purpose. Nevertheless, whilst the primary motivation for our study is simply the pleasure of discovery we would argue that our conclusions have a significance that goes far beyond the Quaker community and those who are interested in that faith group.

This study can also be seen as a contribution to two debates within the field of socio-legal scholarship. The sources of these debates are to be found in two places: first in the pragmatic world of law reform (in particular in discussion about how non-state-centred forms of dispute resolution operate and about how generally applicable they are to wider groups than currently use them) and secondly, in theoretical discussions about the nature of law and legal systems and in particular in arguments about legal pluralism.

3

The Link Between Quakers, Legal Pluralism and Alternative Dispute Resolution

The link between this study and discussion of legal pluralism is relatively plain. Legal pluralism, in its many and varied forms, has been concerned with the different manifestations of law within the same society or the same state. Various writers have described the ways in which different forms of law can exist alongside each other in the same society, sometimes co-operatively and sometimes in conflict, sometimes parasitic one on another and sometimes wholly independent of each other. We will argue that Quaker decision-making and dispute resolution, seen as law or law-like behaviour, is a matter which is of significance for those scholars who are interested in such theories. It is another example of a legal system which exists in a community alongside the state's legal system. More than this, it is a system of law which exists in opposition to the state system, not least in the fact that it lays claim to priority for its values over the commands of the state and expects, in some instances, obedience to its commands rather than the dictates of state law.

> Respect the laws of the state but let your first loyalty be to God's purposes. If you feel impelled by strong conviction to break the law, search your conscience deeply. Ask your meeting for the prayerful support which will give you strength as a right way becomes clear.
> (*Quaker Faith and Practice*, 1995, para. 1.02.34.)

The Quaker community is one which exists in resistance to the state and the state's legal system both in this belief in the limited nature of the state's sovereignty (a belief which on occasion leads to direct disobedience to the state's laws (Dignan, 1983, p. 20)) and, more importantly, in its affirmation (in Quaker law as much as anywhere else in the mores of the Quaker community) of a set of values which contradict those of the state and its legal system. It is thus not merely another example of a legal system that contributes to a state of pluralism but a peculiarly compelling example when one comes to examine questions about the relationship between the various kinds of law and legal systems that one finds in a complex society.

Perhaps less obvious than its theoretical significance in debates about legal pluralism is the potential relevance of this study to those who are interested in the practical day-to-day work of law reform. We would argue that those who are concerned with imminent changes to the British and other modern state legal systems, who favour a move away from the traditional focus of the legal system on courts and lawyers towards greater attention to notions of mediation and conciliation, should pay close attention to the experience of those who have lived under such alternative systems for centuries. The world which some reformers wish to move to and the world that Quakers have long inhabited are, in many respects, similar. Arguments about the desirability of reforms to the legal system which would move the system away from a reliance on courts are often, though not invariably, based on the improvement to the quality of the lives of litigants that such reforms would bring. The lived experience of Quakers, with their generations of knowledge about such a way of dealing with the possibility of discord, should thus be important evidence when law reformers come to make their plans.

In making this link between the concerns of this book and the every-day world of law reform and legal politics we would not wish to give succour to those who argue for the need for 'relevance' to research by making out such a case for this monograph. As Arnold argued over a century ago those who demand relevance in education misunderstand the nature of the educative effort (Arnold, 1960). That which was true then remains true today. (Bradney, 1992, p. 9; Bradney and Cownie, 1996, pp. 18-19). Research and scholarship is justified by its truthfulness or accuracy, not its relevance. Nonetheless, it would be obtuse to ignore the connections between the rarefied world of legal theory and the prosaic world of politics that, in this instance, do exist and can readily be made.

Alternative Dispute Resolution

In a recent pronouncement on the British legal system the present Labour Government has stated that:

> The justice system is top heavy - it is dominated by lawyers, courts, and outdated legal practices and jargon ...
> The Government is seeking to improve the range of options available to people for resolving disputes without a formal court adjudication process.
> (*Modernising Justice*, 1998, p.9.)

This statement reflects a distinctive and deep-rooted strand in Government thinking about the legal system. Rather than seeing law and law reform simply in terms of narrowly conceived notions of courts and lawyers, the legal system, significantly described as 'the justice system', is seen in terms of its wider function in assisting in resolving disputes. Law, on this view, is not about particular actors and particular institutions, however long they have been established in the legal system. Law is seen as being about its function of settling or preventing disputes and bringing justice to the community. Elsewhere, in both speeches and papers, the present Government has consistently put forward arguments for reforms of the legal system which would, in part, move it away from its traditional focus on courts and lawyers. Thus, for example, Lord Irvine, commenting on research by Genn into the Central London County Court mediation scheme, stated that he 'intend[ed] to use the research as a starting point for considering the role that alternative dispute resolution might play in settling civil disputes' (Irvine, 1998).

The position of the Labour Government, which involves a substantial shift of view from traditional attitudes about the nature of the legal system, is not unique in contemporary British politics to the present Labour administration. In his 1994 Hamlyn lectures the previous Conservative Lord Chancellor, Lord Mackay, devoted one of his four lectures to alternative dispute resolution, arguing that 'we should continue to be open to any opportunity to provide informal procedures which lay people can operate themselves without legal assistance ...' (Mackay, 1994, p. 75). Once again this statement reflected a persistent strand in the thinking of the then Conservative administration with a number of initiatives being introduced to try to take the British legal system away from its historic love-affair with courts and lawyers. The Central London County Court mediation scheme, mentioned above, was first started as 'part of an initiative by the [then] Lord Chancellor, Lord Mackay of Clashfern, to improve access to justice' (Lord Chancellor's Department, 1996b). During his period of office as Lord Chancellor, Lord Mackay made a number of speeches stressing the importance of alternative dispute resolution and also during this period the Lord Chancellor's Department published a booklet, *Resolving Disputes Without Going to Court,* which was made available free from County Courts (Lord Mackay, 1996a; Lord Mackay 1996b; Lord Chancellor's Department 1996a). Even the personnel of the legal system whose lives have been intimately connected with being a lawyer and working in courts have not been immune to the charms of a life without courts and lawyers. Lord Woolf, a Lord of Appeal in Ordinary, in his report on the civil justice system, *Access to Justice*, commissioned by the Government, argued that litigation was neither the only nor even always the best way of providing effective mechanisms for the resolution of civil disputes (Woolf, 1995, p.136). Woolf devoted one chapter of his report to an exploration of alternative dispute resolution schemes and made a series of recommendations relating to the monitoring and implementation of alternative dispute resolution schemes (Woolf, 1995, pp.146-147). As we move from one millennium to another policy-makers of all kinds in the United Kingdom are plainly alive to the virtues of dispute-resolution procedures based on institutions which are very different to those which have formed the foundation of British legal systems for many centuries (Fricker and Walker, 1994, p. 29).

An interest in dispute resolution procedures which do not rely on courts and lawyers is not new to the final years of the twentieth century. The prospect of doing away with both courts and lawyers beguiled utopian and anarchist writers of the nineteenth century (Kropotkin, 1970, p. 195; Morris, 1977). Further back in British history Hill notes that a desire to wrest law from lawyers was part of the intellectual foundations of the English Civil War and the subsequent Commonwealth (Hill, 1965, pp. 260–263). In 1652, during the Commonwealth, Winstanley published *The Law of Freedom* in which he advocated that '[n]o man shall administer the law for money or reward' (Winstanley, 1973, p. 379). The centuries' dominance by courts and lawyers does not betoken a universal acceptance of the merits of either. Through the years many have echoed Dick the Butcher's cry, 'the first thing we do, let's kill all lawyers'. The significant change in the last few years in the United Kingdom has not been the fact that people have argued for a move away from a court-centred legal system to a more diverse approach; the significant fact is the position in the state and society held by people who now argue for such a change. The imaginings of utopian writers have remained utopias; anarchism has had relatively little direct impact on the political, administrative and legal history of the United Kingdom (Marshall, 1992, pp. 487-495); the period of the Commonwealth saw no change in the state's focus on the importance of courts and lawyers (Holdsworth, 1924, p. 162); Dick the Butcher's cause was lost with the death of Jack Cade and his failed rebellion, the rebellion itself being the action of those who were 'excluded from the circle of privilege' (Leggatt, 1988, p. 18). Calls for a move away from courts and lawyers in the settlement of disputes in the past have largely been impotent musings by those with little power within the existing political structure of the times. Now, however, those making such calls are in positions of central authority. '[M]odes of dispute management other than lawyer negotiation and adjudication are moving centre stage' (Palmer and Roberts, 1998, p. 2). Changes to the British legal system have already been made and, irrespective of the unpredictable currents of parliamentary and party politics, the idea is now so embedded in the present logic of law reform that further major changes are highly likely to be made in the future.

An interest in the possibilities of dispute resolution procedures which use neither courts nor lawyers is not limited to policy makers in the United Kingdom. It is, rather, a world-wide phenomena. As long ago as 1982 volume two of Abel's *The Politics of Informal Justice* contained studies of non-state dispute resolution procedures systems in five different continents (Abel, 1982). De Sousa Santos's 1977 study of the Resident's Association in Pasargada in Rio de Janeiro, whilst it reveals a dramatic gap between the state view of that body and the actual work which that body does, is, nonetheless, a study of a body set up by the state to help in settling disputes without recourse to either courts or lawyers (de Sousa Santos, 1977). As in the United Kingdom the interest in different kinds of dispute resolution transcends politics. Both liberals and socialists have produced work in the area (Palmer and Roberts, 1998, p. 45). Equally, the interest is not one which has arisen in just the last few decades. To note only a few random examples, Torstein's 1966 study analyses a range of dispute resolution procedures from mediator to judge (Torstein, 1978) whilst Arthurs, writing about English law in the mid-nineteenth century, notes that

> [f]or centuries, businessmen, had eluded the welcoming embrace of the central legal system, organized their affairs according to law which was their own, and settled disputes in forums which they controlled, according to decisional norms and procedures which they consciously contrasted with those of the superior courts.
> (Arthurs, 1985, p. 50.)

Alternative dispute resolution, in all its many guises, is a major subject of enquiry and a major inspiration for policy reform. It is, therefore, unsurprising to find that there has been much research in the area in both the United Kingdom and elsewhere. A number of bibliographies listing such research have been produced (Brown and Marriott, 1993, pp. 425–437; E.S.R.C., 1994, pp. 3–6). Nevertheless, despite the long history of the notion, despite the wide range of political positions which have led people to espouse the notion of alternative dispute resolution and despite the range of countries through which the idea has spread, when the range of research into non-state interventions into dispute resolution is measured against the range of actual activity in the area the former is found sadly wanting (Cownie and Bradney, 1996, p. 134). There are a great many examples of alternative dispute mechanisms in a large number of different jurisdictions throughout the world but there remains much that we do not know about how alternative dispute mechanisms function. The shortfall in research in this area might be taken as indicative of a lack of interest in the area. In part this may be true. Alternative dispute resolution has no more been central to the research agenda of university law schools than, historically, it has been central to the policy agendas of governments. However, not too much should be made of this lack of research. Courts and judges have, historically, been central to both the concerns of government and the university law school. Nonetheless Thompson was forced to write 'I know less about judges than I should, and so do we all' (Thompson, 1988, p. 222). In part our ignorance about matters pertaining to alternative dispute resolution is no more than yet another indictment of past failings in the general research efforts of law schools. As Wilson once observed '[o]ne cause for optimism for the future of [English] legal scholarship is that so little has been tried' (Wilson, 1987, p. 851). Nonetheless the fact of our ignorance remains important. We know very little about alternative dispute resolution and yet policy makers seem determined to bring it into the mainstream of state legal culture.

The research literature that relates to alternative dispute resolution is roughly divisible into three separate areas of concern. First, there are the studies that analyse the variations in the basic conceptual foundations of the different kinds of alternative procedures available. Secondly, there are the studies that the consider the relative efficacy of the alternatives when compared with the traditional forum of the courts. Thirdly, there are the studies that describe, and (sometimes but not always) critically examine, the actual process involved in one or more forms of alternative dispute resolution. Whilst these three areas of concern largely cover the various issues for law reform raised by the existence of alternative dispute resolution the total quantity of research remains rather scant for two reasons. First, there are relatively few such studies in each area of concern. Many forms of alternative dispute resolution have never been investigated, have been investigated only very briefly or have been investigated only by one researcher. Secondly, partly because there have relatively few studies, such studies as there are address the questions raised from a narrow range of perspectives. This is true both when one considers the theoretical basis that underpins the research and when one looks at the research methods that have been used. There are, thus, many gaps in the literature on alternative dispute resolution.

One particular gap in this literature is qualitative research into the experience of those who have been engaged in such forms of dispute resolution. Some studies have been made and some have provided a rich analysis of the area (for example, Yngvesson, 1993). Indeed it has been said that

> since the mid-1970s, anthropological work on dispute processing has increasingly been incorporated into ... the ideologically heterogeneous movements concerned with access to justice and informal alternatives to court.
> (Snyder, 1981, p. 149.)

Nevertheless the number of such studies, even in the context of the relative paucity of material on alternative dispute resolution, remains small. The explanation for this is relatively straightforward. Even though there are many examples of non-state dispute resolution procedures most of them are to be found in a private arena and in each instance they are part of relatively small-scale mechanisms. They arise, for example, in the context of particular retail trade associations. Because they are private and because they are small their activity is not obvious. Thus they do not excite the attention of the research community. In addition such kinds of dispute resolution not infrequently take place in schemes which exist, when measured against the lives of state courts, for a relatively limited time-span. Some have existed for several decades but this is a slight time-scale when compared with the history of state legal systems. Once again, because of this, the research community's attention is not drawn to them. Finally, qualitative research tends to be relatively time-consuming and demands even greater access to the dispute resolution procedure than does other forms of research (Hammersley and Atkinson, 1995, ch. 3). For all ethnographies '[t]he two obstacles ... [are] the money to go and the permission to conduct the research' (Barley, 1983, p. 13). All these factors militate against qualitative research into the experience of such procedures.

Whilst explicable the gap in research into alternative dispute resolution procedures is, from a policy perspective, nonetheless problematic. One strand of the argument for greater recognition of the importance of alternative dispute resolution procedures, and for a greater intertwining of these procedures with traditional state court focused mechanisms or for a substitution of alternative dispute resolution procedures for state courts, is the idea that this will produce greater customer satisfaction (Lowry, 1993, p. 93). Investigation of the experience of those who lived through such procedures is plainly of paramount significance in validating or falsifying such an argument.

It is this gap in the existing research literature which justifies the present study as a contribution to the policy debate on the use of alternative dispute resolution. The Quaker method of decision-taking and dispute resolution is, of course, not typical of the alternatives available. The range of dispute resolution procedures available in both the United Kingdom and elsewhere is so vast that no typology of such procedures would ever allow the validity of any study of a single form of alternative dispute resolution to be sustained on the ground that that particular procedure was typical (Palmer and Roberts, 1998, pp. 18-21). Each procedure is unique and each procedure differs radically from at least some of the other procedures available. The value of this study for the literature on alternative dispute resolution lies in the lengthy history that these Quaker dispute resolution and avoidance procedures have had, the degree to which the method is different from that traditionally found in state legal systems and the degree of access that we, as researchers, have had to the experience of the procedure.

The Quaker approach to dispute resolution and avoidance is not a new or experimental. As we will see in chapter 2 it has existed through centuries, across generations and across countries. In the present day it sustains Quaker faith groups throughout the United Kingdom and, sometimes in rather altered forms, throughout the world. Our study is an ethnography of an individual Meeting. Its results cannot necessarily be generalised in their individual detail for all other Meetings in the United Kingdom. Nevertheless, the culture of the Meeting that we have studied finds its roots in mainstream Quaker thinking. Whilst the Meeting is individual and thus unique the broad trends and currents to be found there are likely to be found elsewhere in other Quaker faith groups. The ethnography thus offers valuable evidence about what it is like to live in a group which uses a form of alternative dispute resolution procedure which has proved its value by its contribution to a community that has such great longevity as a group.

Legal Pluralism

The positivist image of law which long held sway in the common law world pushed non-state dispute resolution to the margins of academic legal concern. Dispute resolution which was not law in the positivist's view of law was not of interest to the academic lawyer. The rise in interest in alternative forms of dispute resolution has coincided almost exactly with an increasing interest in theories of law other than positivism which has finally culminated in the toppling of positivism as the dominant paradigm in academic legal research (Bradney, 1998). One contender amongst the new plethora of theories of law is, in a variety of guises, legal pluralism; the view that law may be a more complex, and a more insidious form than we had once realised has been of increasing interest. Even its detractors note that '[d]espite its relatively recent origin ... the concept of legal pluralism bears the mark of approaching ensconced establishment maturity' (Tamanaha, 1993, p. 192). Seen once as singular and solely the preserve of the state, law is increasingly seen as multiple and arising in many arenas at the same time.

Even if one limits one's argument to Western culture it would be easy to argue that the idea that law is singular and state-based is the result of an ahistorical examination of a particular contemporary moment in history. It would have been a rather odd idea for long periods of English legal history for example. Holdsworth's *History of English Law* tells us that at one time there was not only the common law with its system of courts but also the courts of equity with their law, ecclesiastical courts operating under canon law and courts using the law marchant (Holdsworth, 1922). These were not simply separate systems of courts with a separate technical jurisdiction. They were competitive, contending courts with an overlapping jurisdiction answerable to different authorities. Thus, for example, '[i]n the twelfth century the ecclesiastical courts claimed to exercise a wide jurisdiction' but '[t]hese claims were at no time admitted by the state in their entirety' (Holdsworth, 1922, p. 614). The single monolithic state legal system is a very modern image.

Legal pluralism does not just finds its roots in a re-examination of British, or even more widely Western, legal history. A powerful argument for the cultural imperialism of positivistic views of law has been made. In the nineteenth century and the early twentieth century societies that did not, in the view of Western writers, match Western societies in their form of law simply did not have law.

> Accustomed as we are to look for a definite machinery of enactment, administration and enforcement of law, we cast around for something analogous in a savage society ...
> (Malinowski, 1926, p. 14.)

As a result writers concluded that 'the progress and development of law belongs, for the most part, to a more advanced stage of human society than that which is the subject of this [a study of the anthropology of "savages"]' (Lubbock, 1875, p. 433). Part of the triumph of social anthropology was its early appreciation of the narrowness of this view.

A more enlightened and more intellectually respectable view of law that did not simply see law as being connected with a community's possession of something that could be said to approximate to a bound set of the *All England Law Reports* still involved anthropologists and others in searching for 'the law of' whatever community they were examining. A willingness to consider 'a system of mutual obligations' or 'reciprocity' as the law (Malinowski, 1926, p. 22 and p. 23) the kuta as a court (Gluckman, 1955, p. 9) or military societies as police (Llewellyn and Hoebel, 1941, p. 90) produced a much fuller view of the role of law but still, arguably, failed to live up to the experience of those in many non-Western communities. For them their lives were lived under a multiplicity of legal systems. That had been the experience of their parents and that would be the experience of their children.

Again, as with twelfth-century England, the argument is not simply that such communities experienced separate systems of law with separate jurisdictions, though this has sometimes happened. Lozi law in the twentieth century, for example, had no jurisdiction over capital offences. These were tried under British colonial law (Gluckman, 1955, p. 3). Rather the argument is that law did not emanate from one source or even two or more sources, each covering different areas of life. Law instead was both more permeable and more pervasive (Collier, 1973, ch. 1).

A separate source for arguments about legal pluralism has been studies which originated in urban anthropology. Social anthropology's move from its traditional study of non-Western, non-literate cultures to semi-autonomous communities living in urban settings in complex societies may have been grounded in something that was in part no more intellectually respectable than a shortage of unresearched communities of the traditional type (Basham, 1978, pp. 21–24, 26–30) but the result has been a rich wealth of data on new forms of law within complex societies. Whilst the development of urban anthropology has involved a change in the kind of community studied, the topic for enquiry has often remained the same as it always was; 'traditional anthropological topics ... have been transplanted to urban settings' (Basham, 1978, pp. 29–30). Law and forms of dispute resolution and avoidance have been as much the subject of enquiry in urban anthropology as they were in the earlier studies of those such as Malinowski and Gluckman. As a result de Sousa Santos's study of Pasargada, a favela in Rio de Janeiro (de Sousa Santos, 1977), Mangin's more general analysis of squatter settlements in Latin America (Mangin, 1974) and Burman and Schar's study of popular courts in a South African township (Burman and Schar, 1990), amongst others, have shown how social organization in these communities results in what has variously been described as 'low-level unofficial courts for minor disputes' (Mangin, 1974, p. 345) and 'informal courts' (Burman and Schar, 1990, p. 703). In each case systems of state law continue to exist alongside these newly discovered systems, competing and co-operating with the community's own system in varying ways and at various levels.

Descriptions of different kinds of pluralistic legal systems throughout the world have raised a number of theoretical questions. Two seem to us to be particularly important. First, what criteria do we use in giving the description 'law' or 'legal system' to some things but not to others? Secondly, if we accept that a system of legal pluralism does exist and that this is the normal state of being for any complex society is there any particular hierarchy in the relationship between those laws or legal systems? Is it true to say, as Cotterrell does, that

> [m]odern interpretations of law should incorporate a pluralistic outlook which recognizes in some way the actual and potential variety, complexity, and fragmentation of contemporary regulation. But they must not deny that contemporary regulation is *structured and co-ordinated by centralized power.* (Cotterrell, 1995, p. 307.)

Is it true to say, as Cotterrell suggests, that state law always dominates?

Finding Law

The abandonment of a strictly positivist and strictly Western view of law immediately led to the charge that the law that was now being found by anthropologists had in fact been confused with other social forces. Notwithstanding the success of Malinowski's work many anthropologists continued to use theories of law which found their origins in examinations of Western law, albeit in forms that were more sophisticated and sought some accommodation to the realities of non-Western cultures (Roberts, 1979, p. 192). Indeed, even those who first saw great value in the new examinations of different kinds of law amongst communities not previously thought to possess this social form were sometimes troubled by the 'vagueness' of the law that was revealed (Twining, 1973, p. 151).

These queries about the analytical rigour with which the term law was being used led in turn to two responses. One was to eventually abandon the cross-cultural search for 'law'. Attempts to be both true to the material of the ethnography whilst at the same time using a conceptual schemata which had its origins in Western ideas of law were seen as impossible. 'Law' was the product of Western societies or complex communities or both and to use it in analysis involved

> ... the cardinal error of ethnographic and social analysis: the grossly ethnocentric practice of raising folk systems like the 'law', designed for social action in one's own society, to the status of an analytical system, and then trying to organize the raw social data from other societies into its categories. (Bohannan, 1957, p. 69)

Not only were the schemata of individual Western legal systems seen as being inappropriate concepts for the analysis of other legal systems, the term 'law' itself was perceived as being inherently ethnocentric. If one's interest was in societies *per se* any term which was peculiarly and particularly linked with one kind of society was necessarily of limited utility. It was therefore better to theorise not about law within various cultures but about forms of order and dispute (Roberts, 1979, ch. 2). Discussion should not be discussion of legal anthropology but discussion of political anthropology. 'Disputing displaces law as the subject of study' (Snyder, 1981, p. 145).

This approach has manifest attractions. It dispenses with a whole area of intellectual angst at a stroke. Yet at the same time it is troubling. Disputes occur, are settled, are avoided, in so many different social settings and in many different ways. To categorise and classify the ways of doing this is part of the essence of intellectual enquiry into this area and to abandon law as a tool for that classification is to abandon something that had previously be seen, not just by the law school but by the social sciences generally, as having rich explanatory possibilities. Many of the seminal figures in sociology had seen in law a vehicle for describing and explaining changing social forms (Durkheim, 1933). To abandon its use entirely is a dramatic step.

A second response to charges of inaccuracy or vagueness in the use made of the term law was to attempt to provide a definition of law which was specific enough to separate out law from non-law yet neutral enough to allow cross-cultural application across a range of societies, both complex and otherwise.

These new definitions of law have involved a re-examination of the idea of law. They have often involved abandoning long-cherished elements of Western jurisprudence's concept of law. Thus, for example, Gluckman abandoned the sanction as an element in his definition of law. He defined law as

> ... a set of rules accepted by all normal members of the society as defining right and reasonable ways in which persons ought to behave in relation to each other and things, including ways of obtaining protection for one's rights. (Gluckman, 1955, p. xv.)

Part of this re-examination of the idea of law has involved a re-examination of the way in which law could be said to be about dispute settlement.

State law has usually been seen, both in university law schools and in popular discourse, as being something which is primarily concerned with settling disputes. The courts are central to the legal system (Bailey and Gunn, 1996, pp. 35–36). Legal rules are what we use to settle our quarrels with one another. Law is something we turn to when things go wrong. 'Law' and 'dispute' are virtually synonyms. This connection between law and dispute is wide ranging, being found not only in traditional positivist legal philosophy but also in legal realism. It has had methodological consequences for ethnographers interested in law in different communities. For the legal realist Llewellyn, for example, law was about clearing up 'social messes' and if you wanted to find law it was best to look to see what happened in 'trouble cases', 'instances of hitch, dispute, grievance, trouble', in the community you were interested in (Llewellyn and Hoebel, 1941, p. 21). Yet it has always been clear that, empirically, this linking of law to extant disputes was not a complete picture of law and it has never been clear that, again empirically, this linking was anything other than a misleading picture of law.

It is uncontroversial to note that in many areas of law very few disputes are finally settled in court (Cownie and Bradney, 1996, pp. 23–24). This is so even in the case of those disputes that are characterised by the parties involved as being legal and even in instance of those societies that regard themselves as being litigious (Friedman, 1975, p. 134; Merry, 1990, p. 64). To some extent the link between law and dispute can still be preserved by observing that some disputes are settled in the knowledge of what would happen if the matter went to court, that they are settled 'in the shadow of the law'. Nevertheless empirical evidence weakens the apparently solid link between the idea of law and the idea of dispute resolution.

Examination, even casual examination, of the work of lawyers also casts doubt on the link between law and on-going disputes. Surveys of British lawyers suggest that only a proportion of their work is concerned with settling disputes (Chambers and Harwood-Richardson, 1991, p. 47). British lawyers are not atypical in this respect. Both quantitative and qualitative studies of lawyers elsewhere report the same result (Friedman, 1977, p. 25). There are areas of law and types of lawyer which are wholly concerned with settling disputes but they are unusual. Law is as much, indeed is often more, about avoiding disputes as it is about settling them; it is about establishing patterns of acceptable conduct and acceptable relationships. These patterns will be used when disputes occur as part of the process of settling the dispute but there primary purpose is to prevent the dispute in the process.

The move from seeing law as primarily being about dispute settlement to being, in the first place, about dispute avoidance has important theoretical and methodological consequences. Our definition of law must acknowledge what law does before the dispute as much as what it does at the time of the dispute. We would generally adopt Malinowski's definition of law for this reason, accepting as a working hypothesis that law is

> ... a body of binding obligations, regarded as a right by one party and acknowledged as a duty by the other, kept in force by a specific mechanism of reciprocity and publicity inherent in the structure of the society.
> (Malinowski, 1926, p. 58.)

Our method of looking for law must look not only at law's 'peculiar job of clearing up social messes when they have been made' but, as the oft-neglected (by the authors as much as others) previous sentence in this passage says, law as 'intended and largely effective regulation and prevention' (Llewellyn and Hoebel, 1941, p. 20). For this reason we would argue that Quaker law should be seen more in how Quakers avoid having disputes than in how they settle them when they do occur. For this reason, much of our discussion will focus on the Quaker business method and its relationship to Quaker culture as a whole.

Hierarchies in Law

One way of dealing conceptually with the pluralist nature of law in complex societies and yet preserve much of the purity of the old positivist approach is to accept the reality of legal pluralism but to deny its importance. Legal forms other than state law, it is argued, do exist within complex societies but these forms are of marginal significance affecting few people or affecting people only in areas of social life where state law has chosen not to intervene. Alternatively it can be argued that non-state law legal forms are effective only when they are parasitic on state forms; dependent on the state for either their enforceability or their legitimacy.

The British state, as with all nation-states, claims unlimited power for the legitimacy of its legal system within the confines of its geographical boundaries. Nevertheless, within Great Britain many non-state forms of law either exist within the interstices of power left by the state or involve invoking state assistance at some point. Thus, for example, the operation of A.B.T.A., the Association of British Travel Agents Tour Operators Code of Conduct dealing with disputes between a tour operator and a client, does not run counter to state power but supplements it in an area where the state has not yet fully intervened (White, 1999, p. 311). Equally, the Jewish Beth Din, whilst it is a Jewish court operating under Jewish law, makes its decisions in areas of commercial and contract law in the United Kingdom enforceable by recourse to the 1979 Arbitration Act, a piece of state legislation (Cownie and Bradney, 1996, p. 7). The same points could be made with examples taken from other nation-states.

However, the fact that some non-state legal forms are parasitic on the state and the fact that some use the state legal system in their work does not, of itself, lead to the conclusion that such forms are thereby simply inferior to, or negligible when compared with, state law. Some non-state legal forms are not parasitic on the state. Some non-state legal forms such as Islamic law claim the same sovereignty that the state claims. '[A]ll the affairs of Muslims should be guided by the Divine Book' (Doi, 1984, p. 15). Moreover, even if non-state legal forms are individually of marginal importance when compared with state law (and this has still to be proved) is this so when they are looked at collectively? Does the cumulative effect on interventions by non-state legal forms have more importance than the state system? In any event assessing the relationship between different forms of law means assessing not just claims of power but the realities of power. State law claims an all-powerful ascendancy over people within its boundaries but it is in seeing how that claim is matched in the reality of those people's everyday lives that we can assess the hierarchies of law.

In this context an ethnography of Quakers has a particular value. It does more than describe another legal form. It describes a legal form which claims to challenge state law in the context of a community of people who claim to live very largely within normal society. It might be comparatively easy to show how, for example, an enclosed order of nuns was, at least for much of the time, largely untouched by the state, living their lives according to a different law. But, interesting though this might be, it would be of limited speculative consequence for theories of legal pluralism. The value of using experimental communities such as kibbutizm in constructing social theories about humanity generally has long been the subject of debate. Some have thought that it 'contributed greatly to the elucidation of important theoretical questions' (Weller, 1974, p. 230). Others, however, have been more cautious about the degree to which such evidence can contribute to the discussion of questions of general sociological import (Cotterrell, 1977, p. 250). The more socially isolated and experimental these communities are the less useful they may be in thinking about the nature of society. Thus, for example, the Family, formerly known as the Children of God, choose to live communally according to the Law of Love (Lewis and Melton, 1994). They regard the Law of Love as being more important than anything; more important than state law, more important even than their love for their children (Bradney, 1999, p. 219). That tells us something about what we all might do or be. It perhaps tells us something about the relationship between state law and some numerically rather rare social forms within society. It is more difficult to see how what it tells can easily be translated into observations about ourselves as we are now or those of us who are like ourselves in their social behaviour. Quakers are much more easily ourselves or our neighbours. Quakers do not live enclosed lives. They are educated in the community. They live in the community. They work in the community. They will in some cases be our neighbours. Unlike some Protestant groups who will not be 'yoked with unbelievers' they do not have a philosophy of distancing themselves from the community. Nor are they experimental. Their history stretches back through centuries. Families have lived Quaker lives generation over generation (though some, of course, are new to the faith). Individual local Meetings in many cases have venerable histories. In questioning whether the proposition that 'contemporary regulation is *structured and co-ordinated by centralized power*' (Cotterrell, 1995, p. 307) is true for Quakers and, if not, what is true for them we are looking at a community which is firmly a part of British society. It may not be typical but its position is certainly worthy of consideration.

Quakers and the Pre-Modern World

There is a link between contemporary political interest in the possibilities of alternative dispute resolution and the theoretician's concern with the explanatory power of notions of legal pluralism. As we have seen one reason for the political interest in alternative dispute resolution is the perception that alternative dispute resolution can provide a greater degree of justice and a more user-friendly form of dispute resolution than that that is to be found in traditional courts. One must not take this argument too far. Another less frequently mentioned reason for the politician's concern with alternative dispute resolution is plainly the perception that forms of alternative dispute resolution provide a way of resolving disputes that involves less expenditure by the state (Woolf, 1995, p. 136). Nonetheless, it would be excessively cynical to dismiss entirely the policy maker's expressed interest in the needs of justice. It is here that arguments about alternative dispute resolution and legal pluralism can meet. One strand of analysis within debates about legal pluralism has concerned itself with the way in which communities can themselves generate law that will meet community needs not met by state law (de Sousa Santos, 1977). Such systems are arguably inherently more just and more user-friendly than those to be found within the imposed systems of state law and thus represent the form of dispute resolution which alternative dispute resolution aspires to. In noting this connection between the politician's interest in alternative dispute resolution and the theoretician's interest in legal pluralism we probably take the politician's interest in justice beyond where they would wish to go; to reform the state legal system in order to produce a better standard of justice through alternative dispute resolution is one thing, to accept the authority of non-state generated systems is another. Nonetheless, Cotterrell asks

> Can law help to express community bonds and values, in some sense? ... I take community here to refer to an ideal of social life in which all actors interacting within a social field are able to participate effectively in shaping the conditions of collective life within that field and in which the secure, autonomous existence of all actors within it is guaranteed by operative principles of social justice.
> (Cotterrell, 1995, pp. 300–301.)

We might then ask whether moves towards more alternative dispute resolution and the self-generated law of some forms of legal pluralism are not in fact attempts to answer Cotterrell's question in the affirmative. Cotterrell observes that

> ... [i]t may be appropriate to think of classic legal pluralism ... as a kind of intellectual nostalgia for a fast disappearing or already lost local autonomy in regulation; a nostalgia for the neighbourhood norms of a pre-modern world being replanned out of existence by the law-making activities of modern states.
>
> (Cotterrell, 1995, pp. 306–307.)

Quaker decision-taking and Quaker dispute resolution procedures may, however, be an illustration of the continuing vitality of such pre-modern norms within a community dominated by modernity; a kind of resistance to the tendency of the modern state to gather to itself ever-increasing power.

PART II

QUAKER HISTORY AND QUAKER CULTURE

2 The Historical Development of Quakerism

Origins

Quakers as an organised religious movement have their roots in the teachings and philosophy of George Fox. Born in Fenny Drayton in Leicestershire in 1624, by the time Fox was nineteen he experienced profound spiritual difficulties, which led him to leave home in 1643 and travel widely for a period of about four years, consulting both priests and non-conformist ministers (Punshon, 1986, p. 41). This proved to be a fruitless enterprise, since he could find no-one who could answer his fundamental and challenging questions. However, by the end of 1647, Fox had had a deep spiritual experience, which was to form the basis of his future life as a religious leader.

> When all my hopes in them and in all men were gone, so that I had none outwardly to help me, nor could I tell them what to do, then O then I heard a voice which said 'There is one, even Christ Jesus that can speak to thy condition'. And when I heard it, my heart did leap for joy.
> (*Quaker Faith and Practice*, 1995, para. 19.02.)

Fox soon felt a call to preach, and travelled where he felt called to go, moving slowly through the Midlands and then travelling northwards. In 1652, he entered Lancashire. His diary records that he had a vision at the top of Pendle Hill '... and the Lord let me see a top of the hill in what places he had a great people to be gathered' (*Quaker Faith and Practice,* 1995, para. 19.06).

Shortly after this event, Fox met two people who were to play a significant role in the development of Quakerism; Margaret Fell and her husband, Judge Thomas Fell. Their home, Swarthmoor Hall, was to become the headquarters of Quakerism as it gathered momentum. Margaret Fell quickly became a Quaker, though Thomas Fell never did; as an Assize judge and Vice Chancellor of the County Palatine of Lancaster, it is likely that he felt being a Quaker would greatly hinder his role in public life. However, he supported the new movement, allowing meetings to take place in his home (Foulds, 1960 p.35). The significance of support from a man like

Judge Fell, who had considerable influence in the surrounding area, should not be underestimated, while Margaret Fell's enthusiasm and dedication were unbounded; after being widowed, she was to marry George Fox, and her contribution to the development of Quakerism was extremely important. As the Quaker movement grew, Margaret Fell began to keep in touch with the itinerant Quaker preachers by letter and by maintaining personal contact. She kept an open house for them at Swarthmoor Hall, and also played a leading part in establishing the 'Kendal Fund', which was intended both to meet the costs of the ministry and to support Quakers who were in prison (Foulds, 1960, p. 45).

Fox remained in Lancashire for about a year, and it became clear that a widespread religious movement was springing up throughout the north of England. The movement had a number of leaders and itinerant preachers, who spread its influence; they were engaged in what they called 'publishing Truth'; in other words, preaching the gospel as Quakers understood it. The leaders of the movement included women, for all were regarded as equal before God, and these travelling ministers set up Quaker meetings wherever possible; their work '... enabled a surprising uniformity of faith and practice to be developed very quickly' (Doncaster, 1958, p. 10). Meetings were then left in the care of those who seemed most committed to the Quaker message.

The message which Fox preached, and which his followers embraced, was a radical one. Quakers believed in 'that of God in everyone' i.e. that all human beings have something good, a spark of the divine, within them, whether it is immediately apparent or not. This belief included a radical reinterpretation of the incarnation. God became man not only in the person of Jesus Christ but in the whole of humanity: '... the incarnation was democratised. Jesus was the son of God, but so was George Fox, and so too, in some measure, are we all' (Boulton and Boulton, 1998, p. 221). Quakers did not believe in having priests, since the relationship with God is personal to each individual, and needs no intercession. They were in fact heavily critical of priests, whom they regarded as sources of false interpretations of scripture. Quaker worship was based on a period of silent waiting, during which all present attempted to find God, to be more aware of God, to find God's purpose in their lives (Brimelow, 1989, p. 15). The early Quakers were listening for what Fox called 'the Inward light'; he urged his followers to '... meet together, and know each other in that which is eternal' (*Quaker Faith and Practice*, 1995, para. 2.35). Meetings often lasted several hours and the silence could be punctuated by personal testimony or lengthy extempore sermons, referred to by Quakers as 'ministry' (Punshon, 1986, p. 61).

The seventeenth century was a time of great religious and political turmoil in Britain, with many dissenting sects debating the true nature of religion, and the establishment of the Commonwealth changing the face of British politics for ever. In this context, it is unsurprising that the more radical features of the Quaker message led to persecution from those who felt threatened by it. For example, to proclaim a 'God within' came perilously close to proclaiming one's own divinity, which led George Fox to be accused of blasphemy on several occasions (Boulton and Boulton, 1998, p. 218). Fox's contempt for clerics also led to confrontations with the authorities:

> The thrust of Quaker protest was not against belief in God, but against organised religion that had, in the Quaker view, placed God at one remove from the people. He could only be approached through the proper and widely-recognised channels: the church, her ministers and the appointed sacraments and means of grace. Against this the Quakers called for, and effectively found, an immediate access to God without, they believed, any human intervention. In this way the Quakers claimed that God had brought them out of the darkness of a second-hand religion to the glorious light and freedom of an immediate awareness of his presence.
> (Gorman, 1973, p. 48.)

In addition to their emphasis on a personal relationship with God, Quakers held several other beliefs which the Establishment found challenging. Quakers did not swear oaths, believing that to do so was contrary to the teaching of Christ, since it set up a double standard in truthfulness. They took their obligation to tell the truth very seriously; God is always present, so you should never lie; the concept of oath-taking is therefore made redundant (Braithwaite, 1995, ch. 1). Quaker belief in 'that of God in everyone' also led them to be pacifists; consequently they would not take life at the state's behest in armies. Neither would they pay tithes to a state-controlled church which they believed to be depraved. They challenged what they saw as the extravagance of the secular world by adopting 'plain speech', using the familiar forms of 'thee' and 'thou', instead of the formal 'you', they refused to pay 'hat honour' (i.e. to remove their hats as a mark of respect when in the presence of judges or other dignitaries) and they dressed plainly, without decoration. Finally, to reflect their belief that a church was a community, rather than a building, they had 'meeting-houses' (Punshon, 1986, pp. 61/62). All of these practices emphasised the different way of life the Quakers led. In living out their beliefs in this way, they confronted the lives and beliefs of their fellow-citizens on a daily basis. Quakerism was not a comfortable religion, either for its adherents or for those whom it challenged. Hill argues convincingly that it was these beliefs, rather than their theology, which meant that Quakers so enraged the Establishment of the day (Hill, 1975, p. 233).

It was relatively easy for Quakers to be portrayed as political radicals. It is likely that the movement absorbed many ex-Levellers, and in the early 1650s, many Ranter groups were also absorbed into the Quakers (Hill, 1975, pp. 236-240). In addition, scathing verbal attacks on priests and the imposition of tithes by leading members of the Quaker movement made it likely that they would be associated with radical politics. Hill argues that refusal to engage in hat-honour, which had been a gesture of popular protest since the sixteenth century, reinforced the image of Quakers as threatening to the political establishment (Hill, 1975, p. 247). Once portrayed in this way as dangerous and destabilising influences, Quakers were vulnerable to persecution, retribution and ultimately imprisonment at the hands of a suspicious magistracy.

Early Developments

In 1654 between sixty and seventy Quaker evangelists spread out throughout England in pairs. Known as the 'Valiant Sixty' by modern Quakers, they took their message to all parts of the country. Many of them were to become leading members of The Religious Society of Friends, which was the official title of the Quakers (the term 'Quaker' is said to have come from the taunt of a Justice of the Peace in Derby, who called them Quakers when George Fox told people to 'tremble at the word of the Lord' (Heron, 1995, p. 2).

In some places, the message which Quakers brought was well received; in Bristol and in London, for instance, they quickly became firmly established. However, at times, like other dissenting religious groups in the seventeenth century, they were persecuted for their beliefs. Their belief in the grace of God operating independently of the scriptures, and accessible to all through the Inward Light, i.e. by direct inward revelation, left them open to prosecution under the Blasphemy Act 1650, which carried the possibility of transportation on a second conviction. Their habit of claiming their legal right to speak in churches after the minister had finished opened them to accusations of interrupting services, and this practice was specifically outlawed in 1655, when they were classed with the Ranters as people given to '... rude and unChristian disturbance of ministers and therefore, when behaving in such a manner, to be regarded as disturbers of the peace and proceeded against accordingly' (Foulds, 1960, p. 40).

Frequently Quakers were found guilty of refusing to take oaths. From 1655 onwards everyone who was tried in a court of law to take an oath abjuring the authority of the Pope, so that when Quakers were brought to trial, their refusal to swear this oath was contempt of court, and they could be imprisoned for an indefinite period (Foulds, 1975, p. 61). Many of their practices, such as the use of plain speech, and their refusal to remove their hats, even in court (given that all are equal, this was deemed unnecessary), were also interpreted as contempts, with the same result. Their refusal to pay tithes to a church they regarded as corrupt also resulted in imprisonment for some (Punshon, 1986, pp. 67-68). Quakers were deeply committed to their principles, and stood up for them with an apparent disregard for the consequences; as Punshon comments:

> The internal spiritual assurance that enabled the Quakers to make these quite staggering (and it seems to the world foolhardy) gestures, was a reflection of their message. [Their beliefs] provided an aggressive and uncompromising attitude to all the ways of the world ... The doctrine of perfection as an attainment open to all involved total consistence regardless of consequences, and only by accepting suffering could Quakers practise what they preached. They knew that this was a necessary part of the Lamb's war, and they took it as it came.
> (Punshon, 1986, p. 68.)

Suppression of Quakers after the Restoration was particularly brutal. They were among the foremost targets of the Royalists' drive to make the Kingdom safe against Parliamentarianism. The Fifth Monarchy uprising in January 1661 led to mass imprisonment of Quakers on the basis that they were likely to have been involved. At this point, Fox drew up a declaration to be presented to the King; it was a historic document, which has formed the basis of the Quaker testimony to peace ever since (Sheeran, 1983, p. 14).

> All Bloody principles and practices, we as to our own particulars, do utterly deny, with all outward wars and strife and fightings with outward weapons, for any end or under any pretence whatsoever. And this is our testimony to the whole world.
> (Fox, *Journal*, p. 399.)

The Declaration appears to have had the desired effect, since wholesale imprisonment of Quakers on a massive scale ceased. However, persecution did not stop. Charles II's Lord Chancellor, Clarendon, put through a series of statutes designed to enforce conformity with the Church of England. The Corporation Act 1661 required all holders of civic posts to be communicant members of the Church of England. The Act of Uniformity 1662 required compliance with the Book of Common Prayer, and forbade any nonconformists to live or build chapels within five miles of any incorporated town. The Quaker Act of 1662 provided penalties for maintaining that oath-swearing was unlawful and contrary to the will of

God, for any person wilfully refusing to swear an oath, or encouraging others to do so, and for printing any defence of these views. It also rendered unlawful any Quaker religious meeting of more than five people, other than members of a household; the penalty on first or second conviction was a fine, but the penalty for a third conviction was transportation. However, the most effective means of persecution arose from Quakers' refusal to take the Oath of Allegiance at the beginning of a trial. This was regarded as tantamount to treason, and penalties included imprisonment for life or at the King's pleasure, as well as forfeiture of the felon's estates. Many Quakers suffered considerable hardship as a result of their refusal to swear oaths (Foulds, 1975, p. 116).

The toll taken on Quakers by years of persecution, together with the deaths of a number of leading members of the movement, caused George Fox to realise that a system of disciplined self-government was necessary in order to ensure that the Quaker movement could withstand all the strains it was subjected to. After his release from prison in 1666 he spent the next two years organising a system of church government which was so effective that it has continued virtually unaltered to this day. The structure which Fox put in place consisted of local (known as 'particular') meetings, to which individuals formally belonged. The main administrative unit was composed of representatives from a group of particular meetings, meeting monthly (known as 'monthly meeting'). At a regional level, representatives from several monthly meetings met together in quarterly meetings every three months. The representatives sent to the larger meetings were not appointed permanently; Meetings sent different Quakers on different occasions; it was merely expected that they would choose Quakers who were wise and experienced. By 1678, there was also a Yearly Meeting, which completed the organisational structure with a meeting of representatives from the whole country. Unsurprisingly, Fox did not manage to implement these organisational changes without arousing controversy within the Quaker movement, particularly because they represented a centralising (and therefore standardising) tendency which ran counter to the individualistic nature of fundamental Quaker beliefs, such as the priesthood of all believers (Punshon, 1984, p. 93). However, although divisions occurred, the movement as a whole continued to thrive.

Since Quakers did not see the Bible as the infallible word of God, and personal revelation, rather than the church was the ultimate source of authority, there was clearly a danger that adherents of the movement would substitute their own personal desires for the word of God. Such was the situation with the 'Perrott hat controversy'. Perrott said that he had had a divine leading that Quakers should not remove their hats when they, or other Quakers, were praying, since the practice of removing one's hat in such circumstances was contrary to ideas about equality. Many Quakers followed Perrott, a charismatic leader, but others did not, arguing instead that his ideas should be subjected to the authority of the gathered meeting, which in this case was not in unity about his suggestion. But for Perrott the inspired individual had an authority which transcended that of the Meeting (Halliday, 1991, pp. 10/11). George Fox's reaction to this was to engage in a pamphlet war and finally to denounce Perrott, who eventually went into voluntary exile in Barbados, as the price of his release from Newgate (Sheeran, 1983, p.18).

It was clearly important for Fox to explain precisely what sort of divine promptings Quakers were listening for in their Meetings for Worship. In the writings of the early Quakers it is possible to find much discussion of the concept of 'discernment'. 'Spiritual discernment is the ability to differentiate reliable leadings from unreliable ones' (Sheeran, 1983, p. 22). One early test seems to have been whether one finds the Cross in what one is urged to do; actions from the true spirit were seen as contrary to self-will. Scripture was of limited help, since it is easy to find scriptural authority for many completely contradictory ideas. Often, the early preachers submitted their ideas to each other as a way of testing their spirituality (Sheeran, 1983, pp. 24-27).

One of the ways in which Fox explored this problem was to argue that there were two alternative sources of authority: the first was what he called 'the light of Christ in your conscience' and the other was experience. He qualified the status of conscience and experience by drawing a distinction between 'natural conscience', which was untutored and liable to fall into error, and conscience enlightened by God, which conveyed the truth. Similarly, what was known experimentally was valued only if it was of 'the life'. In order that individuals should not be misled by the promptings of conscience or experience, Fox argued that such promptings should be tested against the collective conscience and experience of the worshipping group (Boulton and Boulton, 1998, p. 215).

It was an important aspect of Quakerism from the beginning that women should play an equal part in the new movement. Fox encouraged the establishment of parallel men's and women's meetings, but did not intend that the women's meetings should be inferior: 'The setting up of separate women's meetings was intended to liberate gift in the service of the church which might otherwise have remained unused' (Doncaster, 1958, p. 17). In fact, the women's meetings soon took on a subsidiary role, but this was far from Fox's original intention. Nevertheless, as time went on, women gradually played a greater part in Quaker life, and this, together with the equal education given to Quaker girls and boys, meant that by the end of the nineteenth century it was realised that separate women's meetings were inappropriate. They were finally abolished in 1896 (Doncaster, 1958, p. 46).

In 1670, as the price of receiving further financial aid from Parliament, Charles II agreed to the passing of the Second Conventicle Act. This was a statute which aimed to destroy Dissent; it introduced a number of new offences, including preaching at a religious gathering, or allowing such meetings to be held in one's premises (Foulds, 1960, p. 104). This offence lay within the jurisdiction of a single magistrate, rather than requiring trial by jury, as had offences under the Quaker Act and other previous legislation which had been used to oppress Dissenters. Since magistrates were frequently of poor quality, their decisions were often arbitrary, and based on ignorance, rather than a correct interpretation of the law. Under the Conventicle Acts magistrates had power to order a search of premises and to use the militia. Frequently, those attending Quaker meetings were subjected to violent assault when they were forcibly broken up, and many meeting houses were destroyed. Those convicted were punished by fines, for which there was rapid distraint.

By 1676 a large number of Quakers were coming to the view that the oppression which they suffered should not be borne passively, but that the Government should be faced with the consequences of its acts. For some time, Quakers had been sending details of their persecution to London, and from 1676 this process became more formalised, with the founding of Meeting for Sufferings, to which each county sent a representative. Meeting for Sufferings met at the beginning of each law term; its purpose was to gather information about the suffering experienced by Quakers, and to help wherever possible, by constantly publishing the details of individual cases and pleading for justice and mercy from magistrates, Members of Parliament, ministers of state and the King (Doncaster, 1958, p. 19). Meeting for Sufferings also co-ordinated the collection and distribution of money to help with legal expenses and the costs of political lobbying.

After the Glorious Revolution of 1689, and the ascension to the throne of William and Mary, the Toleration Act of that year gave Quakers a basic freedom of public worship. However, it did not go so far as to provide for many Quaker practices, including objections to paying tithes and taking oaths. It was not until 1696 that the Affirmation Act allowed Quakers to affirm instead of swearing an oath (Sheeran, 1983, p. 39).

By the time George Fox died in 1691, Quakerism was firmly established, particularly among the middle classes. Fox's achievement in forming an organised religious movement out of the melting-pot of seventeenth-century religious and political turmoil, should not be under-estimated.

The Eighteenth Century - Prosperity and Quietism

However, the new century was to put a brake on the hitherto rapid development of Quakerism. As Gillman points out in *A Light that is Shining,* his introductory text to the Religious Society of Friends, in common with many other charismatic movements Quakerism lost some impetus as the founding members died. '[F]rom being a revival of the true universal church, Friends now saw themselves as a remnant keeping precious their past insights' (Gillman, 1988, p. 40).

It was during the eighteenth century that Quakers took on the distinctive dress and life-style which would characterise them well into the nineteenth century. They continued to adopt both 'plain speech' and 'plain dress'. (The adoption of 'plain dress' involved wearing clothes in dull colours, without lapels or unnecessary frills or buttons.) Both plain speech and plain dress were adopted in order to testify to Quaker beliefs in simplicity, rather than following the dictates of fashion, which was worldly, and to be avoided (Punshon, 1986, p. 129). However, eighteenth-century Quakerism became very inward-looking. Marriage to non-Quakers was forbidden, plain dress became an obligatory uniform, and Quakers were obsessed with the use of plain speech.

It also became the custom to 'record as ministers' those who had something particular to offer, in terms of spiritual ministry. The result was that meetings for worship, lasting two or three hours, would often be completely silent unless one of the chosen ministers decided to speak (and they would only speak if they felt called to do so by the will of God). Hubbard points out that the recording of ministers was accompanied by a formal method of appointing elders, whose function was to advise and counsel ministers. Since this was accompanied by a system of meetings of ministers and elders at Yearly, Quarterly and Monthly Meetings, the spiritual life of the Quaker movement had been handed over to an elite, and like may elites, it tended towards conservatism. Through the questions, known as 'queries' which were answered in writing four times a year by Monthly Meetings, the central Yearly Meeting was able to keep a close eye on the behaviour of individual members of the movement, curbing any tendencies to move away from the norm. Quakers could be disowned for a whole variety of offences, from 'marrying out' (i.e. marrying a non-Quaker) to paying tithes or being made bankrupt (Hubbard, 1974, p. 41).

This period in Quaker history is often referred to as the 'Quietist' period, and is often portrayed as one in which Meetings were dull and ministry uninspiring. However, it would not be accurate to portray eighteenth-century Quakerism in a wholly negative light. It was during this century, for instance, that Quakers became deeply involved in the anti-slavery movement. Their concern first arose in America, but quickly gathered momentum in England, where by 1761 London Yearly Meeting had decided to disown any Quaker involved in the slave trade (Hubbard, 1974, p. 44). Other social concerns at this time led to the founding of Ackworth School in Yorkshire to offer education for children whose parents were not wealthy (Hubbard, 1974, p. 45) and in 1796 William Tuke founded The Retreat, a mental hospital offering an enlightened and humane regime for the treatment of the mentally ill. In the eighteenth century mental patients were either cared for in their own families, often in conditions of great secrecy, or were placed in public institutions, where the conditions were often very harsh, with patients being punished for their unconventional behaviour. William Tuke believed that the Inward Light shone in the insane as well as in the sane, and it was this philosophy which permeated the Retreat's pioneering work in the field of mental health (Foulds, 1960, p. 163).

Other positive developments in the history of Quakerism which took place in the eighteenth century included the establishment of many Quakers as significant contributors to the nation's industrial and commercial life. It had quickly become apparent that Quakerism was a type of religious belief which did not appeal greatly to the extremes of society, neither to the nobility and the gentry, nor to the labouring and servant classes. English Quakerism was largely an urban, middle-class phenomenon. Quaker beliefs were particularly hard to adhere to in a rural context; plain speech struck at the heart of the finely-graded social hierarchy, and refusal to bear arms excluded Quakers from not only the military, but also the social aspects of militia meetings. Quakers offended patriotism, the law and good fellowship in one fell swoop. Given that all this was compounded by a refusal to pay tithes, Punshon argues that for many families, removal to the town '... must have seemed the only way to avoid perpetual, niggardly and debilitating persecution' (Punshon, 1986, p. 108).

The urbanisation of Quakerism was accompanied by the successful establishment of Quakers in trade and commerce. The religious beliefs held by Quakers meant that they did not see a difference between the standards they maintained in their religious and business lives; they adhered strictly to the truth, whether it was to their advantage or not. Quakers also rejected the practice of haggling over retail prices (which was common at that time) and began to gain a reputation for honesty which was to earn them enduring respect within the business community. The prosperity of Quaker families was also increased because their belief in simplicity, not only in dress but in all aspects of life, meant that they did not indulge in conspicuous consumption. Their frugal way of life often allowed them to accumulate capital, and since their career options were limited by the fact that the professions and the civil service were barred to Dissenters, they often used their talents in the commercial world (Punshon, 1986, p. 109). Punshon comments that the Quaker practice of marrying only Quakers also contributed to the prosperity of a number of prominent Quaker families, allowing advantageous financial, as well as familial, alliances to be made. In addition, '... the system of monthly, quarterly and yearly meetings provided an excellent nationwide system of business intelligence and mutual support' (Punshon, 1986, p. 109).

The most famous Quaker entrepreneurs are undoubtedly the well-known confectionery families who dominated the early development of the British cocoa and chocolate industry. Rowntree's, Cadbury's and Fry's were all Quaker enterprises which were established during the eighteenth century (see generally Windsor, 1980). Quakers were also involved in the heart of the Industrial Revolution, as ironmasters. At Coalbrookdale in Shropshire Abraham Darby discovered a way of smelting iron by using coke rather than charcoal. When his son, also called Abraham, took over the business in 1756 he constructed a steam pumping-engine to replace horse pumps, and in his turn furnished the iron industry with a revolutionary innovation which was to completely transform iron production (Windsor, 1980, p. 49). The religious beliefs of the Quaker ironmasters played a significant role in their success. The majority of eighteenth-century iron-working businesses produced shot and cannon for military purposes. Quakers, as pacifists, refused to engage in such business. Instead, they turned to the manufacture of domestic implements. The Quaker ironmasters in Bristol and Coalbrookdale found themselves almost alone in catering for the rapidly-growing domestic market (Windsor, 1980, p. 47).

It is less well known that Quakers were deeply involved in banking, their reputation for honesty proving extremely advantageous in that sphere; both Lloyd's Bank and Barclay's Bank were Quaker in origin. The Lloyd family came from what is now Powys. Realising that there was no bank in Birmingham, Samuel Lloyd II went into partnership with a non-Quaker, John Taylor, and established one in 1765. The firm pioneered the use of the inland bill for small traders and did so well that Samuel Lloyd III was able to set up another partnership in Lombard Street to facilitate the growing business in London. In 1899 these two firms amalgamated, forming the basis of the business which has developed into the Lloyd's Bank we know today. Barclay's Bank was formed out of an amalgamation of a number of different local banks, the majority of which were established by Quakers, such as G. Fox and Co. (1754) in Cornwall, John and Henry Gurney & Co. of Norwich (1775) and J. & J. Backhouse (1778) of Darlington. When the amalgamation took place in 1896 to create Barclay's, it was the leading British joint stock bank (Punshon, 1986, p. 115).

Nor was it only in the commercial sphere that Quakers flourished. Their contribution as scientists was also considerable; Quaker botanists, doctors, clockmakers and instrument makers were all well-known within their specialisms (Raistrick, 1968).

While in terms of prosperity and contribution to the scientific and commercial life of the nation, the eighteenth century was an exciting one for the Quaker movement, in religious terms it was a period of consolidation, rather than rapid expansion. Hubbard sums it up as follows:

> [The eighteenth century saw] a closed and self-sufficient community, preoccupied with the spiritual virtues, and deriving from this preoccupation a great strength, which after achieving substantial social ends, was being turned to maintaining the status quo. But if the fire of Fox and his companions had been banked down, it was not yet extinguished; if the organisation was becoming authoritarian it had not completely rigidified. The eighteenth-century Friends handed on a heritage capable of vigorous and sustained revival.
> (Hubbard, 1974, p. 54.)

Victorian Quakerism - A Time of Change

By the time Victoria came to the throne in 1837, it was clear that a new phase in the development of Quakerism had started. Quakerism was influenced, like all religious movements of the time in England, by the wave of evangelicalism which had its roots in the Methodist movement of the previous century. Quaker evangelicalism, being largely Bible-based, lost sight of the essential Quaker emphasis on the central importance of the Inward Light, i.e. direct revelation open to all. Not all Quakers accepted the new approach, but despite deep spiritual differences between the more conservative and the evangelicals, Quakerism did not suffer any radical splits or schisms. Heron suggests this is because of the cohesive qualities of the Quaker structures and discipline; the testimonies against war and tithes, the training which underlay the silent worship and the quiet decorum which was expected of Quakers (Heron, 1995, p. 11). Nevertheless, the period of evangelicalism did not lead to any great renewal of Quakerism, and by the late 1850s membership had fallen drastically.

In 1859, however, an event occurred which was to be of major significance in the history of Quakerism. A prize of one hundred guineas (equivalent to several thousand pounds today) was offered for the best essay on the topic of the decline of the Religious Society of Friends. A panel of judges was appointed, none of them Quakers (to safeguard their independence), and the prize was awarded to John Stephenson Rowntree for his essay entitled 'Quakerism past and present: an enquiry into the causes of its decline in Great Britain and Ireland'. Punshon describes Rowntree's critique as follows:

> He emphasized the spiritual character of early Quakerism and criticised its subsequent failure to develop creatively its early preaching. He pointed to the disparagement of reason and the Bible, its neglect of prayer, its suspicion of enthusiasm and its elevation of silence above what he considered its proper place to be. He did not like the concentration of power in the hands of elders and overseers and the intolerance of dissent. He pointed to the significance of Methodism as a factor in Quaker decline.
> (Punshon, 1986, p. 191.)

This essay had considerable impact on Quakerism. Yearly Meeting in 1860 made plain dress and plain speech optional, and in 1861 the Book of Discipline was completely revised; over fifty of the more anachronistic rules were removed (Heron, 1995, p. 13).

However, the changes which took place were gradual, and in 1873 when a conference was held 'to deliberate upon the state of our Society in England' Heron notes that the concerns raised included '... decreasing attendance at meeting for worship; lessened interest in meetings for worship for church affairs; the relative decline in membership; the need for more pastoral care; and the religious instruction of the young' (Heron, 1995, p. 14). One of the results of this conference was the establishment of a Home Missions Committee, the predecessor of Quaker Home Service (the Committee of Britain Yearly Meeting which has responsibility for nurturing the spiritual life of all Quaker Meetings in Britain).

In 1884 another event took place which was to change the face of Quakerism for ever. In that year, a book entitled *A Reasonable Faith* was published. Its intention was to call for support from the many Quakers whom the three anonymous authors believed were ready to take a stand against the dogmatic evangelicalism then dominating Quakerism. The distinguishing feature of their arguments was an emphasis on Quakerism as a form of Christianity based not on specific doctrines, but as a way of life based on direct spiritual experience, thus returning to one of the central messages delivered by George Fox. The issues raised by the publication of *A Reasonable Faith* were widely discussed in Quaker circles, and Quaker periodicals were full of arguments for and against the arguments it contained (Heron, 1995, p. 15). More books and discussion followed, and in 1895, the Home Missions Committee asked Yearly Meeting to hold a special conference to discuss the life and work of the Society.

In November 1895, over one thousand Quakers met in Manchester; their deliberations were focused on six topics: has Quakerism a message today?;

the relations between Adult School and Mission Meetings and the Religious Society of Friends; the attitude of the Society of Friends towards social questions; the attitude of the Society of Friends towards modern thought; the more effectual presentation of spiritual truth and the vitalising of meetings for worship. Speakers at the conference put forward views which reflected a liberal view of Quakerism, and of theology, ideas which would remain at the heart of Quakerism throughout the century which followed. Comments about the conference in the Quaker journal, *The Friend,* reflect the fact that such views were by no means universal among Quakers at that time. Nevertheless, ideas put forward at the Manchester Conference laid the foundations of modern Quakerism, and Heron goes to some lengths to try and convey its significance as a defining moment in Quaker history, which he takes as the beginning of his examination of one hundred years of change in the Society of Friends (Heron, 1995, ch. 1). One of the most revealing quotations from the conference proceedings included in Heron's analysis of the events which took place is his quotation from the address given by Frances Thompson, the first address on the subject of Quakers and social questions:

> This belief in the continuous Divine revelation, and in our possible open vision with regard to it, seems to me that which it ought to be our special mission to teach to those around us, and to bring to bear upon the social questions of our time. Are we living up to this belief ourselves? And are we helping others to do so? We talk much of our early Quakers and wish we had their power; we shall not get it by copying their methods and preaching their sermons, though both were suited to the work to be done in their day.
> We shall get it from living in their spirit, and drawing fresh inspiration for ourselves from the same source, for somewhat different work, to be done in a somewhat different day ignoring, as they did, the authority, doctrines and dogmas of men, unless we feel them to be in accordance with the word of truth revealed to our own hearts.
> (Heron, 1995, pp. 22/23.)

The emphasis on direct spiritual revelation, without deference to priests or other intermediaries, and on the necessity of constantly questioning one's ability to live up to this belief, together with the emphasis on social concern and a benevolent attitude to one's fellow human beings, goes to the heart of Fox's message, and clearly reflects a rejection of evangelicalism.

It was during the nineteenth century that the Quaker contribution to the commercial life of Britain blossomed. Quakers were closely associated with the development of the railways. It was three Quaker bankers, Edward Pease, Jonathan Backhouse and Thomas Richardson, who raised the money to finance George Stephenson's first railway line, and the first passenger train in the world travelled along what was known as 'The Quaker Line'. It was another Quaker, Thomas Edmondson, who devised the railway ticket and its associated stamping machine, while the original railway timetable, *Backhouse's Railway Guide,* was produced by yet another Quaker entrepreneur. Quakers were also involved in the English china-clay and porcelain industries, most famously in the person of the Shropshire Quaker, Josiah Wedgewood. Apart from Rowntree's, Cadbury's and Fry's which have already been mentioned, the Quaker food businesses also included Huntley and Palmer's and Carr's, both famous for their biscuits. The well-known shoe manufacturers, Clarks, also evolved from a Quaker enterprise, as did Price Waterhouse and Reckitt and Colman (Windsor, 1980, ch. 2). The list is long and impressive, and it is unsurprising that commentators have linked the commercial success of Quakers with their religious beliefs (see for example, Walvin, 1997 and Windsor, 1980). The story of Quaker commercial success is not unique, in that other religious groups, notably the Jews, have also enjoyed great prosperity. However, it remains true that from the late eighteenth to the late nineteenth century Quakerism was the spiritual home of '... an outstanding commercial elite' (Walvin, 1997, p. 207). From the mid-seventeenth century, Quakers were encouraged to be hard-working, financially prudent and honest in all their business dealings (Walvin, 1997, p. 208). In addition, exclusion from many areas of social and economic life had obliged them to look to their own efforts for education, careers and economic well-being. Quakers also had an effective and supportive network which supported their commercial activity. It provided not only a flow of information, but also sympathetic assistance with financing, in particular from the numerous Quaker banks. It also yielded important links through marriage; some Quaker dynasties spanned entire industries; some brought together expertise from several different commercial sectors (Walvin, 1997, p. 209).

The link between Quakerism and trade is most clearly seen in the 'Advices' on trade which were issued from time to time to remind individual Quakers of the right way to conduct their business affairs. From the time of George Fox, it was impressed upon Quakers that in trade, as in the rest of their lives, Quakers should show forth the truth to the world, and that they should therefore be scrupulous in their business dealings. The advices covered every aspect of business behaviour, setting extremely high standards of integrity in business dealings (Raistrick, 1968, p. 46). The Advices were not merely empty words; they were strictly enforced by the Quaker community, and individuals who failed to live up to them were called to account; ultimately those who were found wanting were disowned (Walvin, 1997, p. 208).

In the last quarter of the nineteenth century, these prosperous Quakers became increasingly active in addressing a wide variety of social concerns. Their involvement with the Adult School movement increased, and this brought them into contact with people quite outside their own social sphere (Gardiner, p. 37). Social concerns among Quakers active in commerce were often reflected in moves to provide better living and working conditions for their own employees; Bournville in Birmingham and New Earswick in York are 'model villages' which sprang out of this concern, and it is well documented that Quaker employers exercised a paternalistic care for their workers which resulted in rates of pay, benefits, welfare services and working conditions in Quaker enterprises which were a vast improvement on those available elsewhere (Walvin, 1997, chapter 11). When Joseph Rowntree launched *The Cocoa Works Magazine* in 1902 to enable him to keep in touch with his vastly enlarged workforce, he made express reference to his belief in combining social progress with economic success. In the same magazine, the list of facilities and organisations open to Rowntree employees is extremely impressive in its length and variety, including as it did '... a library; savings schemes and hospital funds; clubs for singing and music-making, angling, bowling, football and cricket, gardening, photography, cycling and gymnastics for girls'. There were also dress-making classes, and annual trips to Blackpool (Walvin, 1997, p. 185).

Quaker enterprise was not wholly liberal, far-sighted and philanthropic however. Quaker firms were often reluctant to allow their workers to join trade unions, largely because they were contrary to the Quaker way of doing business.

> Unions undermined two tenets of Quaker business ethics. Firstly, they suggested that employees needed representation despite the sympathy of Friends towards workers' interests. Secondly, unionisation created sectional divides which tugged at the Quaker sense of an organic working community. (Walvin, 1997, p. 182.)

Some Quaker entrepreneurs were also opposed to the Factory Acts, and the famous match girls strike took place at the Quaker-owned factory of Bryant and May, when workers were dismissed when they were suspected of giving information to Annie Besant for her exposure of the firm's dangerous practices (Dale, 1996, p. 64).

Meanwhile, the nineteenth century had witnessed a transformation in the religious life of Quakerism, in particular as a result of the Manchester Conference. Heron sums up its contribution as follows:

... it becomes clear that to describe as 'liberal' the era introduced into British Quaker life by the Manchester Conference is inadequate: the religious basis for the era was a reaffirmation of the Quaker form of mysticism. It might be thought of as being 'conservative' without being 'quietist', in the sense that the original dependence on the Inward Light of Christ could be recovered in an active form, appropriate to the new understanding required by both scientific insights and Biblical criticism. The 'shackles' thrown off by this liberation were those of rigid attitudes and spiritually-closed minds. Quakers were being called to a fresh life that was both adventurous and disciplined.
(Heron, 1995, p. 33.)

At the end of the nineteenth century the future of Quakerism therefore looked brighter than it had done for some time. Quakers could enter the new century with optimism, based firmly on the principles of their seventeenth-century forebears. The teaching of George Fox, with its emphasis on 'that of God in everyone' and its insistence on the consequences of that belief on the daily lives of individual Quakers, was re-affirmed.

The Early Twentieth Century

The influence of the Manchester Conference lasted well into the early twentieth century. It was then that Quakers began their tradition of having Summer Schools, to provide continuing religious education and to nourish the spiritual life of their members. The existence of the summer Schools aroused a growing demand for further opportunities for study (Barlow, 1982, p. 5). In response to a plea made by John Wilhelm Rowntree, one of the leading figures at the Manchester conference, George Cadbury gave the house and gardens at Woodbrooke, in Birmingham, as a Quaker study centre. George Cadbury wrote that the object was:

> To provide a place where spiritual and intellectual stimulus, combined with experience in Christian social work can be obtained. In other words - to give to members of the Society of Friends an opportunity for more fully qualifying themselves spiritually, intellectually and experimentally for the work to which, while still discharging the ordinary avocations of life, they have felt called by the Holy Spirit.
> (Gardiner, p. 194.)

The mixture of religious impetus and practical application of knowledge gained has a typical Quaker ethos, and Woodbrooke continues to enjoy a central role in Quaker life, with many people able to take advantage of its short residential courses, meeting with others not just from Britain, but throughout the world. Woodbrooke is open to all, whatever their colour, race or creed. An extract from the 'Statement of Aims' published in 1970, serves to give a flavour of 'the Woodbrooke experience'.

> Woodbrooke provides the opportunity for study in many aspects of Quaker thought and action. We combine exploration into the significance of the history of the Society of Friends alongside Biblical and historic insights. we search into international and social affairs, and draw on literature, science and economics ... The heart of Woodbrooke is the shared experiences of worship, insights and personal encounters. Many of those who come are associated with the Society of Friends, but others, from various churches or none, are always part of the group. As one recent student put it 'Woodbrooke is a place of discovery ...'
> (Barlow, 1982, p. 26.)

The Woodbrooke Extension Committee has also established the annual Swarthmore Lectures, the first of which was delivered by Rufus Jones in 1908. The purpose of the lectures is firstly to interpret further to members of the Society of Quakers their message and mission as Quakers, and secondly to bring before the general public '... the spirit, the aims and fundamental principles ...' of the Quaker movement (see for example Preface to 1996 Swarthmore Lecture, Dale, 1996). These lectures have endured as a source of continuing insights into the development of Quakerism.

The advent of the First World War meant that the Quaker testimony to peace became a significant practical issue, as it had done previously in the Boer War. When conscription was introduced in 1916, over a thousand Quakers and Attenders applied for exemption as conscientious objectors; 279 were imprisoned, of whom 142 were 'absolutists', who felt unable to undertake any form of alternative civilian service (Heron, 1995, p. 34). Throughout the war, Quakers were involved in a number of activities which they undertook as an alternative to military service. Under the auspices of a young Quaker called Philip Noel-Baker, an unofficial body called the Friends Ambulance Unit (F.A.U.) was set up, and staffed with pacifists, both Quaker and non-Quaker, who saw active non-combatant service, mainly in France (Heron, 1995, p. 35). The object of the F.A.U. was to provide an opportunity for rendering voluntary non-combative service '... in the relief of the suffering and distress caused by war' (Braithwaite, 1995, p. 158). Its work included the staffing of hospitals, hospital ships, ambulance trains, ambulance convoys and relief work. In 1916 the General Service Section of the F.A.U. was established, in response to the decisions of tribunals considering the matter to give conditional exemption from military service to some conscientious objectors who were Quakers, or closely associated with Quakerism, and who, for various reasons, could not be absorbed into the ambulance work. The majority of men working in this section were employed in the agricultural sector, but some were employed in education or welfare work (Braithwaite, 1995, p. 158).

After the war was over, there was a joint British-American Quaker programme to provide emergency feeding in Germany on a large scale (Heron, 1995, p. 37). In the inter-war years which followed, many Quakers became involved in work in inner cities, trying to bring about a direct improvement in social conditions. A significant number of Quakers became active socialists, and there were several Quaker M.P.s in the 1920s and 1930s. The Quaker commitment to achieving social change was given added impetus by the Depression, and many charitable initiatives started at that time continued long into the twentieth century (Heron, 1995, pp. 38/39).

The early years of the twentieth century saw some significant progress in the development of liberal Quakerism, when the Rules of Discipline were revised. The 'Discipline' was a generic name for the Quaker rules of church government and the religious principles to which Quakers adhered. They were first brought together in an organised and accessible form in 1738. From 1861, the *Book of Discipline* was divided into separate parts: Christian doctrine, Christian practice and Church Government. Christian Practice was revised in 1911, but Christian doctrine remained unaltered until 1921, when it was renamed Christian life, faith and thought (*Quaker Faith and Practice*, 1995, p. 14). The changes made at this time emphasised the fact that Liberal thought had become predominant among British Quakers. A similar philosophy lay behind the decision at Yearly Meeting in 1924 to abandon the practice of 'recording' Ministers, in an effort to encourage wider readiness among all Members of the Society to offer spoken ministry (Heron, 1995, pp. 41/2). While the early twentieth century did not see the major changes which had taken place in the last quarter of the previous century, it nevertheless saw the consolidation of Liberal Quakerism as the dominant philosophy within the Religious Society of Friends.

The Second World War and the Later Twentieth Century – Liberalism Established

Conscientious objection during the Second World War was treated with considerably more justice than it had been in the First World War. By 1939 the general public was more familiar with the views of conscientious objectors than had been the case in 1916, and there was also a greater variety of alternative service which could be undertaken, although as in the First World War some Quakers were 'absolute' pacifists, and would not undertake any form of alternative service (Braithwaite, 1995, ch. 6). The Friends Ambulance Unit was re-formed, and London Yearly Meeting set up the Friends Relief Service. For most of the war, members of the Friends Relief Service worked in bomb shelters and in evacuation hostels. After the Normandy landings, units of the Friends Relief Service also worked in Greece, Italy and Germany. Heron reports that a Quaker team was one of four sent to the concentration camp at Belsen, where its members worked with the survivors; later, several teams served in the British zone of occupied Germany (Heron, 1995, p. 47). In 1947 the Nobel Peace Prize was awarded to the Friends Service Council and the American Friends Service Committee for their contribution to relief work both during and after the War. In the presentation address, Hr. Gunnar Jahn said

> ... it is not the extent of their work or its practical form which is most important in assessing the services rendered by Quakers to people with whom they have come in contact. It is rather the spirit which animates their work...the Quakers have shown us that it is possible to carry into action something that is deeply rooted in the minds of many people - a sympathy with others, a desire to help others; that significant expression of sympathy between men without regard to race or nationality. These feelings translated into deeds must provide the foundations of a lasting peace. For this reason they are today worthy to receive Nobel's Peace Prize. They have revealed to us that strength which is founded on faith in the victory of spirit over force.
> (Foulds, 1960, p. 290)

The 1950s were a relatively uneventful period for British Quakers, while the following decade saw Quakerism affected by the 'swinging sixties' as much as any other institution. In 1963, a pamphlet entitled *Towards A Quaker View of Sex* was published by the Friends Home Service Committee. It arose out of the work of a group of concerned Quakers, who had met together since the late 1950s to discuss the attitude of Quakers towards sexuality. The authors were prompted to write because of their awareness of considerable confusion experienced by young Quakers growing up in an era of rapidly-changing social mores. The attitude taken in the pamphlet was distinctly Liberal, especially in presenting the view that loving homosexual relationships were not necessarily wrong and its publication provoked a controversy among Quakers which was very much of its time. An influential group of Quakers persuaded the national executive committee (i.e. Meeting for Sufferings) almost to disown the pamphlet outright and several Quakers resigned their membership during the course of the controversy (Allen, 1995, p. 72).

Despite the momentous changes taking place, particularly with regard to social attitudes, as the 1960s came to an end Alistair Heron is clear that British Quakers still held a distinctive 'Quaker Christian position' (Heron, 1995, p. 75). Heron's use of the word 'Christian' as he sums up Quakerism in the 1960s is significant; the distinctive characteristic of British Quakerism in the last quarter of the twentieth century has been its growing acknowledgement of the wide diversity of belief and religious views held by its members, in particular in their differing attitudes towards Christianity. Some Quakers, commonly described as 'christocentric', see the teachings of Christ as central to their faith. Others, known as 'universalists', do not afford Christ a dominant role in their religious belief, regarding him as just one of many great religious teachers, and preferring instead to talk in terms of a belief in 'the numinous', or some power greater than mankind. These differing views were debated at length throughout the latter part of the twentieth century and they continue to occupy the attention of many Quakers today. The Christocentric/universalist debate is reflected in Janet Scott's 1980 Swarthmore Lecture, entitled 'What Canst Thou Say?: towards a Quaker theology'. The central question which she addressed was 'Is the Quaker faith Christian or universalist or both?' In a typically Quaker manner, she sought to elaborate a Quaker theology which has room for both Christian and universalist views. She develops the concept of 'simultaneous models of God', i.e. that there are many ways to see God (she identifies six in particular) and argues that it is possible to hold several of these models at once, since no particular model is to be regarded as essential. 'God is revealed to individuals through models suited to their temperaments and abilities ...' (Scott, 1980. p. 71). One of the main advantages of this thesis is that:

> ... it helps us to answer the Quaker problem of the tension between Christ-centredness and universalism. We may see these as two emphases, two ways out of many in which God is disclosed. Both are significant to Quakerism, but neither is the whole truth. The truth of God is greater than both of these models, and this principle is maintained by the maintenance of the tension which comes from holding both simultaneously.
> (Scott, 1995, p. 72.)

The 1990s saw Quakers struggling with the issue of ecumenism, when they were invited to become full members of the Council of Churches for Britain and Ireland (C.C.B.I.). This proved to be one of the most contentious issues which modern Quakerism has had to face. For many, the necessity of signing documents which used traditional Church language, and which referred to mainstream Christian doctrine, was a betrayal of their distinctive Quaker tradition. For others, to stand apart from the other churches would be just as great a betrayal of the Quaker tradition of tolerance. Whilst it was agreed that Quakers should become full members of the C.C.B.I., this is nevertheless an issue which has continued to trouble many Quakers (see for example Richardson, 1999, p. 23, Edwards, 1994, p. 122).

The 1990s also saw the revision of the *Book of Christian Discipline,* the extracts of writing by Quakers over the centuries which reflects the experience of Quakers over generations. At the same time, *Church Government* was revised; this is the volume which contains the rules which govern the administration and correct holding of Quaker meetings. It was agreed that there should be one volume, entitled *Quaker Faith and Practice,* with a subheading of *The Book of Christian Discipline of the Religious Society of Friends (Quakers)* in Britain. In the new book, matters of church government were integrated with the other extracts, the idea being, as explained in the Introduction to the new volume '... to show the interdependence of our faith and our practice' (*Quaker Faith and Practice,* 1995, p. 14). The revision process took nearly ten years, involving extensive consultation with individual Quakers and with Quaker meetings throughout Britain. Since the last revision had taken place in 1959, social conditions had changed greatly, and the aim of the Revision Committee was to reflect these changes, while preserving the best of the Quaker inheritance from the previous three hundred years. *The Book of Discipline* is the only formal statement of Quaker practice which exists, and as such it provides a direct window into Quaker culture. It contains not only the rules which govern the way in which Meeting for Worship should be run, but also extracts from letters, articles and other texts written by Quakers on a wide variety of subjects, ranging from close relationships and social responsibility to finance and the spiritual journey (*Quaker Faith and Practice,* 1995, p. 10). The inclusion, in particular, of the material in Chapter 22 on 'close relationships' is an indication of how far late twentieth-century Quakerism has moved with the times. Here we find an extract from a document issued by Wandsworth Preparative Meeting which affirms '... the love of God for all people, whatever their sexual orientation ...' and a contribution written by an individual Quaker celebrating his homosexual relationship with his lover (*Quaker Faith and Practice,* 1995, paragraphs 22.16 and 22.29). The inclusion of such material, with its emphasis on respecting and valuing diversity in sexual matters, as in other areas of life, also ties the new *Book of Discipline* firmly to its seventeenth-century roots, reflecting as it does the continuing concern to value 'that of God in everyone', regardless of their gender or sexual orientation. Such complete tolerance is not universal among Quakers, nor was its public expression achieved without much heart-searching; Heron (1995, pp. 118-120) records how Yearly Meeting, when considering this chapter of the *Book of Discipline,* struggled to reach agreement, since some people wished to take a more conservative view than others. However, on being reminded that the *Book of Discipline* 'does not represent a creed: we do not have to agree with every extract - it is an anthology of differing experiences', the meeting agreed to include all the proposed new material, merely adding its own text to the anthology, recording the existence of a wide range of views on these matters:

> The Yearly Meeting has struggled to find unity on this section, which comes so close to the personal identity and choices of each one of us. We are still struggling for the words which will help us, so that we may come to know the balance which allows us both to deal with the personal tensions of our own response to sexuality, and also to see ourselves as all equal in the sight of God. The extracts in this section are an anthology of the evolving experience of Friends and meetings. While our own experience does not identify with every extract, we recognise, in love, the Friend whose experience is not our own. We pray for ourselves, that we may not divide, but keep together in our hearts. (*Quaker Faith and Practice,* 1995, paragraph 22.19.)

The ability to disagree without acrimony, to tolerate that which is often regarded as unconventional, and to seek to find unity within diversity is typical of the best of Quakerism as it enters the twenty-first century.

3 Contemporary Quakers

The Popular Image

Quakers belong to a small Nonconformist denomination, comprising, according to the latest available figures (which state the position as in 1995) about 26,000 people (Brierley and Wraight, 1997, p. 268). This makes them much smaller than either the Baptists (230,000 members) or the Methodists (413,000 members) (Brierley and Wraight, 1997, pp. 249 and 260 respectively). Since Quakers do not believe in proselytising, and maintain a low-key public image, many people today are unaware of their continuing existence.

The word 'Quaker' conjures up an image of a Puritan, deeply religious, dressed in black and white, forsaking all frivolous pastimes and abstaining from alcohol; in short, living a life of unmitigated sobriety. Alternatively, 'Quaker' is associated with a well-known brand of breakfast cereal. Either way, it often comes as a surprise to discover that Quakers have moved on from their seventeenth-century beginnings and that they are alive and well, living in the twenty-first century, outwardly indistinguishable from the rest of the society in which they live.

Nomenclature

While the term 'Quaker' is one which is readily recognisable in society as a whole, many Quakers rarely use the term. The full name of the Quaker movement is The Religious Society of Friends, and individuals belonging to that Society are known as Friends, with a capital 'F'. Thus Quakers will say 'Friends believe that ...' or 'Friends should take action about ...', rather than saying 'Quakers believe that ...' or 'Quakers should take action about...'. Readers of this book will find that the authors have used the term 'Quaker' throughout, since that is a more generally accessible term, but some quotations from Quaker writing, or from the speeches of individual Quakers, may use the term Friend, so it is occasionally retained, particularly if to do otherwise would impair the meaning of what is being said.

47

It is also important to understand the nature of being a member of the Religious Society of Friends. Quakers do not believe in christening or other similar ceremonies. They believe everyone has a personal relationship with God and becoming a Quaker is seen in terms of 'discipleship', following a discipline within the Quaker tradition '... where the way we live is as important as the beliefs we affirm' (*Quaker Faith and Practice*, 1995, para. 11.01).

> Membership does not require great moral or spiritual achievement, but it does require sincerity of purpose and a commitment to Quaker values and practices. Membership is a spiritual discipline, a commitment to the well-being of one's spiritual home and not simply appearance on a membership role ... The process is an important part of the life of the monthly meeting, too; accepting a new member means not only welcoming the 'hidden seed of God' but also affirming what it is as a community that we value and cherish. Quakers once called themselves 'Friends in the Truth' and it is the finding of this truth that we affirm when we accept others who value it into membership.
> (*Quaker Faith and Practice*, 1995, para. 11.01.)

It is currently possible to become a Quaker in one of two ways; by personal application or, for children under sixteen, by admission on the application of parents or guardian (*Quaker Faith and Practice*, 1995, para. 11.05). Applications for membership are made to the relevant monthly business meeting, which will appoint two of its members to visit the applicant. The object of the ensuing interview is to explore with the applicant the responsibilities of formal membership and the commitment which is implied in such an application. The visitors report back to the business meeting, which considers the report and makes a decision about the application (*Quaker Faith and Practice*, 1995, para. 11.07-9).

> Visiting the applicant has a dual purpose. As part of the spiritual journey of the person applying, the visit should be a sensitive exchange of thought between seekers; it should provide an opportunity for, and result in, mutual understanding and enrichment. It also serves to provide clear information to help in making the final membership decision. It should not, however, be undertaken in a spirit of examination.
> (*Quaker Faith and Practice*, 1995, para. 11.13.)

It is no longer possible to become a Quaker automatically, by virtue of being born to Quaker parents. However, the relatively recent abolition of this type of membership means that there are many Quakers living today who became members in this way; they are known as 'birthright Friends'. To lay claim to this label, as some still do, immediately implies that one comes from a family who have been Quakers for some time, perhaps even one of the great Quaker dynasties such as the Cadburys or the Rowntrees. People who have become Quakers by application are known as 'convinced Friends'.

The final item of Quaker nomenclature with which readers should be familiar is the Quaker habit of referring to everyone by their first name and family name only, never using titles of any kind. Thus, 'Mrs Jones' is known in Quaker circles as 'Dorothy Jones', and always referred to as such. When introducing two people to each other, the polite Quaker form would be 'Dorothy Jones, meet Michael Wood'. Quakers do not use first names alone; the etiquette about the use of first names is the same as it is in the rest of society. The practice of omitting the use of titles stems from the Quaker belief in equality (Gillman, 1988, p.50).

Quaker Beliefs

Quakers are often described as Nonconformist Christians, but they differ greatly, not only from the Church of England, but also from the other Nonconformist churches, such as Baptists and Methodists. Quakers have no creed and no priests; they do not sing hymns and do not recite formal prayers. Indeed many Quakers were originally drawn to Quakerism precisely because of the lack of the trappings of the mainstream churches (Hubbard, 1974, p. 105). Quakers believe in the priesthood of all believers - that is to say that a person's relationship with whatever they believe God to be is a matter of direct communication between God and the individual; there is thus no need for priests to intercede.

Embracing Diversity and 'That of God in Everyone'

When asked exactly what they believe, the answers received from individual Quakers are likely to vary a lot. Some Quakers see Quakerism as a development of mainstream Christianity, and will talk, as early Quakers did, of the Inward Light of Christ, which they are seeking to find in their Meetings for Worship. Within Quaker circles, these Quakers are referred to as 'Christocentric'. Other Quakers do not believe that any one religion has a monopoly on truth, and see Jesus as one of many great religious thinkers, standing alongside others, such as Buddha and Mohammed, whose insights they would regard as equally valuable. These Quakers are known as 'Universalists', and they are often cautious about being described as 'Christians'. Their concept of God would tend to be extremely abstract, often amounting to 'a sense of the numinous', rather than any more conventional concept.

The broad range of spiritual beliefs encompassed within Quaker universalism has drawn criticism from others within the Quaker movement, who argue that if universalists had their way, Quakers could believe anything, with the result that Quakerism will stand for nothing, a criticism which universalists have been keen to refute (see, for example, Hetherington, 1993, and Cairns, 1994). The Christocentric/Universalist debate is of continuing concern to contemporary Quakers (see, for example, Denley and Roylance, 1994) and the existence of such divergent views on the essentials of religious belief is one of the hallmarks of contemporary Quakerism. The wide variety of theological beliefs which are held by contemporary Quakers is reflected in this passage taken from a recent Swarthmore Lecture:

> We have the Evangelicals, steeped in the tradition of personal salvation and the New Testament; we have the Quietists, who try to avoid intellectual and creaturely activity, to preserve the 'pure Seed'; the Deists, who are sceptical of the mystical and mysterious and find an abstract, ethical faith both reasonable and natural; the Liberals who have absorbed science, psychology and biblical criticism, and who have combined intellect with a modern mysticism; and, from our most recent times, the Universalists, emphasising the common spiritual thread running through a wide variety of outward forms. Also heavily represented is a strand which has probably always been present – those not really interested in theological matters, and so prepared to go along with whatever is the mode of expression of the time, suspecting that language and ways of thinking are only outward forms which may be detached from the life within, and may be less important in the long run than they seem at the time.
> (Heathfield, 1994, p. 43.)

It is one of the most interesting aspects of contemporary Quakerism that individuals holding all these apparently irreconcilable theological views, often deeply opposed to each other, can co-exist peacefully within one religious movement. Quakerism has its divisions, in terms of belief, but it is not generally riven with schisms or factions, though there have inevitably been occasions when the debate has become very heated. Nevertheless, it would not be accurate to see Christocentric and universalist Quakers as forming two distinct and opposing groups within Quakerism; the position is more complex than that, as reflected in the following excerpt from the *Book of Discipline*, written by three leading Quaker universalists:

> ... The ferment of thought in this post-war period has produced a wide variety of beliefs in our Religious Society today and not a little misunderstanding on

all sides. Intolerance has reared its head. Some Friends have voiced objections to the use of Christian language in meetings for worship and for business; others have been told that there is no room for them in our Religious Society if they cannot regard themselves as Christians. it has become quite customary to distinguish between 'Christians' and 'universalists' as if one category excluded the other.

   This situation has led many Friends to suppose that universalist Friends are in some way set over against Christocentric Friends. This is certainly not the case. Universalism is by definition inclusivist, and its adherents accept the right to free expression of all points of view, Christocentric or any other. Indeed, in London Yearly Meeting there are many universalists whose spiritual imagery and belief are thoroughly Christocentric ...
(Quaker Faith and Practice, 1995, para. 27.04)

Unity in Diversity

The diversity of views held by individual Quakers as to what their exact beliefs are can make it difficult for outsiders to understand the nature of contemporary Quakerism. However, it appears to be true that whatever their particular philosophy, all Quakers will agree that 'there is that of God in everyone'. This is a paraphrase of a saying of George Fox:

Be patterns, be examples, in all countries, places, islands, nations, wherever you come, that your carriage and life may preach among all sorts of people, and to them; then you will come to walk cheerfully over the world, answering that of God in everyone.
(Quaker Faith and Practice, 1995, para. 19.32.)

Today, the phrase 'That of God in everyone' is taken to mean that Quakers believe that all people, however superficially unpleasant, evil or unusual, have something good, springing from 'that which is eternal', within them. It has been described as '... the nearest thing there is to a Quaker dogma' (Leonard, 1995, p. 54), reflecting a belief which is fundamental to the Quaker world view. If everyone is, in this sense, a child of God, then every individual is valuable, and should be treated as such. As a consequence of their deep commitment to the value of each individual Quakers are extremely tolerant, and are firmly against any form of unfair discrimination, whether arising from religion, gender, race or sexual orientation or any other source.

At the centre of Friends' religious experience is the repeatedly and consistently expressed belief in the fundamental equality of all members of

the human race. Our common humanity transcends our differences. Friends
have worked individually and corporately to give expression to this belief. We
aspire not to say or do anything or condone any statements or actions which
imply lack of respect for the humanity of any person...
(Extract from Meeting for Sufferings 'Statement on Racism' 1988, *Quaker
Faith and Practice,* 1995, para. 23.36)

Living Faithfully

One of the most important aspects of Quakerism is the strong emphasis on
faith not as something which is merely a belief, but as something which
constitutes one's whole life. While this is theoretically true of many
religious groups, the Quakers place a particularly strong emphasis on this,
with the result that Quakerism is not merely a belief-system, but a way of
life.

> When I ... encountered Quakers what impressed me most was the way in
> which a spiritual understanding about human beings and our relation to the
> rest of the world was put into practice in so many different ways ... Here were
> people who not only believed that the spiritual dimension of our lives was real
> and important but also that it infused all the other areas of our lives.
> (Halliday, 1991, p. 6).

Part of the reason that Quakerism is so effective in permeating all aspects of
life is that Quakers do not distinguish between the sacred and the secular. All
life is lived as a Quaker; it is never possible to turn one's Quakerism off,
since it is part of the essence of one's being.

Quaker beliefs provide a guide to the way in which every aspect of life
should be lived; their insistence on truthfulness permeates not only personal
relationships, but those at work and at the international level. The same goes
for the Quaker testimony to peace and that to simplicity; there is no hiding
place, no possibility of having a rest for a while; living faithfully as a Quaker
involves deep personal commitment, for the relationship with God, or
whatever is out there, is individual and endless. Quakers are not Puritans, but
there is nevertheless something akin to Puritanism in their uncompromising
acceptance of a demanding and often uncomfortable faith.

> For a Quaker, religion is not an external activity, concerning a special 'holy'
> part of the self. It is an openness to the world in the here and now with the
> whole of the self. If this is not simply a pious commonplace, it must take
> account the whole of our humanity: our attitudes to other human beings in our
> most intimate relationships as well as social and political relationships. It must

take account of our life in the world around us, the way we live, the way we treat animals and the environment. In short, to put it in traditional language, there is no part of ourselves and of our relationships where God is not present. (Harvey Gillman, 1988. *Quaker Faith and Practice*, 1995, para. 20.20.)

Quakers often try to explain their attitude to their religious beliefs by referring to a phrase used by George Fox when preaching: 'You will say, Christ said this and the apostles say this; but what canst thou say? Art thou a child of light and hast walked in the Light, and what thou speakest is it inwardly from God?' (*Quaker Faith and Practice*, 1995, para. 19.07). The point that Fox was making is that it is the responsibility of each individual to live their lives, consistently and without ceasing, in the manner in which their religious beliefs suggest is correct; religion is truly a lived experience, and the significant question is 'What canst thou say?' It is unsurprising therefore, that another much-loved Quaker saying is 'Let your lives speak', incorporating as it does the idea of living out one's principles, experiencing them as part of everyday life (Edwards, 1994, p. 96).

Faith in Action: Concerns and Testimonies

For more than three hundred years Quakers have been at the forefront of those working to eradicate human suffering. Involvement in giving practical assistance to people who are in some way less fortunate arises both from the Quaker belief in the inherent value of all human beings, and from their insistence that faith must be lived.

As Gillman explains, there are two words which Quakers use to describe the practical work which flows from their spiritual insights: 'concern' and 'testimony'. For Quakers, the word 'concern' refers to a 'religious compulsion to act in a certain way, based on a "leading of the Spirit"' (Gillman, 1988, p. 47). A Quaker concern is not just a matter for the individual involved, however; the concern which arises out of the experience of a particular individual is brought before the Meeting to which he or she belongs, and cannot be officially pursued until a course of action is sanctioned by the worshipping group. 'The concern is thus put into focus, refined as it were, in a corporate search for the guidance of God, and the group can then offer moral, spiritual or financial support' (Gillman, 1988, p. 48). The concern is examined very carefully; sometimes the group does not support it, or it may ask for further information before it does so; this process is slow, but since it involves everyone in the decision-making process, a concern which is taken up has the support not just of an individual, but the whole Meeting. Guidance offered about the right way to handle concerns brought forward by individuals seeks to balance the need for caution, ensuring that the concern genuinely springs from 'that which is eternal' as opposed to mere human enthusiasm, while at the same time recognising the desirability of encouraging and supporting new ideas which may truly contribute to human happiness.

> It is ... the practice in our Society for a Friend who, after due consideration, believes that he or she has a concern, to bring it before the gathered community of Friends. This is both a further part of the testing process and an expression of our membership in a spiritual community. It is a recognition of mutual obligations; that of a Friend to test the concern against the counsel of the group and that of the group to exercise its judgement and to seek the guidance of God.
> (*Quaker Faith and Practice*, 1995, para. 13.05.)

Perhaps the most famous example of Quaker social concern resulting in practical action in this way is the work of the prison reformer Elizabeth Fry, who not only improved the conditions of women prisoners in Newgate, but also influenced penal policy across Europe (Whitney, 1937, Rose, 1994) but she is only one of numerous Quakers who have carried out a huge variety of charitable and social work activities. Many academics are familiar, for example, with the Joseph Rowntree Foundation, named after a member of the famous Quaker confectionery family. However, social concern as expressed by Quakers is not limited to great historical figures. In 1987, when Thatcherism was at is height, the Religious Society of Friends (Quakers) in Britain issued a public statement expressing their deep concern about social injustice, just before a General Election.

> Quakers in Britain have felt called to issue this statement in order to address a matter of urgent national priority to promote debate and to stimulate action. We are angered by actions which have knowingly led to the polarisation of our country - into the affluent, who epitomise success according to the values of a materialistic society, and the 'have-leasts', who by the expectations of that same society are oppressed, judged, found wanting and punished. We value that of God in every person, and affirm the right of everyone to contribute to society and share in life's good things, beyond the basic necessities ... We find ourselves utterly at odds with the priorities in our society which deny the full human potential of millions of people in this country. That denial diminishes us all. There must be no 'them' and 'us'...
> (*Quaker Faith and Practice*, 1995, para. 23.21.)

This critique emanated from a group composed of individuals whose commitment to serving the 'have-leasts', in terms both of financial aid and personal service, is very high. No lovers of hypocrisy, Quakers would not ask of anyone else what they would not do themselves.

The Testimonies: Peace, Truth, Simplicity and Equality

The other word, apart from 'concern', which Quakers use when talking about their impetus towards social action is 'testimony'. The Quaker testimonies are particular aspects of their faith about which, over the years, Quakers have made various kinds of formal corporate statement. Sometimes, these statements are very public. At other times they are documents circulated mainly within Quaker circles, often reproduced, in part at least, in *Quaker Faith and Practice.*

Peace Testimony The Peace Testimony arises from the deeply-held beliefs of the founders of Quakerism. Early Quakers were dominated by a vision of the world transformed by Christ, and sought to make this vision real by emphasising Christian practice rather than any particular dogma. They recognised the realities of conflict, but it was in their opinion contrary to the spirit of Christ to use war and violence to deal with it. The Peace Testimony is perhaps the best-loved of all the Quaker testimonies. It has been a source of inspiration to Quakers through the ages, pointing to a way of life which embraces all human relationships (*Quaker Faith and Practice,* 1995, Introduction to Chapter 24). The earliest corporate expression of the Peace Testimony is contained in a Declaration to Charles II made in 1660.

> Our principle is, and our practices have always been, to seek peace, and to ensure it, and to follow after righteousness and the knowledge of God, seeking the good and welfare, and doing that which tends to the peace of all. All bloody principles and practices we do utterly deny, with all outward wars, and strife, and fightings with outward weapons, for any end, or for any pretence whatsoever, and this is our testimony to the whole world ...
> (*Quaker Faith and Practice,* 1995, para. 24.04.)

The Peace Testimony has also found formal expression in further similar corporate statements, often made during times of war. The Napoleonic Wars, the Boer War and both World Wars saw the issue of such statements.

> Issued by Yearly Meeting in London in 1744, during the war of the Austrian Succession:
> We entreat all who profess themselves members of our Society to be faithful to that ancient testimony, borne by us ever since we were a people, against bearing arms and fighting, that by conduct agreeable to our profession we

may demonstrate ourselves to be real followers of the Messiah, the peaceable Saviour, of the increase of whose government and peace there shall be no end. (*Quaker Faith and Practice,* 1995, para. 24.05)

To many Quakers, however, the most important part of the Peace Testimony is its continuing expression through the lives and actions of individual Quakers. Personal witness to peace takes many forms; in wartime, it prompts conscientious objection to military service; in peacetime, it ranges from strong protests about paying taxes for military purposes (including an application to the European Court of Human Rights), through participating in nuclear disarmament protests and working consistently for the relief of suffering caused by war wherever it occurs in the world. Quakers are also at the forefront of attempts to deal with conflict on an individual level, and have initiated many mediation and reconciliation projects. The practical Quaker commitment to peacemaking is well expressed by Adam Curle, who was the first Professor in the School of Peace Studies established, largely through Quaker initiative, at Bradford University.

> I have often been asked how we handle the fact that peacemaking involves a relationship, often a close relationship, with people who are committed to violent solutions to their problems. Do we tell them we disapprove of what they are doing or urge them to repent and desist? And if we don't, how do we square this with our principles? For my part I would reply that I would never presume to criticise people caught up in a situation I do not share with them for the way in which they are responding to that situation. How could I, for example, preach to the oppressed of Latin America or southern Africa? Nevertheless, I do explain that I do not believe in the use of violence as either effective or moral; my job is to try to help people who can see no alternative to violence to find a substitute ...
> (Adam Curle, 1981, *Quaker Faith and Practice,* 1995, para. 24.35.)

Quaker testimony to peace was recognised by the award of the Nobel Peace Prize in 1947 (Foulds, 1960, p. 290) and in the following year by the granting of official consultative status at the General Assembly of the United Nations (Bailey, 1993, p. 104). Quaker influence at the UN is also reflected in the rules of procedure of the General Assembly, which provide that at the beginning of the first meeting of each session of the General Assembly the President shall invite the representatives to observe one minute of silence dedicated to prayer or meditation (Bailey, 1993, p. 101).

Much Quaker peace work is carried on away from the glare of publicity. The world might be surprised to learn how influential the work carried out by members of this small British religious community has been, in conflicts ranging from the Cold War to that in Northern Ireland (Bailey, 1993).

Meetings with diplomats, with world leaders, with non-governmental organisations and with key individuals are ongoing; such is the twenty-first-century witness to the same beliefs which George Fox spelt out so forcibly to Charles II.

Testimony to Truth The Quaker testimony to truthfulness is central to the practice of Quakerism. In theological terms, it has its basis in the teaching of Jesus as related in the writings of John and James 'Let your yes mean yes and your no mean no'. The refusal by Quakers to swear oaths arises directly out of the Testimony to Truth; Quakers believe that you should tell the truth all the time; in that context, an oath sworn on the Bible is meaningless, suggesting as it does that there are some times when one is more scrupulous than others. The paragraph below expresses some of the core issues.

> 37. Are you honest and truthful in all you say and do? Do you maintain strict integrity in business transactions and in your dealings with individuals and organisations? Do you use money and information entrusted to you with discretion and responsibility? Taking oaths implies a double standard of truth; in choosing to affirm instead, be aware of the claim to integrity that you are making.
> (*Quaker Faith and Practice*, 1995, para. 1.02.)

Honesty and integrity are qualities which have always been, and still are, highly valued by Quakers; their appearance in several of the Advices and Queries (one of the most important Quaker texts) emphasises their place at the centre of the Quaker universe. The demanding nature of this testimony is illustrated in the words of John Woolman, an eighteenth century American Quaker who had strong connections with British Quakers.

> A neighbour ... desired me to write his will: I took notes, and, amongst other things, he told me to which of his children he gave his young negro: I considered the pain and distress he was in, and knew not how it would end, so I wrote his will, save only that part concerning his slave, and carrying it to his bedside, read it to him, and then told him in a friendly way, that I could not write any instruments by which my fellow-creatures were made slaves, without bringing trouble on my own mind. I let him know that I charged nothing for what I had done, and desired to be excused from doing the other part in the way he proposed. Then we had a serious conference on the subject, and at length, he agreeing to set her free, I finished his will.
> (John Woolman, 1756, *Quaker Faith and Practice*, 1995, para. 20.46.)

Even in the face of death, the Quaker testimony to truth and integrity prevailed.

Testimony to Simplicity   The Quaker testimony of simplicity began as a protest against the extravagance and snobbery which marked English society in the seventeenth and eighteenth centuries. Quakers rejected extravagances of dress and lifestyle, adopting instead 'plain dress' and 'plain speech'. Plain dress consised of simple clothes in muted colours, while plain speech involved adopting the familiar form of 'thee' and 'thou' instead of the formal 'you'.

The retention of these practices well into the nineteenth century caused much dissent among Quakers, many believing that their continuance had become an obsession, and that Quakers themselves were ironically in danger of placing too much emphasis on outward appearances and too little on the practice of their faith. Plain speech and plain dress were made optional in 1860 (Punshon, 1986, p. 190). However, the belief in simplicity survived the controversies over the nature of its expression to become one of the enduring Quaker testimonies.

> ... In whatever form this [testimony] is maintained today, it must still be seen as a testimony against involvement with things which tend to dilute our energies and scatter our thoughts, reducing us to lives of triviality and mediocrity ...
> (*Quaker Faith and Practice*, 1995, para. 20.27.)

Testimony to Equality   It was the testimony to equality which gave rise to the Quaker attitude towards 'hat honour', which caused so much controversy in the seventeenth century. At that time, it was customary for men not to wear their hats in the presence of social superiors. Since Quakers regarded everyone as equal, they were not prepared to take their hats off to satisfy what they saw as mere worldly convention (*Quaker Faith and Practice*, 1995, para 19.39 and 19.40).

Nowadays the testimony to equality covers a wide range of issues, focussed on the belief that all human beings should be treated without discrimination.

Faith in Action: Quaker Marriage Ceremonies

A good example of the distinctive nature of contemporary Quakerism can be seen in the procedures which are adopted for a Quaker marriage. Many Quakers are tolerant of the fact that many couples choose to live together, rather than to undergo a formal marriage ceremony; they are also sensitive to the feelings of same-sex couples, for whom a legal marriage is not possible, and there is dicussion in *Quaker Faith and Practice* of the possibility of holding a 'celebration of commitment' for such couples (*Quaker Faith and Practice,* 1995, para. 22.45). If a marriage is to take place, however, it has a distinctive Quaker form.

Quakers have their own Registering Officers, and the religious ceremony gives rise to a legally-recognised marriage. The ceremony takes the form of a Meeting for Worship, with people gathering as usual for a period of silent contemplation. In keeping with the testimony to simplicity, any wedding clothes and floral decorations are likely to be appropriately low-key. There is no priest, of course, so the couple marry themselves. When they feel it is right to do so, they stand and exchange declarations of marriage in the form laid down by law. Each person in turn makes a promise: 'Friends, I take this my Friend ... X ... to be my wife, promising, with God's help, to be unto her a loving and faithful husband, so long as we both on earth shall live'. Once both partners have made their promises, they are married; rings play no part in the ceremony, though they may be exchanged. A certificate confirming the declaration is signed by the couple and two or more witnesses, and this is then read aloud to all those present. After the wedding is over, it is customary for everyone who was present when the declarations were made (i.e. all the 'congregation') to sign the certificate (*Quaker Faith and Practice,* 1995, paras 16.06 and 16.36).

Meeting for Worship and the Centrality of Silence

When Quakers gather for Meeting for Worship (the Quaker equivalent to a church service) they do so in silence, and they continue to sit together in silence, unless someone is moved to speak (Quakers call these extempore talks 'ministry'). The silence is used for meditation, in the sense of concentrated thinking, and Quakers will talk of 'centring down' when they are in Meeting for Worship, though they do not use any particular meditational techniques, and indeed, would not regard their form of silent worship as meditation at all, in the strict sense of the word.

> [Early Quakers] made the discovery that silence is one of the best preparations for communion [with God] and for the reception of inspiration and guidance. Silence itself, of course, has no magic. It may be just sheer emptiness, absence of words or noise or music. It may be an occasion for slumber, or it may be a dead form. But it may be an intensified pause, a vitalised hush, a creative quiet, an actual moment of mutual and reciprocal correspondence with God.
> (Rufus Jones, 1937, *Quaker Faith and Practice,* 1995, para. 2.16.)

Silence lies at the heart of Quakerism. For Quakers, silence is not merely an absence of noise, but a creative, active experience. If it is to offer the spiritual refreshment which Quakers seek, it involves concentration, commitment and self-discipline on the part not only of the individual, but the worshipping group as a whole.

> So one approaches, by efforts which call for the deepest resources of one's being, to the condition of true silence; not just of sitting still, not just of not speaking, but of a wide-awake, fully aware non-thinking. It is in this condition, found and held for a brief instant only, that I have experienced the existence of something other than 'myself'. The thinking me has vanished, and with it vanishes the sense of separateness, of unique identity. One is not left naked and defenceless, as one is, for example, by the operations of the mind in self-analysis. One becomes instead aware, one is conscious of being a participant in the whole of existence, not limited to the body or the moment ... It is in this condition that one understands the nature of the divine power, its essential identity with love, in the widest sense of that much-misused word.
> (Geoffrey Hubbard, *Quaker Faith and Practice*, 1995, para. 26.12.)

The communal experience of sitting together in Meeting for Worship is also a fundamental part of Quakerism. While worship can be experienced at any time, in any place, individual experience is not enough; '...in a meeting held in the Spirit there is a giving and receiving between its members, one helping another with or without words. So there may come a wider vision and a deeper experience' (*Quaker Faith and Practice*, para. 2.11). 'Quakers do not begin with a theory. They begin with an event in which, ideally, the presence of God is experienced by each person as part of a group experience' (Sheeran, 1983, p. 5). '... I and all the others in the room, in a great variety of ways, have been making a "spiritual" journey to the deepest parts of ourselves' (Gorman, 1978, p. 11). A meeting where everyone present feels in touch with their spirituality is described as a 'gathered' meeting.

> The meeting comes to be truly gathered when most, if not all, of those present have themselves been drawn into the very depths of themselves so that even their thoughts have been stilled and their minds, while by no means empty, are in near perfect rest. ...The meeting's corporate awareness of this state may only be glimpsed for brief, fleeting moments, or may last for shorter or longer periods. Because of its nature it cannot be adequately described, it can only be silently experienced, but it can be known by its fruit, and this is a deep sense of organic unity, so vastly different from an imposed uniformity.
> (Gorman, 1978, p. 40.)

When Quakers minister in Meeting, they just stand and talk to everyone who is present in the room, using everyday language and talking about some subject that they feel is important. They will only stand up and talk in this way, however, if they believe they are moved by God to do so. Quaker ministry is in no way charismatic – there is nothing like 'speaking in tongues'; a Quaker Meeting for Worship is a place of intense silence, punctuated occasionally by the spoken word. Indeed, it is not unusual in many Meetings for no ministry at all to be given in the whole hour of worship on a Sunday morning. If ministry is offered, all those present will use the silence to think deeply about what is said, and others may feel prompted to speak on the same topic. It is important to realise, however, that spoken ministry offered in a Meeting for Worship is offered as part of a religious experience, and not as an opportunity for debate. Speakers may in fact disagree with one another, but Meeting for Worship is not the place to express those disagreements.

> In my young tempestuous days, I heard many things in the Friends' meeting that I disliked and some that seemed to me quite false, and I felt the need to answer them. I was taught, and I believe correctly, that to insist on answering then and there would be to destroy the meeting; and that we all sit under the baptising power of the spirit of Truth, which is its own witness. We sit in silence so as not to trip over words; and we trust the good in each other which is from God, so that we may know the good from the evil.
>
> (J. Ormerod Greenwood, 1980. *Quaker Faith and Practice*, 1995, para. 2.68.)

Topics of ministry may include current events which are causing concern – war, famine, corruption, or thanks may be given for friendship, family relationships or kindnesses received from strangers. Other possible subjects for ministry are personal ethics – the difficulty of knowing what is right, or of standing up for one's principles, or more overtly religious topics – the meaning of a particular part of the Bible, or of some saying of Mohammed. But the essence of a Quaker Meeting for Worship is the silent waiting upon God, and it is the depth of that silence which leaves the deepest impression upon anyone who participates.

Key Texts

Quaker Faith and Practice

Although Quakers do not have a creed, and do not use any set form of service, over the years they have gathered together in a volume currently entitled *Quaker Faith and Practice* their rules of procedure, such as the correct holding of Meetings for Worship and the procedure for becoming a Quaker, as well as texts which are more spiritual in nature, recounting the lived experience of individual Quakers through the ages, and covering topics such as 'approaches to God – worship and prayer', 'personal journey', 'close relationships' and 'social responsibility' (*Quaker Faith and Practice*, 1995). *Quaker Faith and Practice* contains, therefore, comprehensive and readily accessible statements about Quaker beliefs which together form a record of the corporate testimony of contemporary Quakers in Britain.

The subtitle of *Quaker Faith and Practice* is *The Book of Christian Discipline of the Religious Society of Friends (Quakers) in Britain.* The word 'discipline' is used in the sense of 'discipleship'. 'A disciple is one who learns, and a discipline is what is required of us if we are to learn' (Halliday, 1991, p. 15).

> The promised reward of this discipline is very clear in Fox's famous words ... be obedient to the Lord God and go through the world and be valiant for Truth upon earth; tread and trample all that is contrary under ... Be patterns, be examples in all countries, places, nations, wherever you come, that your carriage and life may preach among all sorts of people, and to them; then you will come to walk cheerfully over the world, answering that of God in everyone.
> (Halliday, 1995, p. 15.)

Quaker Faith and Practice collects together the writings of Quakers about their experience as Quakers, their relationships, their struggle to ascertain 'the will of God' and to witness to the testimonies. It is a thorough exploration of the discipline involved in being a Quaker today, but while it contains material which is rigorous in confronting the dilemmas facing modern Quakers, it also contains passages of great beauty and lyricism, which have an appeal reaching out far beyond the confines of the religious community from whence they come, especially in the chapters about personal and social relationships:

> Love is the will to nurture life and growth in oneself and in another. Love is personal; it is the sacred trust of living things. Likewise, love is neither need nor dependency. 'I need you' is not the same as 'I love you'. Need as the basis of a relationship may lead one person to suffocate another through demands. Need may drive me to manipulate, intimidate or coerce you into fulfilling me. Love is so vastly different! It is freeing; it acknowledges the separateness of the beloved. It treasures the unique otherness of the beloved that is each one's contribution to the relationship. Love calls for submission and sacrifice. It does not seek to possess, but rather to empty itself in nurture of the loved one.
> (Donald A. Green, 1982, *Quaker Faith and Practice*, 1995, para. 22.42.)

Advices and Queries

Every year at Yearly Meeting, when Quakers gather together on a national basis, there is an 'Epistle' sent from Yearly Meeting to all the Preparative (local) Meetings. It is a specially-composed letter which reminds individual Quakers of their responsibilities, and brings to their attention some aspect of the Quaker witness. It was out of the spiritual content of some of the early Epistles that the 'Advices' were born. The 'Advices and Queries' form a separate part of *Quaker Faith and Practice*. Their inclusion is intended to be a reminder of the insights gained by Quakers over the years and an invitation to consider their application today, and they are offered as spiritual guidance. The full text of the Advices and Queries is preceded by one of the best-loved of all Quaker texts, part of an epistle 'to the brethren in the north' issued by a meeting of Quakers in 1656.

> Dearly beloved Friends, these things we do not lay upon you as a rule or form to work by, but that all, with the measure of the light which is pure and holy, may be guided; and so in the light walking and abiding, these may be fulfilled in the Spirit, not from the letter, for the letter killeth, but the Spirit giveth life. (*Quaker Faith and Practice*, 1995, para. 1.01.)

The presence of this text at the very beginning of the Advices and Queries underlines the fact that these insights are just that, not a creed or a set of rules (which would be anathema to Quakers), but ideas to consider for the purpose of living a richer and more spiritual life. Yet, typically, they raise deep and serious questions, which, if acted upon, may lead to fundamental changes in the lives of individuals. The Advices and Queries themselves consist of forty-two short numbered paragraphs, addressing all aspects of individual and corporate Quaker life. Their subject-matter gives a clear picture of Quaker values.

> 17. Do you respect that of God in everyone though it may be expressed in unfamiliar ways or be difficult to discern? Each of us has a particular experience of God and each must find the way to be true to it. When words are strange or disturbing to you, try to sense where they come from and what has nourished the lives of others. Listen patiently and seek the truth which other people's opinions may contain for you. Avoid hurtful criticism and provocative language. Do not allow the strength of your convictions to betray you into making statements or allegations that are unfair or untrue. Think it possible you may be mistaken.

> 27. Live adventurously. When choices arise, do you take the way that offers

the fullest opportunity for the use of your gifts in the service of God and the community? Let your life speak. When decisions have to be made, are you ready to join with others in seeking clearness, asking God's guidance and offering counsel to one another?

38. If pressure is brought to bear upon you to lower your standard of integrity, are you prepared to resist it? Our responsibilities to God and our neighbour may involve us in taking unpopular stands. Do not let the desire to be sociable, or the fear of seeming peculiar, determine your decisions.
(*Quaker Faith and Practice*, 1995.)

The Structures of Modern Quakerism

Organisation

The structure of the contemporary Quaker movement is relatively simple. Individual Quakers belong to a local meeting, which holds a religious service at least once a week, on Sunday mornings, and which is the centre of 'grassroots' Quaker activity. Once a month, each local meeting holds a business meeting, known as Preparative Meeting (originally because its major business was to prepare answers to questions sent to it from the next tier of Meetings, known as Monthly Meeting). Preparative Meetings are grouped together in groups of four or five, and representatives from each of the Preparative Meetings are then sent to a regional business meeting, which takes place once a month and is known as Monthly Meeting (individual Quakers who are not official representatives may also attend these meetings). Quakers from groups of Monthly Meetings attend a larger regional meeting called a General Meeting, which takes place several times a year, but not at any specified interval. This is not a business meeting, but an opportunity for discussion and for a broad oversight of Quaker life within the area. Quakers also meet nationally once a year in Yearly Meeting; all Quakers can attend if they wish, and representatives from Preparative Meetings are also sent. Yearly Meeting is the authoritative body of Quakers in Britain, and can make corporate pronouncements on behalf of the whole movement. Yearly Meeting is a business meeting, and the many regional Monthly Meetings form a crucial link between Yearly Meeting and individual Quakers in their Preparative Meetings (*Quaker Faith and Practice*, 1995, chapters 4-6).

Meeting for Sufferings

The other important part of the national Quaker structure is known as Meeting for Sufferings. This originated in the seventeenth century, at a time when Quakers were suffering considerably from religious persecution. It was London-based, but included representatives from each of the counties, as well as some individuals. Meeting for Sufferings received information about individual cases of persecution, and its job was to put the case of Quakers before Members of Parliament, a task which it carried out very efficiently. It was also given the job of trying to obtain relief from the oath, in which it was successful, the result being the Affirmation Acts of the late seventeenth and early eighteenth centuries. Later in the eighteenth century, Meeting for Sufferings campaigned with great effectiveness for the abolition of the slave trade. During the nineteenth century, there was a significant increase in the work of Meeting for Sufferings, and it established a large number of committees to ensure that its increased workload was met. In 1888 it was Meeting for Sufferings which established a Peace Committee, and subsequent committees were formed to express Quakers' views on opium trading and on betting and gambling (*Quaker Faith and Practice*, 1995, para. 7.01).

During the twentieth century, Meeting for Sufferings played a major role in drawing together and relating to one another the different strands of Yearly Meeting's business (an early example of 'joined-up thinking'). All Standing Committees of Yearly Meeting are appointed by Meeting for Sufferings, and it gradually became a sort of executive body of Yearly Meeting, which was able to act between the actual annual meetings. All monthly meetings send a representative to Meeting for Sufferings. The actual work of Meeting for Sufferings is carried out by four Standing Committees, known as the Central Committees. These are Quaker Home Service, Quaker Peace and Service, Quaker Social Responsibility and Education and the Administrative Committee. All members of the Standing Committees are appointed for limited terms by Meeting for Sufferings, and apart from the Administrative Committee they all have a Representative Council, the members of which are appointed by Monthly Meetings. The function of the Representative Council is to provide a two-way channel of communication between individual Quakers and the central bodies (*Quaker Faith and Practice*, 1995, para. 7.01).

Quaker Home Service (QHS) supports and strengthens the life of local meetings, offering support, training and the promotion of good practice on a range of concerns, including working with children and young people and the carrying out of special tasks such as oversight or eldership. QHS is also responsible for what Quakers refer to as 'promoting outreach'. This refers to the way in which Quakers make it known to the rest of society that they exist. Since Quakers are deeply opposed to any kind of proselytising, their outreach is very low-key, and mainly restricted to posters and leaflets giving information about the Quakers, as well as responding to enquirers and appearing at relevant exhibitions (*Quaker Faith and Practice*, 1995, para. 8.05).

Quaker Peace and Service (QPS) has as its primary function work for peace and against violence, helping to build institutions of peace at all levels, from neighbourhoods to the international level. It also promotes non-violent alternatives to conventional weapons of war and all kinds of violence, promoting human rights and sustainable development (*Quaker Faith and Practice*, 1995, para. 8.06).

Quaker Social Responsibility and Education (QSRE) exists as a direct result of the Quaker belief that spiritual understanding demands expression in society. 'The more deeply we live out our faith, the more surely that faith will be nurtured' (*Quaker Faith and Practice*, 1995, para. 8.07). It supports a range of concerns, and provides a resource centre enabling Quakers to study and pursue their concerns about social and educational matters.

The Administrative Committee acts as employer on behalf of Meeting for Sufferings in relation to all the staff who comprise the permanent secretariat of the three main Central Committees. It also has responsibility for the library which is housed in Friends' House on Euston Road in London (the permanent headquarters of the Quakers in Britain), as well as for finance, fundraising and communication services (*Quaker Faith and Practice*, 1995, para. 8.08).

'Office Holders'

The Clerk Quakers have no priests, and this, together with a strong belief that all are equal in the sight of God, means that anyone who holds any kind of special responsibility is not (theoretically, at least) a member of a hierarchy, but is an ordinary person, simply selected for their ability to carry out a particular task. Every Quaker meeting, from the local meetings, right up to Yearly Meeting, has a Clerk, and usually at least one Assistant Clerk. The Clerk is like a General Secretary, convening and chairing business meetings, carrying out administrative tasks such as writing letters on behalf of the meeting and ensuring that the meeting is enabled to play its part in Quaker life as a whole. However, because Quakers do not differentiate between the sacred and the secular, and their business meetings are also Meetings for Worship, although the Clerk does not have a spiritual role in the way that a priest does, nevertheless, it is important that anyone appointed as Clerk should have '... a spiritual capacity for discernment and sensitivity to the meeting ...' because part of their role is to '... set the pattern of worshipful listening which should characterise ... meetings for church affairs ...' The Clerk must be experienced in Quaker culture and in particular the way that Quakers hold their business meetings, so that they can assist the worshipping community '... to discern God's will and recognise the way forward' (*Quaker Faith and Practice,* 1995, paras 3.12-3.15).

Elders and Overseers Apart from the Clerk, other individuals within a Meeting will be asked to serve as Elders and Overseers. All monthly Meetings appoint Elders and Overseers for each Preparative (i.e. local) meeting. The Elders look after the spiritual life of the meeting. They have a particular responsibility for the right holding of Meetings for Worship, including the responsibility to nurture helpful ministry, ensuring that the method of conducting business meetings is understood and that all in the meeting are given opportunities to deepen their knowledge and understanding in spiritual terms (*Quaker Faith and Practice,* 1995, para. 12.12). There are usually two Elders present at every Meeting for Worship, and their practical task is to shake hands with each other at the end of the meeting, to signal that worship has come to a close.

Whereas Elders have responsibility for the spiritual life of the meeting, Overseers have a pastoral role. Overseers ensure that newcomers are welcomed, make opportunities for everyone to get to know each other and ensure that pastoral needs are met – that the sick and elderly are cared for, that parents of young children are supported and that children are welcomed. Overseers also give advice and information about how to apply for membership, ensure that those intending to marry understand the principles on which the Quaker understanding of marriage is based and encourage caring friendship within the Quaker community (*Quaker Faith and Practice,* 1995, para. 12.13).

In the case of both Elders and Overseers, Quakers are clear that appointment to one of these offices does not mean that the individual concerned is elevated to a higher position, but merely that they are recognised as having the capacity to offer a particular kind of service to the worshipping group (*Quaker Faith and Practice,* 1995, para. 12.07).

The functions of these two offices is summed up in *Quaker Faith and Practice* as follows:

> Traditionally the first concern of Elders is for the nurture of the spiritual life of the group as a whole and of its individual members so that all may be brought closer to God and therefore to one another, thus enabling them to be more sensitive and obedient to the will of God. So the right holding of our meetings for worship will be their particular care. The chief concern of

overseers is with the more outward aspects of pastoral care, with building a community in which all members find acceptance, loving care and opportunities for service.
(*Quaker Faith and Practice,* 1995, para. 12.11.)

In Chapter 7 we consider the extent to which the position of Clerks, Elders and Overseers set out in *Quaker Faith and Practice* is an accurate reflection of reality, and explore the extent to which they can be seen as having a leadership role.

The 'Ffriendly fringes'

The 'Ffriendly fringes' is a phrase invented by a member of the Preparative Meeting which we studied to describe all the informal groups which take place within the Quaker community. Locally, these may include activities such as the arts circle, the painting group, various music groups and a range of peace-related activities, as well as discussion groups, Bible study groups and other meetings of a more religious nature. The double 'f' in friendly is taken to indicate that, in this Meeting at least, some people participate in these activities who are neither Quakers nor Attenders, but who enjoy participating in some Quaker activities.

On a national level, this kind of activity is reflected in the Listed Informal Groups, which are listed in the *Annual Book of Meetings.* This is a volume produced every year, giving brief details of all the Quaker Meetings in Britain. The Listed Informal Groups are about forty in number and range from the Fellowship of Black Friends and Their Families to the Quaker Esperanto Service, the Quaker Vegetarian Society and the Quaker ethics and Genetics Network.

There are also various Quaker publications; the most widely available of which is the weekly journal, *The Friend.* In keeping with the Quaker abhorrence of proselytising, no Quaker publication has an evangelising purpose. The journals keep Quakers in touch, and allow space for debate and exchange of ideas, while pamphlets and other material are produced for those seeking information about Quakerism (known within Quaker circles as 'enquirers').

PART III

THE LIVED QUAKER EXPERIENCE

4 Quaker Decision-Making

Introduction

This chapter looks at the theory of Quaker decision-making. The actual practice in the Meeting which we studied is discussed in Chapter 8. Quakers approach the making of decisions in the same way as they approach all other aspects of their life, as something to be considered in the light of God's guidance. This applies to any decisions they make: in their personal and domestic lives, in relation to the business of their meetings and in their public life. The ensuing discussion will focus on Quaker business method (i.e. decision-making) in the context of the monthly business meeting held at local level, known as Preparative Meeting, but it is important to remember that the theory of decision-making set out in this chapter is widely applicable to decisions taken by Quakers.

Business Method

Quaker business meetings reduce formality to a minimum. Silent worship precedes and follows the business, a constant reminder that these are Meetings for Worship for Business, not just business meetings, in accordance with Quaker belief that it is impossible to separate the sacred and the secular. The meeting, unhampered by many rules of procedure '... is left free to follow the leadings of the Spirit' (Pollard *et al.*, 1949, p. 42).

The basis of Quaker decision-making is that it involves decisions taken with the agreement of all present, in the light of God's guidance. This does not mean that everyone has to completely agree with every aspect of the decision, but it does mean that everyone must feel it right to let the decision go ahead, even if there are bits of it which they might have expressed differently, or changed in some way. Quakers often speak of achieving 'unity' to describe the situation which is arrived at when the decision is taken. Use of the word 'unity', rather than 'unanimity' is significant. Everyone must be content with the decision and be confident that it is the right thing to do (and for Quakers, the right thing to do is that which is right in the light of God's guidance, which is what they are seeking in their periods of silent worship). However, it is not necessary that everyone should be unanimous in every particular.

> In our meetings for worship we seek through the stillness to know God's will for ourselves and for the gathered group. Our meetings for church affairs, in which we conduct our business, are also meetings for worship based on silence, and they carry the same expectation that God's guidance can be discerned if we are truly listening together and to each other, and are not blinkered by preconceived opinions. It is this belief that God's will can be recognised through the discipline of silent waiting which distinguishes our decision-making process from the secular idea of consensus. We have a common purpose in discerning God's will through waiting and listening, believing that every activity of life should be subject to divine guidance ...
> (*Quaker Faith and Practice*, 1995, para. 3.02.)

It is the belief that seeking the will of God has a part to play in arriving at the agreement of all present which is one of the main features distinguishing the Quaker method of decision-making from that of any secular group which chooses to make its decisions by consensus. Early Quakers were not very precise in their descriptions of the will of God, the 'Inward Light' or the 'Light of Christ', as they often called it, but they were sure that there was only one Light. This meant that if everyone followed the Light, everyone would be led to the same conclusion, i.e. into 'unity'.

> This belief in only one Light underpinned the authority of the gathered meeting, for this was a meeting where individual Friends, following their individual apprehensions of the Light, were led into a common place. Here the meeting was in Truth. Individual leadings were to be tested against the corporate discernment and were ultimately subordinate to the authority of the gathered meeting.
> (Halliday, 1991, p. 10.)

The corporate authority of the meeting is as strong today as it was in the seventeenth century. Decisions are taken not because individuals acting alone think that God's guidance draws them in a particular direction, but because the gathered meeting thinks that a decision is right.

> [Quaker decision making involves a] need for humility and patience, a willingness to contribute what is given to us, and to be receptive to what is given through others. This involves discipline: a sustained alert sensitivity, and, sometimes, a restraint on one's own desire to press a point of view.
> (Doncaster, 1958, p. 71.)

Meetings for Worship for Business not only begin and end with a period of silent worship, but at any time during the meeting anyone present can suggest that a further period of silence be held. Business meetings are also conducted in accordance with Quaker beliefs about how people should treat each other, respecting everyone as valuable, even when expressing opposing points of view, and subjecting everything that is said to serious and prayerful consideration. This is a context of faith and practice, in which the participants behave in a very different way from people engaging in the cut and thrust of debate.

> Each vocal contribution will be something added to the material in the minds of Friends, a fact or an insight or a judgement sincerely given, not in argument or debate, not deliberately criticising a previous contribution, but a statement of truth as seen by the speaker, having significance just insofar as the truth in it is communicated to the group. Silence between such contributions is not a mere pause waiting for words, but a creative element allowing change and growth. (Doncaster, 1958, p. 68.)

It is a process of decision-making which demands considerable self-discipline. However enthusiastic one is about a particular proposal, or however deeply one disagrees with it, the method demands that every contribution made to the discussion must not only be listened to without interrupting, but should, once it has been made, be considered carefully before any reply is made. Since the purpose of the meeting is to take the right decision, in the light of God's guidance, there should be no attempt to influence the outcome by lobbying beforehand (*Quaker Faith and Practice*, 1995, para. 3.04.)

The duty to consider with care all contributions made does not preclude disagreement. The decision-making process is also intimately bound up with the Quaker testimony to truth, which means that it would be wrong to give assent, unless agreement is truly felt to be the correct course. At the same time, there is an emphasis on the value of each individual, and on acknowledging that truth can come from unexpected sources (for example, from people with whose views one generally disagrees).

> ... [Our business method] demands that we shall be ready to listen to others carefully, without antagonism if they express opinions which are unpleasing to us, but trying always to discern the truth in what they have to offer. It calls, above all, for spiritual sensitivity. If our meetings fail, the failure may well be in those who are ill-prepared to use the method rather than in the inadequacy of the method itself.

It is always to be recognised that, coming together with a variety of temperaments, of background, education and experience, we shall have differing contributions to make to any deliberation. It is no part of Friends' concern for truth that any should be expected to water down a strong conviction or be silent merely for the sake of easy agreement. Nevertheless we are called to honour our testimony that to everyone is given a measure of the light, and it is in the sharing of knowledge, experience and concern that the way towards unity will be found ...
(*Quaker Faith and Practice*, 1995, para. 3.05.)

The belief that everyone has a 'measure of the light' is significant. 'Light' to the early Quakers meant Christ; it was his power and spirit which everyone had in some measure, and it was that which they were seeking when making decisions. That is still true for contemporary Quakers, though they would not all necessarily identify the Light exclusively with Christ; belief in divine guidance of some form is a basic conviction which, it has been suggested, has practical consequences. 'It is not easy to give way to someone else or to another point of view; but if one believes that in some way the spirit of God is being liberated in a meeting, one's resistance is weakened and one is alert to find the truth in an unacceptable point of view' (Doncaster, 1958, p. 65).

Clearly, there will be times when it is not possible to reach the unity which it is desired to achieve. In that case, the decision should be left for another time. There is no possibility of solving any impasse by putting the matter to a vote, since Quakers do not vote. '...We do not vote in our meetings, because we believe this would emphasise the divisions between differing views' and inhibit the process of seeking to know the will of God ...' (*Quaker Faith and Practice*, 1995, para. 3.06). Clerks of meetings are reminded that they should not allow decisions to be held over just because it is an easy option, but there may be good reasons for doing this, such as the need for more information, or that everyone needs time to go away and think further about the matter under consideration (*Quaker Faith and Practice*, 1995, para. 3.07).

The Quaker belief in the priesthood of all believers, and their emphasis on decisions taken on the basis of what individuals believe to be right, in the light of God's will stress the importance of the individual. Yet at the same time, decisions are only taken if everyone who is present is content to agree with them; decisions are thus a corporate affair. It is a significant aspect of Quaker business method that it is the corporate discernment of the gathered meeting which possesses the ultimate authority, and not the insight of any one individual (Halliday, 1991, p. 10). The resulting tension between the individual and corporate aspects of Quaker business method are often seen as fruitful: 'The visions and concerns of individuals prevent the Society from being over-traditional and static; the insights of a gathered group prevent it from moving over-hastily in unconsidered enthusiasm' (Doncaster, 1958, p. 63). Quaker business method is not intended to be about everyone present '... falling in courteously with the opinions of the most fluent'; rather it is about everyone contributing what they can (which may be merely keeping silent) and being open to what can be learnt from the contributions of others (Loukes, 1970, p. 141).

The Role of the Clerk

Every Quaker business meeting has a Clerk, whose job is to prepare the business, conduct the meeting, draft the minutes and follow up any decisions which need to be implemented. Usually, the Clerk is assisted in these tasks by an Assistant Clerk; the intention is that the Assistant should be involved in all the Clerk's duties as much as possible. Sometimes assistant clerkship is regarded as a training for future clerkship, but that is not necessarily the case (Redfern, 1993a, p. 7).

The Clerk of a Quaker meeting has a lot of responsibility, but is in theory merely a member of the meeting who has been chosen to undertake this task by virtue of their suitability for it. Unlike the ministers of other Christian denominations, the Clerk has no special religious standing, though they are expected to have considerable spiritual sensitivity (*Quaker Faith and Practice*, 1995, para. 3.12). In preparing the business and introducing it to the meeting, the Clerk is expected to act as '... a servant of the meeting ...' (*Quaker Faith and Practice*, 1995, para. 3.13). Clerks are expected not to state their personal views on matters, but to lay them before the meeting in an objective yet informative fashion, to exercise a 'discipline of detachment' (*Quaker Faith and Practice*, 1995, para. 3.13). If either the meeting or the Clerk wishes that he/she should become more involved in the discussion, it is good practice for the Clerk to leave their position at the Clerk's table and to become an ordinary member of the meeting for that item; the Assistant Clerk can then draft the minute (Redfern, 1993a, p.23).

During discussion, the role of the Clerk is to discern what Quakers habitually refer to as 'the sense of the meeting', so that when discussion ends, it is possible to draft a minute which accurately reflects the corporate view. If the Quaker practice of decision-making is to work effectively, the Clerk needs to be able to discern the sense of the meeting accurately, in other words, to discern where the will of God is leading; this process demands much from the Clerk, in terms of spiritual sensitivity. Clerks must be aware not only of what has been said, but by whom it has been said, and also of the likely views of those who have remained silent; all this is not a simple matter of calculation, but a complex matter of judgement. 'The sense of the meeting depends on the weight of utterances, not on their number' (Doncaster, 1958, p. 68). *Quaker Faith and Practice* makes it clear that it is the Clerk who should '... set the pattern of worshipful listening which should characterise our meetings for church affairs' and emphasises that '[t]he meeting is likely to repose great trust in you, and you bear an important responsibility in enabling the meeting to listen and wait for God's guidance in its deliberations' (*Quaker Faith and Practice*, 1995, para. 3.13).

In addition to possessing the necessary spiritual qualities, the Clerk has to ensure that the meeting is run, in procedural terms, in accordance with Quaker practice, since that is what ensures that the will of God will be found: 'Your experience in the ways of Friends and your understanding of the Quaker business method are very important in helping the meeting to discern God's will and to recognise the way forward' (*Quaker Faith and Practice*, 1995, para. 3.13). The method of making the decision, and the belief that God's will will be discerned if it is followed correctly, are indissoluble.

In his *Handbook for Clerks* Keith Redfern's comments on the nature of clerkship clearly reflect the fact that the Quaker business method relies heavily on Clerks having a knowledge of what might best be described a 'Quaker culture' – not only the formal rules of procedure, but the unwritten rules and ways of behaving: 'Many aspects of clerkship cannot be taught and no-one can expect to learn to be a clerk simply by reading this booklet' (Redfern, 1993a, p. 7). Redfern, having been appointed by the Central Committee of Quaker Home Service to take forward its concern for revitalisation of Meetings for Business, is in a strong position to make such comments. During 1992 he visited 55 Monthly Meeting Clerks, conducting semi-structured interviews with all of them, often meeting them together with their local Preparative Meeting Clerks. Redfern produced both a Report based on his interviews (Redfern 1993b) and a *Handbook for Clerks* (Redfern, 1993a). While both these are primarily concerned with Monthly Meetings, Redfern himself says that much of their content is also applicable to Preparative Meeting Clerks (Redfern, 1993a, p. 8). In his *Handbook* he reinforces his comments about the need for experience of Quaker business methods by cautioning against the importation of secular practice:

> It is important to remember that what may be efficient and useful practice in another context may not necessarily be in keeping with the spirit of Quaker business method, and the temptation to introduce new methods for reasons of expediency should be considered very carefully.
> (Redfern, 1993a, p. 8.)

His report also draws attention to the concerns expressed by some of those whom he interviewed about a lack of knowledge among some Quakers about Quaker business method (Redfern, 1993b, p. 21). Unsurprisingly, this seemed to be a particular problem among Attenders, as opposed to Members. Quakers have no structured way of passing on cultural norms, relying on individuals to learn 'the Quaker way of doing things' by a mixture of experience, attendance at discussion groups and other such activities and by private reading and study.

The writing of the minutes of a Quaker business meeting reflect a marked difference from general business practice. At the end of discussion the Clerk drafts a minute and then reads it out to see if it is acceptable. While the Clerk is writing, the duty of the meeting is to remain quiet. The suggested minute is then read out, and alterations made if necessary, until all present are satisfied that the minute accurately record the decision which has been taken. This can be a lengthy process, but it has been suggested that it ensures that the views of all are taken into account (Decisions, 1998, p. 6). Once a minute has been approved in this way, it must not be altered, except to make minor amendments of spelling and punctuation (*Quaker Faith and Practice*, 1995, para. 3.15).

> Acceptance of a minute must be a deliberate act. Even if it is not thought necessary to read out the whole of an agreed draft minute again at the moment of acceptance, the meeting must be sufficiently aware of its terms from the preceding exercise to be conscious of uniting to accept it ...
> (*Quaker Faith and Practice*, 1995, para. 3.15.)

Clerks are called upon to exercise considerable skill in order to ensure that they carry out their task effectively. While sufficient time must be devoted to thinking about the business in hand, business meetings should not be unnecessarily protracted. The Clerk may have to exercise a disciplinary function, to prevent individuals from speaking for too long. The performance of any such function, while its actual form may vary from Clerk to Clerk, will be carried out in accordance with Quaker practice. Sheeran notes that in London Yearly Meeting (the annual national meeting of Quakers in Britain) if anyone speaks for too long, the Clerk will stand up, to signify that the speaker should sit down: '... this movement is so much a part of Friends practice that the offender is likely to hear "the clerk is standing" [from other Friends present]. Such a remark is ignored at one's peril' (Sheeran, 1983, p. 93).

The Elements of Quaker Business Method

It has been suggested that 'The successful conduct of a Quaker business meeting thus requires rigorous self-discipline, profound humility, patient charity and faithful obedience ...' (Doncaster, 1958, p. 72). These are qualities which, it seems, must be found solely within the participants in the meeting themselves. However, a more searching analysis suggests that the right conduct of Quaker business meetings, though it relies heavily on the personal discipline of participating individuals, also relies on the corporate discipline of the assembled meeting and the techniques used in Quaker business meetings (Halliday, 1991, p. 21), and it is the interaction of these three ingredients which brings about success.

Personal Discipline

An important part of the personal discipline is the cultivation of the ability to know when one is being prompted to do something spiritually (or, as Quakers might say, by the Inward Light) and when it is mere human desire. Halliday argues that this involves living a full and active spiritual life which is firmly grounded in a Quaker context - not just a contemporary context, but including an awareness of Quaker history and Quaker culture. Knowledge of Quaker language is important, and it must be made to have real meaning for the individual, aided by an understanding of its place in the historical development of the Quaker tradition. Understanding the language is itself a discipline, part of the learning process, the spiritual journey (Halliday, 1991, pp. 29/30). Understanding of Quaker language must be accompanied by a grounding in Quaker tradition and practices. The Quaker business method is seen as an integral part of Quaker spirituality.

> Our Meetings for Worship for Church Affairs are far more than a committee tacked on to the main body for dealing with finances and nominations; they are an integral part of the worshipping life of the meeting. Friends have long held that one cannot separate the secular from the sacred: this testimony finds its expression in the spiritual insight Friends have brought to their work for peace, for green concerns, for disadvantaged people and to every aspect of everyday life. Quaker business method is about bringing this insight to the administration of our own affairs and making them an integral part of the spiritual life rather than a drain on it.
> (Halliday, 1991, pp. 31/32.)

Corporate Discipline and Techniques

However faithfully individuals conduct their lives as Quakers, individual endeavour alone is insufficient to guarantee the success of the Quaker business method. It is the meeting which makes decisions, on a corporate basis, and the 'gathered' meeting, composed of individuals who come together to share real spiritual depths, is fundamental to the success of the method (Halliday, 1991, p. 40). A Quaker business meeting is an integral part of a worshipping community, composed of individuals who know each other well and trust one another on a spiritual level. This is a community in which people have been able to '... meet together and know one another in that which is eternal ...'. 'The Quaker method is not simply a technique; it is a faith which finds expression in a method' (Doncaster, 1958, p. 73).

It is the fact that a Quaker business meeting is composed of individuals who all believe that in coming together they will be able to seek the will of God for the decisions they have to take which makes it work. Shared assumptions, shared modes of behaviour and shared expectations as to the quality of the decisions which will be made, all contribute to the success of the Quaker business method.

Another important part of corporate discipline is what lawyers might call 'knowledge of procedure and procedural rules'. Halliday argues that this knowledge is crucial: 'If, as a community we are to come to a communal decision we must share the basic understandings of how business is conducted' (Halliday, 1991, p. 49). In his list of the techniques employed by Quakers which assist their business method, he identifies sitting in a circle or square, speaking briefly unless the subject really demands otherwise, not repeating what has been said before, addressing the meeting as a whole rather than one individual, and drafting and approving the minutes in the meeting. There are also strong conventions about what is not to be done, such as holding private conversations or reading the agenda or other papers while others are talking. These conventions are not merely matters of courtesy:

> [They] are essential to the purpose in hand. They contribute to the unhurried deliberation and corporate searching which are the hallmarks of Quaker decision making. If we really are to search for the will of God for the meeting rather than just a consensus decision then we are embarked on a spiritual rather than a secular quest. The techniques I mention above are all part of that quest.
> (Halliday, 1991, p. 50.)

Since knowledge of Quaker conventions and practices is so vital to the success of the business method, it is unsurprising that those studying it, such as Halliday, should express concern that there is no official method for handing this knowledge on to newcomers. Most Quakers appear to assume that it will be picked up by osmosis, or that if people want to know, they will ask; knowledge of Quaker business method is not necessarily discussed when people apply to become Quakers, and Halliday argues that there is a marked reluctance to correct these who do not use the method correctly (Halliday, 1991, p. 53). Yet, as Redfern points out, if clerks are appointed who are inexperienced in Quaker business method, it can have severe consequences both for the individuals concerned, and the Meeting they are supposed to be assisting (Redfern, 1994, p.26).

The lack of any systematic method of ensuring that Quaker techniques and practices are adhered to is a very significant problem for the Quaker movement as a whole. Its business practices are one of its most distinctive features. They also involve active participation by every individual in a process which demands that they 'act like a Quaker', thus providing an excellent experiential induction into Quaker culture. But these practices will only continue to work in the way they were intended to, and can only act as an experience of Quaker culture, if their distinctive nature, and particular modes of behaviour, are transmitted successfully to newcomers.

Conclusion

The Quaker business method is not infallible. Its dependence on the 'gathered' meeting means that if this depth of corporate spiritual experience is not achieved, the decisions taken will be poorer. Quakers struggle to achieve their ideals, like many other bodies, and they make mistakes (Decisions, 1998, p. 9). However, perhaps the main advantage of the Quaker business method is that '... it can achieve a unity which incorporates the minority position' (Decisions, 1998, p. 7). In a Quaker decision, there are in the end no deep divisions, no winners and losers in the conventional sense. This is not because people have compromised, but because the group has reached 'unity'. It is a method which assumes ownership of the decision by all who are present. Everyone's view is taken into account, everyone who has something to say is listened to, and their ideas are considered seriously. Even someone who disagrees, but says they are willing to put that aside because they believe the decision is right for the group remains part of the group.

In a meeting rightly held a new way may be discovered which none present had alone perceived and which transcends the differences of the opinions expressed. This is an experience of creative insight, leading to a sense of the meeting which a clerk is often led in a remarkable way to record. Those who have shared this experience will not doubt its reality and the certainty it brings of the immediate rightness of the way for the meeting to take.

(*Quaker Faith and Practice*, 1995, para. 3.06.)

5 Method

Introduction

This chapter is concerned with the general background to our analysis of our Meeting. In it we will outline what we take to be the overall value of an ethnography and then go on to discuss the means that we used to gather information for this ethnography.

Ethnography

As with any ethnography this book has both limited and immense ambitions. Its core is no more than our observations of one local Quaker Meeting. We do not claim that that Meeting is typical of other British Quaker Meetings. Indeed we would suggest that there are a number of features, such as its comparatively large size, which are important to our Meeting which would make it unlike many other Meetings. Equally, our observations are of a Quaker meeting in Great Britain and British Quakers account for less than 10 per cent of all Quakers (Heron, 1995, p. 111). 'Quakers today are not simply watching pictures of famine on their televisions; they are farming the inhospitable altiplano in Bolivia; they are facing drought in Turkana' (*Quaker Faith and Practice*, 1995, para. 28.13). Quakers elsewhere often have very different traditions to those to be found amongst British Quakers (Punshon, 1986, p. 253). Even amongst British Quakers Heron, amongst others, has noted that 'variation in practice is very great indeed' amongst Monthly Meetings (Heron, 1995, p. 148) and we would expect no less variation in practice amongst the individual local Meetings, of which our Meeting is but one example, that comprise each Monthly Meeting. Moreover, we would not contend that our observations of Quakers would necessarily hold good for other social groups. Again, on the contrary, we would suggest that there are a number of features, some general to Quakers and some particular to our Meeting, which would make them unlike many other social groups. An ethnography in the end speaks only of the thing observed. What we report we hold to be true for our Meeting during the time we observed and analysed it. Nevertheless, we also

83

think that there is something which is of general instruction in that which we have observed in our Meeting.

This book is not, in itself, a grand theory of the relationship between individuals, societies and dispute avoidance and dispute resolution. Yet this modesty should not distract from the ambition of any work of ethnography.

> Let's begin with the goal of scientific anthropology: to describe and explain the regularities and variations in human behavior ... If we are to understand this diversity, we must begin by carefully describing it.
> (Spradley, 1980, p. 13.)

Grand theories, which do explain the regularities and variations of human behaviour, must be grounded at some stage on empirical observations. If sociology and anthropology is not to be astrology then empirical observations must have their place. Each observation reported is small in its individual import but together they form at least part of the basis for the theory that follows. What we make of those observations, how we disentangle, if we can, the observer from the observed, the intellectual connections we make between observations and the connections between connections, may all be more important than the observations. Nevertheless, empiricism has its place. Indeed 'contra the theoretician, the observer should always have the last word' (Levi-Strauss, 1967, p. 12).

Ethnography makes large claims for the quality of its observations. If this book succeeds it succeeds because, as Kaberry said of Malinowski's work, it provides an 'actuality of relationships and richness of content' and enables the reader to come 'to know the inhabitants...as actors in a changing scene' (Kaberry, 1960, p. 71). What Malinowski was able to do with the Trobriand Islanders justifies in large part anthropology's claim for a separate disciplinary status. An ethnography is more than a quantitative description of the members of a community. It is an attempt to portray the felt life of the community and translate that life into terms that are comprehensible to those who are not of the community; it seeks 'to grasp the actor's point of view' (Kuper, 1996, p. 34). Moreover, it seeks to find not a single truth, whether that be the rules of behaviour within a community or the actual behaviour of that community, but, rather, the 'multi-layered character of ethnographic reality' (Kuper, 1996, p. 16); the complex and contradictory amalgam of behaviour, attitudes, customs and rules that constitutes the community. This is qualitative research in one of its purest forms; an attempt to step into the mind of others. The facts we present are meaningless unless we are also able to give a sense of the lived experience of our Quaker Meeting. The difficulty in doing this both in a theoretical and a practical sense and the difficulty of successfully reporting results in a way which is comprehensible to non-Quakers but faithful to the original material can scarcely be over-estimated.

Understanding the world-view of a group is always difficult even for the most diligent and empathetic outsider. There are large-scale problems such as the effect, if any, of the gender of the observer (Brandes, 1992) and small-scale problems such as the difficulty of taking adequate notes in the particular circumstances of the group studied (Flood, 1983, p. 146; Holdaway, 1983, p. 10). Some anthropologists have challenged the degree to which traditional studies can indeed succeed in seeing the world through another's eyes (Clifford, 1988; Kloos, 1996, pp. 184-185; van Maanen, 1995, pp. 1-4). Because of these difficulties each ethnography has to answer the question how far was it possible to successfully counter the problems of ethnography in the case of this individual study? This chapter is our answer.

Insider and Outsider Research

This study is a joint work by one person (Fiona Cownie) who is, was and hopes to continue to be a participating member of the Meeting which we studied and one person (Anthony Bradney) who is not and who has no desire to be a Quaker. This is also a study written by an academic couple (Collier, 1998, p. 39; Ferber and Loeb, 1997). As will be seen below these biographical facts are important when looking at the research methods which were used in preparing the book.

The reason why the above is important can be illustrated by looking at the problem of Quaker language. One of the more obvious problems in any ethnography involves having to come to grips with a new language (Burgess, 1984, pp. 93-94). The understanding of the language that the ethnographer needs is not just at that level of comprehension which is necessary to gather basic information. Their level of fluency and sophistication must be such as to be able to interpret nuances of meaning so as that they can ascertain motivation and psychology within the community studied. Reading some of the more venerated anthropological studies one marvels at the ability of anthropologists to learn languages to this level in a mere six months (Kuper, 1996, p. 27) or determine the accuracy of a translator, again to this degree, largely by measuring the relative sentence length that the translator used when first speaking in the language of the community and then speaking in the anthropologist's own native language (Llewellyn and Hoebel, 1941, p. 30). Taking some anthropologists at their own estimation one might think that the first requirement for any anthropologist is a facility with languages hitherto known only to the hero of the Doctor Doolittle stories (Lofting, 1922). A reading of the seminal studies in anthropology would suggest that:

[o]nce in the field, he [the anthropologist] transforms himself into a linguistic wonder-worker. He becomes fluent in a language much more difficult for the Westerner than French [although before he failed to master French], without qualified teachers, without bilingual texts, and often without grammars and dictionaries. At least this is the impression he manages to convey.
(Barley, 1983, p. 44)

Evans-Pritchard is unusual in confessing the difficulties of acquiring the language of the subject of one's study.

[T]he whole of my first and a large part of my second expedition were taken up with trying to master the language sufficiently to make inquiries through it, and only those who have tried to learn a very different tongue without the aid of an interpreter and adequate literary guidance will fully appreciate the magnitude of the task.
(Evans-Pritchard, 1940, p. 10)

In truth of course anthropologists frequently accept a very poor level of language knowledge as being sufficient for their purposes. Malinowski, for example, was willing to accept 'conversational command' as sufficient for the start of his enquiries (Hoskins, 1993, p. 96). This is so not just because of the individual failings of anthropologists but because of the inherent limitations of, and barriers created by, language. In his study *Coral Gardens and their Magic,* Malinowski begins a section of the book entitled 'The Translation of Untranslatable Words' with the observation

Let me start with the apparently paradoxical and yet perfectly plain and absolutely true proposition that the words of one language are never translatable into another.
(Malinowski, 1935b, p.11)

Steiner has argued that '[p]oetry will not translate', that at best 'poetry may be paraphrased, imperfectly mimed' (Steiner, 1970, p. 21). He goes on to argue that the reason for this lies not in the special nature of poetic language but in the nature of language itself. The argument

cuts much deeper than verse. It implicates even rudimentary acts of linguistic exchange, the attempt to translate any word or sentence from one language to another. A language is not a passive representation of reality, it does not restrict itself to being a mirror. It is an active world image, selecting certain possibilities of human analysis and behaviour, certain ways of initiating, structuring and recording experience from a total potentiality of

representation. Each language cuts its segment of reality.
(Steiner, 1970, p. 22)

The average anthropologist's linguistic knowledge of the community they
have studied is much less than that that is the case for the average translator
of poetry. If poetry translations must always be partial failures despite the
linguistic knowledge of their translators it seems reasonable to infer that this
is even more so with the act of translation that lies behind ethnographies.
But if anthropologists are to produce ethnographies, if they are to do their
work, they must presume there is some possibility of communication and
that failed translations will still be efficacious to some extent. What
anthropologists aspire to and what they attain is often very different. But
this failing does nothing to undermine the initial proposition. To produce an
ethnography you need to understand the language of your community at a
very sophisticated level. Language remains a problem and arguments over
its use lie at the heart of some of the seminal disputes in anthropology
(Gluckman, 1955; Bohannan 1957; Bohannan, 1965b; Gluckman, 1969;
Moore, 1978, pp. 227-231).

The difficulty presented by dealing with an unfamiliar language is
obvious in traditional accounts of non-literate societies usually conducted in
Africa, Asia or South America by anthropologists from France, the United
States or Great Britain. The language of those studied is not only different
to the language of the observer; it lacks even the faintest of familial
similarities with the observer's own language. Language is, however, also
problematic in ethnographic studies done within complex societies even
where the observer ostensibly speaks the language of the group studied. De
Sousa Santos's classic study of Pasargada is a study of a Brazilian favela in
Rio de Janeiro where the language of the favela is Portuguese. De Sousa
Santos is himself Portuguese. He has written of his study, 'I felt at home in
Pasargada for many reasons: my nationality, language and class origin' (de
Sousa Santos, 1977, p. 8). Nevertheless in an essay on the background to
his study de Sousa Santos described how an early attempt to start his study
led him to a favela other than that which he later described as Pasargada. He
was approached by members of the community who asked what he was
doing. He explained he was doing research using the Portuguese term
'investgacao'. Upon so doing he was escorted out of the favela at gun-point.
Later he learnt the Portuguese term 'investgacao' translated as 'police
investigation' in the language of the favela (de Sousa Santos, 1981, p. 272).
Language, where nuance is vital, can be just as problematic in studies in
complex societies as it is in studies elsewhere. In his study of American
hoboes Spradley found that their argot was 'a rich repository which [held]
the key to our understanding of their culture' but which, although it was a

dialect of English, he nevertheless had to 'decode' (Spradley, 1988, p. 131); Patrick found that being '[b]orn and bred in Glasgow' and having 'two years part-time work' with boys from a Glasgow street gang was insufficient linguistic preparation to easily allow him to follow what they said (Patrick, 1973, p. 15).

Language is a problem in the study of Quakers. As we have already seen in Part II of this book Quakers have their own terminology. Notwithstanding their own perceptions (Heron, 1995, p. 125) they do have peculiarities of speech. Quakers are 'Friends' (that is members of the Religious Society of Friends (Quakers) in Britain). They hold Meetings which are in 'right ordering' (that is properly conducted according to a range of formal and informal rules). Meetings for worship are sometimes 'gathered' (spiritually satisfying for the participants). Friends read or hear things that 'speak to my condition' (give spiritual insight). Friends say 'hope so' in order to indicate assent to a course of action but only in a business meeting and not in any other context. These phrases and many others constitute a Quaker language. Like any other language it can be learnt. However, to come to the study, as does the participant Quaker author of this book, with a knowledge of that language that is bred of an education at a Quaker boarding school from the age of 11 and membership of the Society for many years is an inestimable advantage; to learn a language is one thing, to be a native speaker is another. As with language so with other aspects of Quaker culture.

This study is, in part, an insider account of Quakers with all the advantages that that implies (Roseneil, 1993). As an insider within a community one begins one's research not only with an immense knowledge-base of institutions but also with an already existing sense of the 'imponderabilia of actual life' (Malinowski, 1953, p. 18). If

> [t]he essence of participant observation is the prolonged participation of the researcher in the daily life of the group ... and his or her attempt to empathize with the norms, values and behaviour of that group ...
> (Punch, 1993, p. 185)

the insider is in many ways in the best position to achieve this. This study is in no sense autobiographical; still less is it simply an unmediated description of an anecdotal experience of Quaker life. Nevertheless, a long-standing previous acquaintanceship with Quaker life answers many questions about how the observer can comprehend the community's own view of the material present. It provides a starting-point for our analysis, a beginning for our sense of what are the important questions to ask and what are the important aspects of Quaker life to examine and record. Finally, previous ethnographies have noted a tendency in a host community (conscious or unconscious) to manage access to material so that the ethnographer is either led away from that which the community wishes to conceal or is confirmed in the view the community detects they wish to hold (Hocking, 1993, p. 99). Inside knowledge is a good, though not a certain, guard against both these possibilities. This is an insider study with all the advantages that that brings in allowing the research the deepest access to the community studied (Burgess, 1984, pp. 21-25). Moreover it is insider account where the insider is a complete participant in the sense of the phrase as used by Gold though without the element of deceit involved in Gold's account of that role (Gold, 1957, pp. 219-220).

Being a member of the community you are studying is not however an unalloyed advantage for an anthropologist. For an insider 'there is a danger of missing the sense of wonderment and discovery' (Douglass, 1992, p. 129). To see ourselves as others see us, to see our difference to others, can be as hard as seeing into the mind of another. In a discussion of her research into Greenham Common, also a piece of insider research, Roseneil notes the potential difficulty of being too close 'to see the sociological significance of that which appears [to the insider observer] completely normal, or to be able to form criticisms' (Roseneil, 1993, p. 192). Similarly Muetzelfeldt notes of his research into Friends of the Earth, also a piece of insider research,

> [t]he usual problem for anthropological fieldworkers is to achieve sufficient intimacy with the people in the situation being studied. In my case, the problem was the opposite: to achieve sufficient distance from them.
> (Muetzelfeldt, 1989, p. 51)

As importantly, Levi-Strauss has noted the danger of anthropologists becoming wholly engrossed in the communities they have studied, the danger of 'the complete absorption of the observer by the object of his observations' (Levi-Strauss, 1967, p. 26). Others have noted examples of ethnographers 'going native' and seeing the world only from the perspective of the community they have studied (Punch, 1993, p. 186). When it happens this is unfortunate. Anthropologists should not be publicity agents for the subjects of their study. They should be able to see both what the community says it does and what it actually does (Kuper, 1996, p. 15). They should describe both because it is in the combination of both, not in one or the other, that we find the life of the community. To see a community's professed mores and its actual lived life, which differs from those mores, in your own community can be difficult. Other studies have noted the tendency for individuals in a community to be perturbed by attempts to investigate matters which may show a community in a less than perfect light (Llewellyn and Hoebel, 1941, p. 30). The insider who is an ethnographer may share these tendencies.

The difficulty in being dispassionate about your own community may be heightened when the individual has elected to join the community in question rather than being a member because of an accident of birth. Quakers are now all Quaker by convincement (Hubbard, 1974). You cannot now be born a Quaker even if you are born into a Quaker family of the greatest of antiquity. You must, normally after the age of 16, elect to join and then be accepted into membership of a Monthly Meeting (*Quaker Faith and Practice*, 1995, paras. 11.06 and 11.20). Moreover a Quaker's membership of their community is not something which is usually taken lightly. In a loose sense we all belong to many communities. Some are constituted by our work, some by our place of residence, some by the family into which we are born, some by our choice of recreation and so forth. Not all of these would constitute communities sufficient for the purposes of ethnographic study but in a complex society such as Great Britain what they all share is the fact that, for most people, membership of them is always largely voluntary. We take up and continue our membership in the light of our own perceptions of our best ends (although that perception can, of course, be the result of social forces and pressures of which we are unconscious). In Great Britain membership of a religious group is often seen in this same light by those who are not themselves believers. Knott has written that in looking at academics' attitudes towards religious belief 'one sometimes gets the feeling that religion is like stamp-collecting or playing squash, a minor hobby' (Knott, 1986, 4). In modern England for many believers that perception will often be accurate. Religious beliefs if held at all are usually lightly held.

> In 1991 forty per cent of people questioned in a British Social Attitudes Survey said that their religious beliefs made no difference in their lives. In 1993 25 per cent of people questioned in a British Social Attitudes Survey said they never or virtually never attended church, or meetings associated with their religion.
> (*Social Trends*, 1996, p. 225)

Membership of a religious group for these people frequently signifies little lasting about behaviour or belief. Either few obligations are seen as being entailed in claiming to belong to a particular religious tradition or those obligations are easily set aside in the face of countervailing demands. But for committed believers, and many, probably most, Quakers are committed to their belief in this sense, religion is not seen as being voluntary. Religions choose them, not they it (Dummett, 1986, pp. 10-11). One member of our Meeting noted that Meeting was for them and their partner 'a spiritual anchorage and socially our main anchorage too'. Belief in such a context is a command which comes before other demands and which is an important part of the believer's sense of self. If anthropologists in general find difficulty in writing about the full measure of the subject of their study, sometimes being more enthusiasts than analysts, how much more difficult the task is for the person writing about a community that they have made a conscious choice to become a part of because they believe that it offers the best possible spiritual and emotional support for them. Moreover, the Meeting that we discuss in this book is the participant author's Meeting. This creates a two-fold difficulty. It is normal in anthropological research to enter the field and then withdraw from it before undertaking the analysis. Other accounts of insider research have stressed the especial importance of this withdrawal in the cases of insider research (Muetzelfeldt, 1989, p. 53). However, in this instance, the participant author has no wish to withdraw from the Meeting that she considers a necessary part of her spiritual life. Secondly, the events discussed in this book are truly ones that the participant author took part in. The discussions were discussions that she had a free and equal say in. The issues were ones that she held views about. As with any other member of Meeting her presence in Meeting affected what happened. In no sense was she at any stage simply a value-free sociologist noting what was happening before her eyes. And all this is in the context of a study where question of the balance between leadership and consensus (or leadership by the Spirit) and between individuality and community was part of our research agenda. Holdaway had the problem that he was a police-sergeant in the community he was observing (Holdaway, 1983). How far was he, by the use he made of his power as sergeant, creating the events that he was later to write up as an ethnographer? How far was the participant author altering what was happening in front of her because of the research agenda that, as researchers, we both possessed? It is here that we find the advantage in this study not just being by both someone who is an insider but also by someone who is an outsider.

The advantage of being an outsider in studying a community is in seeing that which seems different. What one sees as everyday behaviour can become extraordinary when seen through the eyes of another who has not seen this behaviour before. It is therefore important to specify in what way and to what degree this study is indeed in part a study by an outsider because the outsider status of the non-participant observer in this instance is to some extent questionable. An outsider whose wife is a Quaker in the Meeting studied and who knew some of the members of Meeting studied long before the study took place, as is the case here, may not be seen by everybody as being a study by an outsider at all. Indeed a case for arguing that both authors are in some senses members of the community studied could be made. The membership list for Meeting notes the fact that a Quaker is married (though not the name of their spouse) if there is a spouse who is not a member of the Meeting. Non-Quaker spouses or partners are frequently invited to the Meeting's social events (though in the case of this non-Quaker author less frequently attend). In our personal experience legal advice, as well as advice about universities for children, is sought almost as readily from the non-Quaker spouse as from the Quaker. Members of Meeting have eaten in our house. We have dined with them. In such a case a non-participant may not be a member of the Meeting but one is less an outsider than many others. One might then ask whether or not the consequences of tact and involvement might blind this kind of outsider to the realities of the interaction of the community just as easily as the insider is blinded. Indeed in our preliminary discussions about this study with Meeting even one member of Meeting queried whether the non-participant author could be said to be truly independent of Meeting. To answer this one needs to specify the nature of being an outsider and what one means by independence in this context.

The direct observations in this study were made by the participant member. All interviews were conducted by that person and all observations of both meetings for worship and business meetings were made by that same person. The non-participant author has attended only two Quaker meetings in his life. The first was a Quaker Meeting specially drawn up by Meeting in order to mark the marriage of the two authors of this study. A Quaker marriage ceremony would have been inappropriate because in such a ceremony both spouses have to say that they are marrying with 'divine assistance' (*Quaker Faith and Practice*, 1995, para 16.36). As an atheist the non-Quaker author was not willing to say that which he held to be palpably untrue. The Meeting held was thus unique and therefore in many respects atypical. The second Quaker meeting the non-participant has attended was the Preparative Meeting at which the authors of the study sought and received the Meeting's permission to carry out the research. Thus, whatever personal knowledge of members of Meeting the non-participant might have, there has been no religious involvement with the Meeting or participation in what the Meeting would see as being its most central and significant moments. As importantly there is a clear philosophical divide between the non-participant author of this study and the members of Meeting.

Being an atheist, as the non-participant author is, does not prevent you from being a Quaker. Many Quakers attach no special importance to either the Christian message or to the creed of any other religious tradition, seeing instead a general immanence of spirit in everything (Dandelion, 1996, pp. 156-162). Krishnamurturi's dictum, 'the truth is a pathless land', is sometimes cited. Some Quakers, both in the Meeting we studied and in general, describe themselves as atheists. One member who was interviewed for this book simply and straightforwardly said in the interview 'I don't believe in God'. Laplace's remark that he had no need of the hypothesis that God exists has been cited with approval in an article in one of the leading Quaker journals, *The Friend* (Hewlett, 1996). However, whilst Quakers are divided on the existence, nature and importance of God as we have seen in Part II all Quakers see an importance in membership of the community of Quakers. Whilst sometimes intensely individualistic in their beliefs Quakers are always members of a community. Membership brings 'corporate insight' (Heron, 1995, p. 91) which is why Quakers continue to belong to the group. It is in this aspect that the non-participant author differs most markedly from the group studied. Quakers of whatever persuasion take sustenance from their Meeting. They strive to reach agreement with other members of the group and believe in the authority of decisions taken by the group. Membership of Meeting is important to them. Most, perhaps all, will agree that 'the group often has a wisdom which can seldom be justified on logical grounds but which is, nevertheless, superior to the wisdom of the individual' (*Quaker Faith and Practice*, 1995, para. 12.08). On the basis of the theoretical position taken in previous work by the non-participant author he would argue that in this Quakers are both psychologically and philosophically profoundly mistaken in this priority given to the group (Bradney, 1993, ch. 2). He would contend that ethical decisions, and in consequence of ethical decisions all decisions, have to be made by an individual who, in the existential mode, takes sole and total responsibility for those decisions. Groups, including Meeting, are usually a hindrance not a help in this decision-taking.

The other factor which guarantees that the non-Quaker author remains an outsider is his refusal to subscribe to the most fundamental tenet of Quakerism. If there is any credal statement for Quakers it is the proposition that 'there is that of God in every man' (Hubbard, 1974, p. 73). The non-participant author, once again on the basis of previous work, would hold that this is either not true or that, if it is true, nothing of significance follows from it. He would prefer Salman Rushdie's comment '[w]e have to learn how to be human. Some of us get there and some of us don't' (Akhtar, 1989, p. 31). It is these disagreements which makes this study truly in part a study by an outsider. For the purposes of this book the point is not the accuracy or even the value of the theoretical stance taken by the non-participant author. It is rather the fact that in consequence of that stance Quaker instincts, Quaker motivation, Quaker methods remain as unacceptable to the non-participant author after the study as they were before it; although now known they still seem unfathomably strange.

Collaborative Research

One final point needs to be noted. Collaborative research is always difficult and in some senses always suspect. If work is divided up and parcelled out between authors it is not truly collaborative. The result is simply a collection of essays by two or more people bound into a book and there is no particular value in the 'collaboration'. If it claims to be the joint thoughts of two people then it raises the question of how ideas, which seem inherently individualistic, can come from more than one mind. This is still more the case when, as in this instance, the two authors claim a fundamental difference in perspective and further claim that that fundamental difference is central to the work that they are writing. On this matter we have can say only one thing. Here the fact of our marriage and the fact that we have worked in the same department for many years seems pertinent. We have literally lived this research for the last five years. Our discussions of Quaker methods go back far further than that. Whilst we have produced other work, individually and together, during this time this research has been an important part of our lives. This has been more than an interchange of drafts of chapters. In our understanding of the working of Meeting at many points we can no longer see where one person's ideas start and another's stop. Our perceptions which started as an insider on the one hand and an outsider on the other have become conjoined in a single view of the nature of Quaker life in the Meeting we have studied. We continue to differ, as we doubtless always will, about the value of that life. In this sense this work is a collaboration.

Meeting's Co-operation

Before we began this research we discussed what we would like to do with a number of members of Meeting. Later we approached Preparative Meeting and explained what we wanted to do. We explained both the way in which we intended to gather information and what we proposed to do with it. We also explained the purpose of our research and the debates that we saw it as being a contribution to. We only began our research in earnest after Preparative Meeting had given its consent. If that consent had not been given we would have abandoned the project. We are in consequence very grateful for Meeting's co-operation in this venture. Some members of Meeting saw their consent as contributing to Quaker 'Outreach', the Quaker attempt to explain to the outside world what Quakers think and how Quakers live. Others thought that Meeting might find out something about itself when the results of our observations were available. We hope both groups will find their hopes fulfilled.

'[E]thnographic research always pries into the lives of informants' (Spradley, 1980, p. 28). We have tried to keep the level of our prying to a minimum and to reveal through publication only those results which are necessary for our arguments. We have not identified our Meeting. Nothing follows from its name. Similarly we have not identified those individual members of Meeting whose remarks we quote. We wish, in so far as it is possible to do so, to preserve the privacy of Meeting from the outside world. We also wish to preserve the privacy of individual members of Meeting from each other. We could have changed the names of those who we quoted as is commonly done in studies such as these and then attributed those names to quotations. However, this would not have ensured anonymity for those who we quoted. The numbers in Meeting are small. Attributing a series of remarks to a particular person would have made it easy for other members of Meeting to identify that person, particularly if characteristics of previous office within Meeting or employment or the like were added. For this reason, very occasionally we have had to make small adjustments to the reported background of an interviewee in this book in order to preserve their privacy.

Preserving the privacy of individual members of Meeting both from the outside world and from each other has presented a number of problems. Unlike most other researchers we have worked in the knowledge that our book would be read by those who are the subject of the study. Protecting privacy has meant that it is difficult to portray an idea of the individual characters of Meeting. Equally, it has meant that we have been unable to discuss in detail particular grievances that have arisen in Meeting. Our concern with protecting privacy has meant that some common methods in legal anthropology were not open to us. For example, many studies in legal anthropology over the decades have used a form of the trouble-case method, focusing on particular disputes as a way of explaining the nature of the law within the community in question. This method was not open to us. Using the trouble-case method in a small community is only possible if you are unconcerned about the privacy of your subjects. It is regrettable that some detail is absent from this study and we accept that it detracts to some extent from the depth of the picture that we are able to draw. Nonetheless, in this instance, we would accept that the right to privacy laid out in the Socio-Legal Studies Association's Ethical Statement (S.L.S.A., 1999, p. xxii) should be upheld. Finally, we should note that this concern about privacy is one which is seen as pressing by us as authors rather than as being important by members of Meeting. In early discussions about this project the view that privacy was unnecessary was put to us by a number of members of Meeting. Our view, on the basis of our reading and our knowledge of reactions to other studies, is that there is always some potential risk for a group and for individual members of that group when they agree to a study such as this. Day-to-day behaviour can seem less innocuous and more threatening or unacceptable when set down on paper (Whyte, 1984, p. 205). Collins' PhD thesis on Dibdenshaw Meeting does identify members of Meeting and does attribute remarks to those members. Even though that thesis has never been published this invasion of privacy did cause difficulties in that Meeting (Collins, 1994). Publication is a further risk (Hammersley and Atkinson, 1995, pp. 269-273). The degree of that risk is greatly increased if the identity of the group or, more importantly, the members of that group is known. We were not willing to increase the degree of risk.

Period of Study

We first began this study in 1994 when we sought Meeting's co-operation. The period of study is important in an ethnography. The shorter the period of study, the less convincing the ethnographer's claim to a rich and full picture of the community they have studied. The duration of the study is a little less important in this instance because of the insider knowledge of one of the authors. We have not, of course, spent the last five years continuously in the field. We have not had the opportunities of prolonged intense involvement that were, for example, afforded to Malinowski (Malinowski, 1953, p. 16). We have had teaching and administrative commitments in our Faculty, we have produced (individually and together) various other essays and books on topics not directly related or not related at all to this project, we have both been involved with professional associations and, very occasionally, we have had a private life. We did, however, find the period of time over which this project has extended an advantage in two respects. First, it allowed us to gather more data than would otherwise have been possible. We were able to significantly alter direction and to go back and gather new material where we became aware of gaps and faults in our work. Malinowski, amongst many others, has noted that as one progresses in field work one becomes aware of early errors. In *Coral Gardens and their Magic* he entitles one section 'Some Detailed Statements About Errors of Omission and Commission' (Malinowski, 1935a, pp. 462-482). Even when one has the opportunity to correct initial mistakes the result is far from perfect. Like Malinowski we still feel our data is far from perfect. Nevertheless we feel that the time the study has taken has enriched it. Secondly, after we had alerted Meeting to our work by asking its permission to undertake the research we were then able to allow time for members to forget what we were doing and resume their normal lives. We did not feel under any ethical duty to continually remind Meeting or its individual members what they had agreed we could do. In the early days of our research members of Meeting would bring stories saying, 'this will interest you'. Some openly wondered how what they were doing would look to an outside audience. An observer effect was clearly present. More latterly, however, the few who have expressed interest have said, 'whatever happened to that research you were doing'. This study has taken longer than we anticipated. We would argue that that extra time strengthens rather than weakens it.

Sources of Information

We take the information for our analysis of Meeting from three main sources.

First, for a period of 12 months the participant author kept a diary detailing what happened and what was said at the weekly Meeting for Worship, the monthly Preparative Meeting, meetings of Elders, meetings of House Committee and the meetings that she had in consequence of being Assistant Clerk for the Meeting at that time. This diary describes only a small fraction of the things that happened at Meeting during this period. There were committees whose meetings were not observed and gatherings of Quakers from the Meeting that were not attended. That which was not seen exceeded that that was seen. This is always the case with any ethnography. To claim that it is physically possible to observe all the activities of the community that one is studying is to put the status of that group as a community into question by saying that it does so little, meets so infrequently that one person can see (or have reported to them) everything. As Malinowski's diary of his period in the Trobriand Islands demonstrates there is selection in what one chooses to look at and selection in what one chooses to record (Malinowski, 1967). Almost inevitably, there is regret in what one finds one has not observed or not recorded (Malinowski, 1935a, pp. 462-482).

There was, of course, deliberation in what we chose to observe for the purposes of the diary. The weekly Meeting for Worship and the monthly Preparative Meeting are the core of the corporate face of Meeting. Meeting for Worship is in many senses the reason for Meeting existing whilst Preparative Meeting is the venue for all important business decisions. Preparative Meeting is the place to which other committees that were not observed reports. Elders are responsible for the spiritual life of the Meeting and are the only people who have any official disciplinary role in Meeting (*Quaker Faith and Practice*, 1995, para. 12.12). Whilst Elders are not seen as having a 'higher position' (*Quaker Faith and Practice*, 1995, para. 12.07) the fact that they should be 'known and accessible' to members of Meeting

(*Quaker Faith and Practice*, 1992, para 12.06) suggested that their meetings would be of particular interest for this study. The Clerk of Meeting is responsible for the administration of Preparative Meeting and the Assistant Clerk works with them. Again there is no suggestion that either the Clerk or Assistant Clerk are thereby superior to any other member of Meeting. Indeed *Quaker Faith and Practice* does not use the upper-case when referring to either office emphasising the instrumental or service character. (The upper case is generally not used in descriptions of offices and positions in Quaker literature indicating the non-hierarchical nature of the faith.) Nonetheless the Clerk 'bears the final responsibility for preparing the business, conducting the meeting and drafting the minutes' whilst the Assistant Clerk should 'share in all the clerk's duties as much as possible' (*Quaker Faith and Practice*, 1995, para 3.12). Their work thus gives them a centrality to the life of Meeting which is once more of particular interest for this study. Finally House Committee, whose functions are largely concerned with the maintenance of the Meeting House, is illustrative of the more mundane side of Meeting's life being concerned with decision-making which is often more technical than principled in its nature.

After an initial analysis of the diary noted above at a later stage in the study the participant author conducted a series of 19 semi-structured interviews with members of Meeting. In combining interviews and participant observation in this study we hoped that 'the data from each can be used to illuminate the other' (Hammersley and Atkinson, 1995, p. 131). These interviews lasted between 45 minutes and three hours. Interviewees were selected as being representative of a cross-section of Meeting using our own knowledge of Meeting and the opinions of members of Meeting that we talked to. The oldest person that was interviewed was 86 and the youngest 36. This age profile roughly reflects that of Meeting. The interviewees had been Quakers for very varying times. In some cases they had been born into Quaker families when Quakers still had the notion of birthright Quakers whilst in others their experience of being a member of Meeting was of less than two years. Most had been Quakers for many years. This is generally reflective of our Meeting which does attract new members but only at a rate in the single figures each year but also loses very few members. Three of the interviewees were Attenders whilst the others were Members. Approximately one third of Meeting are Attenders and our sample is thus somewhat biased to the experience of Members though we found little difference of significance in the answers of Attenders and those of Members. All the people who were questioned had some experience of holding office in Meeting or serving on one of Meeting's various committees. Once again there is some bias in this since not all Attenders in Meeting have been a member of a committee or have held any kind of office. This bias was deliberate. One of the focuses of this research is the Quaker business method and it was therefore important that our interviewees had some experience of that method. Nine of those interviewed were or had been involved with Quakers at a level beyond Meeting and the Monthly Meeting of which it is a constituent part. The ages of this small group reflected the age range of those interviewed as a whole. This group could judge Meeting's behaviour in the light of an experience of wider Quaker practice. Whilst we put no more weight on the answers given by this group than we did the answers given by everyone else we were conscious that there was a utility in answers that could see things in a broader light. Six of those interviewed were male. As compared with the gender balance in Meeting this means that the group interviewed is somewhat biased towards women but, for reasons we discuss in Chapter 6, we do not believe that gender is a significant issue in this study. Questions in the interviews focused on issues that had arisen as a result of the diary that had been kept as well as matters that had seemed pertinent to us when we first began the study. Most interviews were conducted in the houses of the interviewees although some were conducted in our own house. In all cases interviews were taped (with the permission of the interviewee) and in addition a note was taken of the interview. An attempt was made to ask all interviewees all questions but in some cases this proved to be impossible.

Finally, during the period of the study the participant author was also, at various times, Assistant Clerk, Convenor of House Committee, Convenor of a special committee set up to consider the future of House Committee, a member and sometimes Convenor of committees to appoint three successive Wardens and an Elder. In the case of the first two sources of information, the diary and the notes and tapes of interviews, the information was equally available to both authors. In the case of this third source the information obtained was in the first instance available to the participant author. However, our ongoing conversations about Quaker life and its relevance to our scholarly concerns about the nature and practice of law meant that behaviour in these venues was constantly coming to the fore. The less formal observations made in these areas have to some extent informed our analysis.

Verification

Checking the validity of observations made in an ethnography is almost as difficult for the authors of a study as it is for its readers. In the end for us there is only our Meeting and only that Meeting at the time that we observed it. Observations of other Meetings and analyses of Quakers in general can, in the final analysis, neither confirm nor deny the validity of our work. Even later observations of the same Meeting would be observations of another Meeting. For some writers, even observations made at the same time could not necessarily be used to verify or falsify our account. Pitt-Rivers has suggested that, in the end, all ethnographic analyses are personal directed towards the larger intellectual concerns of the observer.

> [F]ieldwork is an intensely personal and intuitive affair and no man can grasp all the aspects of a given society, nor hope his account, however clear his vision and however aware he may be of his prejudices, will survive the passing of his age ... All fieldwork responds to a problem, originating in the fieldworker's own society, which is ultimately assuaged, if not resolved for him, by the unique perspective that anthropology contributes.
> (Pitt-Rivers, 1992, pp. 136-137)

Nevertheless the history of previous enthnographies suggests that simply taking a work on trust is dangerous. The controversy over the accuracy and even the good faith of Mead's observations of adolescent Samoans for example indicates that for both author and reader some attempt should be made to verify findings (Freeman, 1983). Even Llewellyn and Hoebel, whose work The Cheyenne Way is far from a model of methodological integrity, sought to cross-check their material with earlier work by George Bird Grinnell (Llewellyn and Hoebel, 1941, pp. 38-39).

There has been comparatively little sociological or anthropological enquiry into contemporary British Quaker life. There are much richer veins of material which look at the history of Quakers and at their theology. These, however, are only of tangential value to this study. We have looked at two published book-length studies of Quakers and two unpublished PhD theses. Of the published studies one by Dandelion, is a sociological account of the theology of modern British Quakers (Dandelion, 1996). There is thus a difference in methodological perspective and critical focus when compared with our own study although part of the data source for this study was a period of limited participant observation at two Meetings (Dandelion, 1996, p. 30). The second published study, by Sheeran, is based in part upon participation observation of Quakers in Philadelphia Yearly Meeting (Sheeran, 1983). One of Sheeran's central interests is decision-taking amongst Quakers. There is thus a close similarity between his work and our own. We found his book particularly beneficial in the early stages of our own analysis. Nonetheless too close a similarity between our work and his should not be expected. As we have observed earlier the British Quaker tradition and Quaker traditions elsewhere are not the same. Sheeran himself notes that, for example, the different history of American Quakerism has involved a different historical relationship between central and local Quaker bodies (Sheeran, 1983, pp. 109-110). In addition Sheeran's study focuses much more on the work of the Clerk and the making of minutes than we do, looks both at central as well as local decision-taking and does not attempt any ethnographic account at all. Of the two recent PhD theses that focus on Quakers, which we located with the assistance of the librarian at Woodbrooke College, one by Pluss, *A Sociological Analysis of the Modern Quaker Movement,* is a sociological account which attempts to situate contemporary British Quakerism within a generally Durkheimian framework (Pluss, 1995). We found Chapter 5 of this of assistance. The other thesis by Collins, *The Sense of the Meeting: An Anthropology of Vernacular Quakerism,* is an ethnographic account of Dibdenshaw Meeting (Collins, 1994). Although we only discovered this work very late in our study we found it to be a valuable account which prompted us to return to our data to ask new questions. It also confirmed for us our pre-existing view that modern British Quakerism functions differently in different local meetings.

6 Meeting

The Failure of Legal Anthropology

This ethnography suffers from the fault of all ethnographies whose concern is with just a single issue in the community that is being studied. By directing the reader's attention to factors pertinent to that one issue the reader's attention is focused and, in the context of anthropology, therefore, because of that focus, distorted. The ethnography looks not at the way in which the community lives and sees the world but at one aspect of the community's interaction. Yet it is central to modern anthropology to argue that the whole life of the community is interconnected and that if one is to understand one aspect one must understand the whole (Malinowski, 1935b, pp. 454-455). It is, after all, this attempt to study 'peoples' rather than 'people', cohesive semi-autonomous communities rather than individuals, that separates social anthropology from sociology (Lewis, 1976, p.16). To argue that the issues that we have chosen to focus on, Quaker dispute settlement, dispute avoidance and decision-making, are things which are of defining importance for the group itself, although true, does not meet the point. Nor is it sufficient to point to the fact that there is a long tradition of legal anthropology which, either in its writing or in its reading, suffers from precisely this fault of particularisation. It is true that many people have written works solely concerned with legal anthropology before. It is still more true that many readers, interested in law or dispute settlement, have read only the works of an author concerned with what they thought was their interest and neglected the wider oeuvre of the author. Many in law schools will have read Malinowski's *Crime and Custom in Savage Society*, a few *The Sexual Life of Savages* and virtually nobody *Coral Gardens and their Magic*. Malinowski may have attempted 'synchronic analysis', relating each level of society and each institution one to another, (Malinowski, 1935b, pp. 454-455), and thereby made himself an anthropologist but few of his readers in law school will have attempted it in their reading of him. Nevertheless multiplying previous error is not usually seen as the best means of reducing it. Nor, finally, does it help, in this instance, to abandon the traditional rule-centred paradigm's interest in the search for law in one's chosen community in favour of the more open process paradigm's concern

103

with dispute settlement (Comaroff and Roberts, 1981, pp. 5-17). Such an approach may be less ethnocentric but is does not cure the, literal, partiality of the analysis.

The problem of the law school's partial use of social anthropology is part of a wider problem in the law school's use of the social and humane sciences. Overcoming the narrowly focused positivistic research paradigm in law may have made life intellectually more interesting but it is has not made it any easier (Bradney, 1998). The positivist research agenda was clear even if, at the end of the day, it proved capable only of giving substantial answers to trivial questions and trivial answers to substantial questions. Methods and disciplines from outside law which are now used in law schools have a way of enforcing their own agendas on the law school. Questions and links which could once be dismissed as 'not being our business' now force themselves on our attention (Travers, 1993). If we use social anthropology or sociology or philosophy or literature in our examination of law or dispute settlement we are challenged to say why we are using some of it and not all of it and to show that, in using some of a discipline but not all of it, we are not thereby misusing the concepts and methods of that discipline. Hurried comments about the time available to today's ever busier academic are not intellectually convincing as an answer. If we cannot make the efforts necessary to do all of the work that has to be done we should make way for those that can.

Our solution to this problem for legal anthropology and the use in law schools of anthropology is this chapter. In it we have set out a description of our Meeting and its life. This description is not directly concerned with decision-taking or dispute settlement. Rather it provides the context for that which follows. We will have much to say about the way in which Quaker culture transforms what are, on superficial examination, very similar activities to those that occur in communities outside Quaker circles. Our description of Meeting and its activities in this chapter together with our description of Quaker history, contemporary Quakers and the theory of Quaker decision-taking in Chapters 2 to 4 constitute our attempt to substantiate this argument. The brevity of the description does not give as rich a picture as we would have wished. It does, however, do something to bring Meeting out of the shadow of our otherwise ever present research concerns. The chapter is set in the present tense and where figures are quoted they were true for Meeting at the time that we were writing. Where, however, there have been any significant changes to Meeting during the time of our study we have noted that fact.

Meeting

The Meeting that we studied is located in a city of approximately 300,000 inhabitants. It is the only Meeting in that city though there are a number of other Meetings, all of which are much smaller, in nearby local towns. Our Meeting together with these other nearby local Meetings constitute a Monthly Meeting. The total number of members of our Meeting varied slightly during the period of our study but was always in the order of 200 people. This is rather large for a Quaker Meeting. The other adjacent local Meetings were of the order of 30 to 50 people.

There are no geographical jurisdictions for Quakers. People may join any Meeting they wish to if that Meeting will accept them. Thus it is not surprising that a number of members of our Meeting came from outside the city in which the Meeting was found nor is it surprising that in some cases their homes were closer, sometimes considerably closer, to other Meetings. Slightly more surprising is the fact that, with the exception of one couple, those living within the city and its environs within which our Meeting is situated had not chosen to worship at other local Meetings. Although some people who were interviewed expressed disquiet at the size of Meeting, expressing the wish for a smaller Meeting, the continued size of our Meeting attests to a comparative success in its being attractive to Quakers.

Quaker Faith and Practice notes, '[t]oo large a meeting can ... cause ... difficulties in pastoral care, and in achieving a sense of community' (*Quaker Faith and Practice*, 1995, para. 4.31). The tension between the desire for the intimacy of a small Meeting and the size created by a successful Meeting in the case of our Meeting may in part be dissipated by the fact that some groups meet for worship outside the normal venue of the Meeting House and the normal time for weekly worship, 10.30 a.m. on Sunday. One small group has met each weekday in one of two adjacent member's houses for 12 years. This group is not in any sense schismatic. Most members of this group continue to worship regularly at the Meeting House on Sundays. The group meets simply because its members feel a need for a communal experience of worship on a daily basis. Another small Meeting is held in another member's house every Saturday. Yet another group meets elsewhere in the city. Meeting for Worship at the Meeting House is not only the relatively large 10.30 a.m. Sunday Meeting. During school term-time there is a Meeting for Worship on Wednesdays at 12.45 p.m. For a number of years during the period of our study there was an 8.30 a.m. early morning Meeting for Worship on Sunday at the Meeting House in addition to the 10.30 a.m. Meeting but this has now been discontinued because of lack of interest. More recently a small group has taken to holding a Sunday weekly Meeting for Worship not at the Meeting House but at another property owned by the Meeting. The time of this Meeting overlaps with the time of the Meeting for Worship at the Meeting House in a way that enables those attending the small meeting to complete their worship and then return to the Meeting House in order to socialise with other members of Meeting in the normal manner. Those attending this Meeting for Worship are not necessarily out of sympathy with the main Meeting. One person who attended the new Meeting for Worship said that they were 'torn between' the two Meetings and that although they saw the disadvantages in a large Meeting they missed attending it. However, one of our interviewees, who did not themselves attend this Meeting for Worship, described this separate Sunday Meeting for Worship as being a place for those who were disaffected with Meeting. At present the directory for Monthly Meeting lists the existence of this new Meeting, giving a map of its location, the time of its weekly Meeting and the address of a person to send correspondence to, but notes that all those who use this Meeting are members of our Meeting. Those who use the new Meeting have the letter W attached to their names in the directory. At present there are nine such people. In time this Meeting may prove schismatic but at present it could as readily be regarded as illustrative of the process of adaptation which enables our Meeting to survive as a community whilst catering to the differing individual needs of its members. We have regarded those people who attend this meeting as continuing to be part of the community of our Meeting and some are included in those that were interviewed.

The city in which our Meeting is located is divided into 18 postal districts. Slightly over 50 per cent of the members of our Meeting live in just one of those postal districts. Whilst some postal districts contain a higher level of residential accommodation than others this concentration into one postal district does not suggest a random distribution of Quakers throughout the city. Closer examination of the residential choices of Quakers in our Meeting is even more striking. Twenty-one of the Quakers living within the postal district favoured by our Meeting live in nine streets which are immediately proximate to each other. A number of interviewees described this area as the 'Quaker acre'. The Meeting House for our Meeting is within the favoured postal district but not within the Quaker acre. A further 30 Quakers live in the streets that stretch the two miles between the Quaker acre and the Meeting House. This remarkable residential concentration cannot go unremarked.

In part this concentration can be accounted for by the fact that Quakers not infrequently marry Quakers and that children of Quakers, once they reach the appropriate age, not infrequently themselves become members. Thus one house may have two or more members in it contributing to the combination noted. However, only 17 households within the chosen district contributed more than one member to Meeting. In any event the effect of family membership would, on a random basis, produce pockets of Quakers throughout the city not a concentration into one postal district. The concentration that has occurred is in part enhanced by members selling houses privately to each other rather than putting them up for sale on the open market. Houses that become Quaker houses within the chosen district and still more within the Quaker acre are thus more likely to stay Quaker. One house within the Quaker acre is currently in its third generation of Quaker owners. Yet the total number of such private sales within Meeting is small, most Quakers buy or rent homes in the normal manner, and it does not answer the question why do Quakers congregate together in this fashion?

A resident of the city in which Meeting is located would have no difficulty in answering the question, why do Quakers live where they choose to live. The area chosen simply represents some of the more attractive housing in the city in question. The area is of a mixed character and divides into three well-known residential districts. The housing is varied in size from small two bed-roomed terraced houses up to substantial family homes. A lot of it is Victorian or Edwardian though there are some more modern properties dating from the 1950s onwards. It is mainly located in comparatively safe leafy streets with acceptable local schools. A very large percentage of the properties are in good condition. There are several nearby large municipal parks which are well maintained. There are good local shops and there is easy access to the city centre. It is not quite the most expensive housing in the city but it is very close to being that and, although the cost of housing in the area varies depending on the size of the house in question and the precise location of the house in the area, in all cases houses of the same size are readily available elsewhere in the city for much lower prices. Some of the more affluent business people choose to live slightly outside this area of the city but the particular occupational and social groups, drawn from the relatively prosperous middle classes, flock to the same suburbs chosen by Quakers. Social workers, teachers and professionals (including university academics) frequent the areas. The fact that Quakers have in large numbers the desire to choose these areas in which to live and the means to realise these desires says something about the Meeting as a community.

British Quakers are not a representative cross-section of British society. This generalisation holds good for our Meeting. Whilst some come from working-class backgrounds none of the members of our Meeting could, by reference to the usual indicators, be said to be truly working class at present. Their incomes, education, employment and way of life are mostly solidly middle-class. Indeed the lack of variation in their choice of employment is striking. In deciding who to interview for this study one factor we did not take account of was the employment of the potential interviewee. However, when we reviewed the employment of those that were interviewed we found that 15 of the 19 people described themselves as being teachers in some kind of sense. It is true that the precise nature of their work as teachers varied considerably. Some were teachers in secondary or private schools, some were teaching on a private part-time basis, some taught in colleges, some were university academics and some had retired from teaching. Nonetheless the choice of a form of teaching as a suitable occupation is indicative of the kind of world-view to be found in Meeting. The point can be taken further. Comparatively few of the Meeting work in the private sector. Those that do are, in the main, professionals. Most have chosen occupations that give the worker a relative degree of autonomy and a sense of ownership of their job. Moreover, most jobs are ones where it is clear what the worker has themselves created and where that which has been created can be justified in social and theological terms. Put simply, few in our Meeting chose to work in a Fordist work-place.

What you do, to members of Meeting, is more important than what you earn, and it is important that you do something that is, in a Quakerly sense, 'worthwhile'. However, Quakers usually have the educational background and the personal traits which will mean that, even if they do not maximise their earning capacity, they will still be materially comfortable when compared with the average in society. Later in this chapter we will argue that Meeting is in some ways a diverse and heterogeneous place. It is important that we also note what unites it. What is significant here is not just the earning capacity of those in our Meeting. This varies considerably. Some are unemployed, some live on private income and others have the range of salaries that one would expect with the range of occupations they had chosen. On average most in our Meeting are comfortably off, perhaps very comfortably off, compared to the average in the population, without being overly affluent. Their choice of housing indicates that Quakers have at least in part the same desire as other members of the population to live a pleasant and secure material existence yet they repeatedly opt for occupations which are in no financial sense profit-maximising. How you live your life is more important than the money that you make from it.

Age is a regular subject for debate amongst Quakers (Heron, 1995, p. 139). For some years there has been concern about the relatively small number of young and relatively large number of older Quakers. For example when Dandelion carried out a survey of Quakers he had questionnaires returned by 274 Quakers over 61 but only 112 by Quakers under 30 (Dandelion, 1996, p. xiv). In Heron's 1991 survey of Attenders in Yorkshire General Meeting 9.8 per cent of his respondents were aged between 20 and

29 whilst 16.1 per cent were aged 70 or over (Heron, 1992, p. 12). Our Meeting contains Quakers of all ages, some of whom have their own children of varying ages.

Quakers have a somewhat ambivalent attitude to the relationship between children and Meeting. As we noted earlier children cannot normally apply for membership until they are 16. Nevertheless Monthly Meeting is recommended to think of having a 'Children and Young People's Committee' (*Quaker Faith and Practice*, 1995, para. 4.03) and one of the tasks for local Meetings is taking a 'special responsibility for the children within its care and for their parents'. (*Quaker Faith and Practice*, 1995, para. 4.38c). In our Meeting infant children are frequently 'welcomed' to Meeting (*Quaker Faith and Practice*, 1995, para. 10.09) in a ceremony which is not theologically a baptism but which an outsider would see as taking the place of a baptism. Children can also go to 'Children's Meeting' which involves attending the first 10 minutes of the Sunday Meeting for Worship and then having their own separate Meeting (which takes more the form of a Quaker Sunday School). Children, like non-Quaker partners, are welcome at Meeting's social events. Monthly Meeting's directory lists 33 children of members of Meeting placing an asterisk against their names denoting 'children under 16 who are not members'. We have not included these children in our figure of 200 within Meeting as a whole. Children and their needs are both a unifying and a dividing force within Meeting. For parents with children the needs of their children can take them away from Meeting. At the same time when our interviewees were asked about the presence of groups within Meeting a number suggested that parents with children formed a specific group because of their common concerns.

At the opposite end of the age spectrum many in Meeting are of retirement age. Those who are of retirement age have a considerable influence in Meeting. At the time of writing this book of the 13 people holding offices in Meeting listed in the directory only two were not of retirement age. This influence is well-recognised by Meeting. One interviewee said of this age group 'a lot of the energy and power in the Meeting lies with them'. The free time that retirement can bring is doubtless one reason for the influence exercised in Meeting by those who are retired. However other factors associated with age are also important. Those who have retired frequently have much greater experience of Quaker life than those who are younger. Some were born into Quaker families at a time when one could be a birthright Quaker. Some of these families are notable in Quaker history. Other retired Quakers have belonged to our Meeting or to other Meetings for many years. Some have served on national committees. Some have contributed to and continue to contribute to debates in Quaker journals about matters of policy and theology. Taken together they carry with them a knowledge of Quaker culture that can be persuasive especially in the case of those who are relatively new to the Quaker tradition. That which is in 'right ordering' is sometimes simply a question of knowing the appropriate rules but it can also be a matter of intangible spirit. Equally, their knowledge of the history the Meeting is extremely extensive and that can also help give their views greater weight in Meeting.

The city within which Meeting is located is of the most cosmopolitan cities in England. It includes those whose parents were from Poland, the Ukraine and Italy as well as large numbers who are first, second or third generation immigrants from Kenya, India, Uganda, Pakistan and the West Indies. Meeting does not reflect this ethnic diversity. During the period of our study numbers from the ethnic minorities involved in any way with Meeting never exceeded single figures. Frequently there was no ethnic minority presence. This is not to say that all members of Meeting are British born. For example, a number of members of Meeting were people who had come to Great Britain as a consequence of the upheavals attendant on the Second World War. However, to being middle-class Meeting adds the fact that it is white. One interviewee said that Meeting still seemed to have the social mix that was true of the city in which it is located in 'the 50s...[there is a] difficulty for me [in] that Meeting is all white'.

The reason for this lack of ethnic diversity cannot be said to lie simply in the Christian antecedents of Quakerism. The West Indian population is largely Christian in its traditions. Moreover, within the city in which our Meeting is located, Jehovah's Witnesses have been relatively successful in recruiting from the ethnic minorities. More important in the creating the monotone hue of our Meeting is probably the non-aggressive character of Quaker evangelising. 'It is not the habit of Friends to try to win converts by persuasion nor to preach the merits of their ways against those of others' (Hubbard, 1974, p. 214). In the case of our Meeting evangelising consists of little more than providing written information about Quakers, appearing in the local media and having a stall at the local City Show. Meeting has to be found by those seeking it in both the physical sense and the spiritual sense and although newcomers are welcomed Meeting does very little to advertise its existence. Those from ethnic minority backgrounds, particularly those from Asian backgrounds, have less cultural reason to have any awareness of the existence of Quakers than do those who come from the indigenous white cultural traditions. This may explain Meeting's ethnic mix.

As we saw in Chapter 2 Quakerism has had a long history of equality between the sexes and this is reflected in our Meeting. There are slightly more female members of Meeting than there are male members. At the time of writing this book seven out of the thirteen office-holders listed in the directory were men. Six out of nine Elders (who have an ostensible

Mile End Library
Queen Mary, University of London
Christmas Vacation 18th Dec - 9th Jan

Extended vacation loans
Ordinary loans borrowed or renewed
from 20th Nov
will be due back on Friday 14th Jan
One Week Loans borrowed or renewed
from 11th Dec
will be due back on Wed 12th Jan

Borrowed items 30/11/2010 16:20
XXXXXX1062

Item Title	Due Date
* Living without law : an ethr	14/01/2011

* Indicates items borrowed today
PLEASE NOTE
If you still have overdue books on loan
you may have more fines to pay

Item Title	Due Date
* Living without law : an ethn	14/01/2011

disciplinary function) at this same time were women. Women have held all the various positions within Meeting as have men. Quaker women like women in general continue to face discrimination in general society and this discrimination may in turn reflect on the way in which they can participate in Quaker life. Quaker mothers, for example, probably find life just as difficult as do mothers in general. Moreover, it would be wrong to suggest that general gender issues have no relevance to the day-to-day life of Meeting. The Catering Committee had only one male member at the time of writing this book. Our Meeting is not atypical of other Meetings in this respect. Heydecker in a study of Monthly Meetings noted, for example, that women were as likely as men to be Clerks of Meeting but men were 3.5 times more likely than women to be Treasurers of Meeting (Heydecker, 1986, p. 36). Meeting does not operate on the basis of patriarchal assumptions but that does not mean that some taint of partite does not find its way into some parts of Meeting's culture. In a meeting of Elders observed during the period of our study one female Elder said they found both Preparative Meeting and Monthly Meeting 'very un-Friendly and, as a woman, very male'. Nevertheless, within the Meeting itself gender did not seem to be a significant issue. Hampson's observation

> Clearly when as a feminist one meets the Quakers it is a delight. There is so much with which one feels at home, which needs no explanation.
> (Hampson, 1982, p.124)

would be as apt a comment on our Meeting as it is on Quaker culture as a whole.

Meeting currently has 30 members who are married to non-Quakers, a figure which has varied little during our study. The directory does not note how many members have a non-married partner who are not Quakers. It does list 117 members without any indication of a partner. Many of these are single but some do have non-Quaker partners. Quakers with a non-Quaker partner are in a different position with regard to Meeting as compared with those who have Quaker partners. As we noted earlier, like many religious traditions, for many years Quakers did not marry outside the faith and disowned those of their members who did. This has long since passed and no Quaker that we know of in our Meeting would wish to see its return. Nevertheless a union with a non-Quaker does carry with it problems. Attendance at Meeting for Worship, business meetings and some social events takes the Quaker away from their partner. Sunday, for most Christian religious traditions in the United Kingdom, including the Quaker tradition, is a day of worship. For the secular majority it is a time for recreation and shopping. If the non-Quaker partner is of another religious tradition times of worship are unlikely to coincide with that of their Quaker partners. If the non-Quaker partner is secular Meeting for Worship cuts across what is a prime part of what little time most couples have together. If there are children who need looking after the situation becomes still more difficult. Accommodations can be made and the tolerant nature of the Quaker faith makes the matter less fraught than in the case of similar situations in many other faiths but if both in a couple are Quakers no accommodation needs to be made.

Whilst our Meeting is ethnically homogeneous, theologically it is divided. As we have noted earlier in Chapters 2 and 3 Quakers have no creed. What you are required to believe is extremely limited. Indeed it is sometimes difficult to see any requirements at all. When discussing a draft of a new edition of *Quaker Faith and Practice* one member of Meeting asked if there was anything that would lead to Meeting terminating someone's membership of Meeting. After some discussion joining the I.R.A. was the only bar to membership that was suggested. (Lisburn Meeting refused an application for membership from a person who was involved in Republican politics in Northern Ireland (*The Friend*, 1996, p. 23).) Some people in our Meeting hold joint membership of both Meeting and some other Christian church. Others always preface their statement of Quaker allegiance by linking it with another religious tradition. ('Hello, I'm Pat. I'm a Zen-Quaker.') Most significant of all, some in our Meeting are Christocentric whilst others are Universalist. As we saw in Chapter 3 Christocentric Quakers hold to the primacy of the Christian faith. Universalist Quakers look for truth in many different religions and do not regard Christianity as having special significance over other faiths. This theological diversity needs to be underlined. What is significant about it is the importance that most Quakers will attach to their beliefs. These beliefs may sometimes be vague, having little by way of specifics and absolutes in terms of what one should or should not do (although this is not always the case and depends upon the individual Quaker) but, vague or not, the members of Meeting attach great value to them. And what they believe they differ about. The differences matter to people and are sometimes genuinely painful. Some years ago, long before we began our study, differences between Christocentrics and Universalists caused discord in Meeting although this is now no longer, in the main, the case. These theological differences have continued for years and do not prevent the continuance of Meeting. Meeting is not of course a fixed entity. People join and leave and some leave because of dissatisfaction with the spiritual life of Meeting. Yet Meeting, although it is a faith community, is not a group of theologically like-minded souls united in their views which periodically rids itself of those who dissent. Rather it seeks to accommodate and accept difference.

Most people who become members of Meeting stay in membership for a prolonged period of time although other events in their life may alter the part they play in the life of Meeting from time to time. This is true whatever category of member they be. In Chapter 3 we referred to the distinction made by Quakers between those who are Members and those who are Attenders. In our Meeting there are broadly speaking three categories of people who use the Meeting House for worship. There are those who come once or for a short period of time or extremely spasmodically and who have no other connection with Meeting, there are Attenders and there are Members. Both Members and Attenders are listed in Monthly Meeting's directory. It is these people who we regard as members of Meeting and constituting the community that is Meeting. (For this reason we have used the upper-case M and A when referring to Members and Attenders in the Quaker sense reserving the lower-case m for members in our more inclusive sense. Quakers do use the upper-case in their own writings.) Attenders have an 'a' against their names in Monthly Meeting's directory. Meeting has 73 Attenders at present.

Whether any distinction can or should be drawn between Members and Attenders is a question which is fraught with difficulty. On the one hand the distinction is one which is written into *Quaker Faith and Practice*. In some cases Members have rights that an Attender does not have. For example, Members have a right to attend Monthly Meeting but Attenders can be present only with the permission of the Clerk of Monthly Meeting (*Quaker Faith and Practice*, 1995, para. 4.05). Attenders are, however, by no means excluded from the life of Meeting or pushed to its periphery. For example, three of the present members of Children's Committee are Attenders as are two of the members of the Catering Committee. Some Attenders are long-time members of Meeting and clearly play a settled and valued part in Meeting. In recent years there seems to have been a tendency to appoint more Attenders to committees, a tendency which may not be unconnected with difficulties in finding people with the time to spare for committee membership. However, '[t]hose nominated to serve as clerk of meeting, elder, overseer, treasurer, registering officer or as member of any nominations committee should be in membership [Members in our sense of the term]' (*Quaker Faith and Practice*, 1995, para. 3.24i). As we have seen above some small but important parts of the life of Meeting are forbidden to Attenders although on a personal level we could detect no sense of alienation from Meeting amongst Attenders.

In its administration as in its theology very little is compulsory in Quaker life. Local Meetings are, for example, told which offices are 'generally found most helpful' (*Quaker Faith and Practice*, 1995, para. 4.39). However, Meetings are generally free to organise themselves in a way that is appropriate to their size and resources. In this respect our Meeting is in the main wholly conventional in its approach to its administration. Meeting has a Clerk (which on two occasions during our study was an office jointly held by members of Meeting) and an Assistant Clerk. It currently has a Notices Clerk who is responsible for seeing that notices of events and appeals are made at the end of Meeting for Worship. (This was previously the responsibility of the Clerk and Assistant Clerk.) There is a Treasurer who currently has an assistant as well as there being a separate office of Assistant Treasurer. There are two Collectors who are responsible for gifts that members make to the Society. Meeting has an Auditor who has an assistant. There is also a Clerk of Elders, a Clerk of Overseers who has an assistant, a nominated member to be contacted in the case of a death in Meeting and a Children's Convenor. Finally, Meeting has formal representatives to keep it in contact with four outside Quaker bodies.

In addition to individual offices there are nine committees or groups with constitutional status within Meeting. Two groups, Elders and Overseers, are formally constituted under the authority of Monthly Meeting and include people not only from our Meeting but also from other local meetings which are a part of Monthly Meeting. However, our Meeting's Elders and Overseers are noted as a separate group in Monthly Meeting's directory. Indeed, because two of the other Meetings which form Monthly Meeting with our Meeting do not appoint Elders, whilst the only other constituent Meeting appoints only two Elders, the ten Elders from our Meeting dominate meetings of Elders; a matter which one Elders' meeting we observed found problematic. The Committees cover the various aspects of Meeting's life. Some committees have titles which are self-evident in their description: Catering Committee, Children's Committee, Finance and Premises Committee and Funeral Committee. Appeals Committee is concerned with advising the Meeting about the charitable side of Meeting's life. Nominations Committee is concerned with who should be put forward for offices or membership of a committee. Outreach Committee is responsible for providing information about the Meeting in particular and Quaker life in general to non-Quakers. Finally, Wardenship Committee is responsible for the relationship between the Meeting and its two paid employees the Warden and the Deputy Warden. None of these committees have any final authority, existing only to make recommendations to Preparative Meeting.

In all there are 91 offices or places on formal committees in Meeting. Some people hold more than one office either because of their degree of activity or because one office puts them *ex officio* into other roles. Nevertheless the number of offices and places on committees both signifies the degree of involvement of so many members with their Meeting and puts a strain on that involvement. An office is usually held for three years and is perhaps renewed for a further three years. 'It is generally undesirable for someone to hold an appointment for more than six years continuously although there may be exceptions' (*Quaker Faith and Practice*, 1995, para. 3.23). Finding people to fill these places is, in the first place, the job of Nominations Committee. 'The great responsibility resting on nominations committees ... cannot be too strongly stressed' (*Quaker Faith and Practice*, 1995, para. 3.24b). The Committee's membership has to be seen to be both representative of the Meeting and knowledgeable about the various capacities of people in Meeting. As is recommended by *Quaker Faith and Practice* Nominations Committee at our Meeting currently has a membership drawn from a range of age-groups. However, it is also noticeable that, whatever their age, during the period of our observations most members of Nominations Committee have generally had a rather deeper knowledge of Quaker practice and/or the Meeting's history than is true for the average member of Meeting. When this has not been so there has been adverse comment by other members of Meeting.

In addition to the formal institutions of Meeting there are the 'Ffriendly fringes'. These comprise a large number of special interest groups which exist sometimes on a permanent and sometimes on a short-term basis. In some cases their members include people who are not otherwise at all involved in Meeting and who do not attend the Meeting House for worship. These outsiders are, however, sympathetic to both Quaker social objectives and also to their working methods. Hence members of fringe groups may either be 'Friends' (Quakers) or 'friends' of Quakerism. A good example of such a group is the Peace group which includes a significant number of non-Quakers. As a group it is nonetheless of great importance to Meeting, the name of its contact being listed in Monthly Meeting's directory. The activities of these groups covers a range of matters but tends to fall into either areas of cultural interest (there is an Arts Circle, an Art group, two Recorder groups and a group which meets to discuss novels), discussion groups concerned with more general matters, some of which may have been raised by central Quaker authorities (thus, for example, one group met fortnightly for nearly a year to discuss booklets produced by Quaker Home Service and Woodbrooke College on questions of Quaker identity), or groups concerned with theology (there is a Bible study group and a prayer group). Other groups are more *ad hoc*. For example, one group meets on an occasional basis to discuss topics taken from *The Friend*, a Quaker journal. Membership of each of these groups is small but they are a flourishing part of the life of Meeting. As one interviewee put it, 'they help glue Meeting together'.

A description of the existence of committees and groups within Meeting says nothing about the degree of their activity. Typically committees meet once a month although some, such as Children's Committee, will meet informally more frequently. Other groups will meet at least once a month but some meet more frequently. The Art group, for example, meets on a weekly basis. In addition to the various committees and groups Meeting also organises other activities. Speakers are invited to meetings which are often open to the general public but are intended primarily to be of interest to members of Meeting. Like the groups described above these other *ad hoc* activities cover a wide spectrum of social, cultural and theological areas. In total the range of activity does much to add to Meeting's own sense of its community.

Quaker Meetings normally appoint Overseers. The full list of responsibilities for Overseers takes over two pages in *Quaker Faith and Practice*. The main focus of their work is pastoral both with respect to those within the Meeting and those who are enquiring about membership or attending Meeting on an irregular basis. Meeting has always, through Monthly Meeting, appointed Overseers during the period of our study. However, more latterly Meeting has also been divided into a number of Colour Groups. The division was largely done on a geographical basis although one group was drawn up so as to include members with children or who were known to like children The function of these groups is in part simply social, a recognition of the size of Meeting and the difficulty in getting to know every member well, but was also seen as being pastoral. The success of these groups has been patchy. Some seem more active than others and they have not in practice involved everybody. This in turn has created a difficulty for pastoral care within Meeting. Since not all Colour Groups function in the way that was intended they cannot fully cater for pastoral care. Yet for one interviewee

> the Colour Groups redeemed Meeting for me. The Colour Group was my way of getting to know a few Friends - certainly I feel I know them well.

Whatever their merits, given the existence of Colour Groups, Overseers are now uncertain of their role. Indeed, one of our interviewees, a Member for some four years, when asked what the role of Overseers was replied that they were rather uncertain because the work of Overseers had not impinged on them very much; another interviewee, who had been an Overseer, simply said 'there isn't really a role'. The role of Colour Groups and Overseers is the subject of continuing debate within Meeting.

Finally in the life of Meeting there is Meeting for Worship. The 10.30 a.m. Sunday Meeting for Worship at the Meeting House remains central to the life of Meeting. The Meeting House itself is a relatively large building.

Purpose-built in 1955 it is made out of brick. Our Meeting neither has the problem of maintaining historic but now unsuitable premises nor of being housed in physically defective quarters as do many Meetings in Great Britain. Adjacent to the Meeting House is a small three-storey block of flats owned by the Quaker Housing Association. These flats and the Meeting House share a small car-park and the Meeting House has a garden behind it. On the ground floor of the Meeting House there is a large Meeting Room, a small Meeting Room, a library, a kitchen, a large lobby, a toilet for use by the disabled and two other toilets. Upstairs there is an office, an activity room, a small coffee room and a committee room. In addition there is a one bed-roomed flat which is the private quarters of the Meeting's Warden, a person employed by Meeting to look after the Meeting House. The Meeting House is used by Meeting both for Meeting for Worship and for a range of other Quaker purposes. It is also heavily used by other bodies. Such use quietens the consciences of those Quakers who are concerned about the large amount of capital which is tied up in the Meeting House which could otherwise be put to what they might regard as a more worthy use. Rooms, including the room that is used for Meeting for Worship, can be hired. The hire-charge for the rooms depend partially on the nature and financial situation of the groups who wish to use the rooms. Most of the outside use is by charitable or voluntary bodies. There is no religious discrimination in the way rooms are hired out. Until recently, when they acquired their own premises, the local Progressive Jewish Synagogue met at the Meeting House. Some use has been made of the Meeting House by bodies who seek to make a profit but in the past this has sometimes caused a problem. At one time a person offering supplementary tutoring for school children used the Meeting House. From small beginnings the business expanded rapidly making more use of an ever-increasing number of rooms. This greater use represented a larger profit for Meeting. However, the increased use presented Meeting with two problems. First, Meeting was advised by the local authority that a significant use of its premises for profit-making purposes would adversely effect its Council Tax position. Secondly, some people in Meeting were concerned about the connection between the Meeting House and a business which was being pursued solely for profit. (The business, together with its location at the Meeting House, was widely advertised in the local neighbourhood.) After discussions Meeting eventually asked the business to discontinue its use of the Meeting House. Larger commercial concerns are routinely refused use of the Meeting House on first enquiry.

The large Meeting Room is used for Meeting for Worship. This is not its exclusive function. The large Meeting Room is hired out in the same way that any other room in the Meeting House is hired out. No sense of the sacred attaches to the room. When it is used for Meeting for Worship it is furnished with benches set in a square with a table in the middle. The table always has flowers on it and copies of the Bible and *Quaker Faith and Practice* are scattered round. Meeting begins at 10.30 am on a Sunday. Some people come by car but, because they live reasonably proximate to the Meeting House, in clement weather many will walk OR cycle. A Doorkeeper is there to greet people when they arrive. They will also let children out of the Meeting after the first ten minutes. Two Elders sit on a bench opposite the clock in Meeting. They will eventually draw an end to Meeting for Worship by shaking hands, usually after a period of about 60 minutes. The number attending Meeting varies. During the period of 12 months of intensive observation for this study it averaged approximately 80 people. More recently the average number has been closer to 60. Attendance tends to be higher in the winter months than it does at the height of summer. Meeting for Worship does not always take the same form. In particular the relationship of silent ministry to spoken ministry varies. People speak during the period of Meeting about events of the moment or things they have seen or thought about. Some quote poetry or the Bible. Meeting is not a place for argument. There is never direct contradiction of previous ministry. Most ministry is relatively short. For most people their time is spent in silence. When the Elders have signified the end of Meeting for Worship the Clerk will read out any notices that have been sent in during the week. Most of these will pertain to the activities of one of the formal or informal groups mentioned above but others will refer to national Quaker activity or other matters which might be of interest to Quakers.

Attitudes towards Sunday's Meeting for Worship vary. Members of Meeting are not required to attend Meeting. Even the most prolonged absence would be a matter for no more than pastoral concern. It would not in itself lead to a person being required to discontinue their membership of Meeting. Some people view regular attendance as being very important and one interviewee said that they would never fail to attend simply because 'they'd rather not go'. Another said that they went to Meeting 'because I need it. It's almost a habit'. On the other hand another interviewee, a Member not an Attender, said that their attendance at Sunday Meeting for Worship varied and that they found Sunday morning a good time for other activities. Such an attitude does not necessarily betoken a failure to be involved in Meeting. The same respondent, at the time that they were interviewed, was a member of one of the more important committees of Meeting and also held another office in Meeting and was active in both roles. Unsurprisingly, many interviewees stressed the reflective purpose of Meeting. This was true for those who were clearly Christocentric, for those who were Universalist and those whose theological position was uncertain.

However, the precise description of this reflective purpose of Meeting varied. For some it was a spiritual time but others found the word spiritual 'difficult' and talked in terms of a search for 'insight'. These differences in nuance reflect the deep-rooted theological differences within Meeting that we have already averted to. Many interviewees noted that Meeting for Worship had a purpose beyond the one that was purely religious. One person said that they went to Meeting for Worship because, amongst other things, 'I feel like I belong to a family' and others noted Meeting for Worship's value in establishing a feeling of solidarity and community in Meeting. One interviewee said of themselves and their partner that Meeting was 'both our spiritual and our social anchorage'. The reflective and social sides of Meeting for Worship are not always seen as being different. One interviewee, who saw Quakers as containing a wide range of viewpoints, saw Meeting for Worship as a place

> for everyone to come closer to a common way of doing things ... not through arguing ... [but] gradually influencing each other.

The importance of Meeting for Worship can change for members. Thus one member said that it once been the focal point of their life but that now, although it was still important, it was less central. Another member said that at one point it was important socially, and they had then attended frequently, but that it was now more important for religious reasons but they attended less frequently than they once had.

People's personal experience of Meeting for Worship varies. Some approach it an almost formal manner and were able to describe techniques that they used to focus on a search for insight or to 'centre down' on the religious experience they sought. Others described instances of themselves 'day-dreaming' in Meeting and sometimes of simply being 'bored' and 'waiting for it to end'. Several people mentioned sometimes sleeping in Meeting. One interviewee said that there were three reasons why people came to Meeting for Worship; to worship, to meditate or to listen and think. This analysis, and the theological differences it implies, accords with both our own observations and our other interviews. Everybody who was interviewed saw Meeting for Worship as being valuable in general, although not everybody saw every Meeting as being successful, but there seemed to be a divide between those who saw its value as being in the search for something positive and those who saw the value as its being a space to withdraw from the everyday concerns of the world.

After Meeting for Worship there is tea with biscuits and orange juice for any children. This takes place in the small Meeting Room and the lobby during winter but in summer people may move out to the garden and patio area. Most people will stay for anything up to an hour. This is a period for socialising. A particular effort is made to greet those who are just attending their first Meeting. Many interviewees seemed to see staying for tea as being almost as important as the Meeting for Worship, some saying that they stayed for tea but 'didn't drink tea'. Meeting is more than just a theological group, it is also a social community. *Quaker Faith and Practice* has a passage in it which says that '[t]he spiritual life of a meeting is greatly helped if its social life is vigorous, and its members take a warm personal interest in one another's welfare' (*Quaker Faith and Practice*, 1995, para. 10.17). (Socialising is not, however, compulsory; one interviewee, a long-standing and active member of Meeting, said that they rarely attended Meeting's social events, observing that they were 'just not a sociable person'.) We have already noted that the times of the small Sunday Meeting for Worship now being held elsewhere have been arranged so as to allow those attending that Meeting for Worship to also attend tea at the Meeting House. During tea people will discuss forthcoming meetings, bring others up to date on their own lives and share information about others in Meeting; a mixture of gossip and pastoral concern.

'Bring and share' lunches are organised after Meeting for Worship on an *ad hoc* basis. The lunches, held in the small Meeting Room, will not finish until between 1.30 p.m. and 2.00 p.m. Not everybody who has been at Meeting for Worship will attend the lunch. The lunches are often linked to some event that is occurring that afternoon at the Meeting House, the idea of the lunch being in part the possibility of a prompt start for the event at 2.00 p.m.

In most months Meeting holds a Preparative Meeting. Preparative Meeting's function is both to consider matters for the later Monthly Meeting, to receive reports from Meeting's own committees and offices and to consider matters of interest to Meeting. Preparative Meeting does not occur in July because of the large number of people absent on holidays. Meeting has experimented with the time of Preparative Meeting in order to try and maximise attendance. At times it is held after Sunday's Meeting for Worship. At other times it has been held in the evening on Sunday or on a weekday. Despite its importance in the functioning of Meeting attendance at Preparative Meeting is usually very low with numbers of between 15 and 20 being common and lower figures not unusual.

As we noted above Meeting is a member of a larger group of Meetings, Monthly Meeting. As an external body Monthly Meeting falls outside our study but it is important to realise that the needs of Monthly Meeting also fall on our Meeting. Monthly Meeting has its Meetings, its officers, its committees and its life and since our Meeting is far larger than the other local Meetings the burden of providing the personnel for Monthly Meeting falls very heavily on it.

Meeting regards itself as a community. During the period of our observations one person began their Ministry in Meeting for Worship with the statement 'I have been thinking about the community we have here in Meeting, how everyone is valued' and that view would be widely shared amongst members of Meeting. An interviewee described Meeting unprompted as 'a ready-made community'. We have sought to show that Meeting is something more than a group of people who meet together for worship. If this is all they were they could not be said to constitute a community for ethnographic purposes. However Meeting is far more than either its Sunday act of worship or indeed the sum of its other acts of worship. Meeting operates in the context of the history we have explored in Chapter 2 and in the context of the wider Quaker world that we have seen in Chapter 3. The groups, committees and events which are part of Meeting reflects the intricate social life of a group of people who are in many ways diverse and individualistic. It is a religious community and that is reflected in some of its groups and groupings but it is more than a religious community. It has its political concerns and its cultural interests. Members have personal friendships with each other which come out of knowing each other at Meeting. It is an old community. At times during our study three generations of Quakers from the same family have met for worship. Many more members, however, are first generation Quakers and they bring diversity to the community. It is that combination of diversity and continuity that contributes to the particular spirit of Meeting. A community is often brought together in part because of what makes them different from outsiders. It is easy to say that Quakers are different, and therefore a community, because of their religion. But their religious beliefs, diverse within Meeting as they are, also bring with them or reflect a different set of cultural attitudes towards things which have totemic significance within British society at the beginning of twenty-first century. Each war which Britain participates in, each time British armed forces are used in support of British foreign policy, is of course a redefining moment for Meeting and vigils for peace are held in the local city centre. Material wealth is more likely to be a matter for embarrassment not celebration. One interviewee noted that their partner, also a member of Meeting, was uncomfortable with their wealth although they had no more than a normal professional income. Conformity to many of the norms of British society is regarded with suspicion within Meeting. The acknowledgement of the fact that British society is not rightly ordered, that it is not just and that it is not caring of humanity is taken as the accepted norm within Meeting and attempting to change those facts is seen as being the personal responsibility of each member of Meeting. Most Quakers in Meeting meet non-Quakers every day of their lives. In many cases they have to work with them. Whilst they may find their chosen form of employment more congenial than most they will still have to work in a non-Quaker manner. The fact that they are Quakers and the difference that this means is thrust against them every day. And their community, comfortable and secure as it is, is nonetheless a community committed to resistance. Once again Meeting is aware of its position. In the same Meeting for Worship from which we quoted above another member of Meeting said in ministry

> We have been reminded of both the social and spiritual dimensions of our Quaker community. It seems to me that both of these things bring with them responsibilities – if our community is really a place where everyone is valued and where everyone feels valued, then we all have a responsibility to achieve that and not to leave people out. Equally, if Meeting for Worship is to be a truly spiritual experience, we all have a responsibility for it, not necessarily by Ministry, but by our presence and our ability to centre down in worship.

Moore defines the proper subject as for ethnographic analysis as being

> the small field ... studied in terms of its semi-autonomy – the fact that it can generate rules and customs and symbols internally, but ... it is also vulnerable to rules and decisions and other forces from the larger world by which it is surrounded. The semi-autonomous social field has rule-making capacities, and the means to induce or coerce compliance; but it is simultaneously set in a larger social matrix which can, and does, affect and invade it ...
> (Moore, 1978, pp. 55-56)

From the description above it is clear that Meeting enjoys the position of semi-autonomy that Moore describes. The vigorous social interaction amongst the members of Meeting ensures its survival. It also makes Meeting an important, and in most cases primary, point of reference for the lives of individual members of Meeting. It is a community in the fullest anthropological sense. Members take not only their religion from it, they frequently take much of the rest of their social life from it. Nevertheless Meeting does not exist in isolation and the particular relationship that Meeting has with wider society is somewhat different to that described by Moore. For Meeting the 'larger social matrix' which impacts upon it is not just more general British society but also the wider Quaker Community. The Quaker way of life that Meeting lives is taken from that wider Quaker community. The way in which Meeting lives the Quaker life is local. As we have already observed no two Meetings are ever exactly the same. Again, as we have already observed, Quakerism is rarely precisely prescriptive either as to the behaviour of members or the behaviour of Meetings. Quakerism is more about general modes of thought than it is about particular commands. But, this notwithstanding, Meeting not so much 'generates rules and customs and symbols internally' as takes those rules and customs and symbols from the wider Quaker community and gives them its own particular twist. What our Meeting does is, in the British context, recognisably Quaker. At the same time it is also recognisably special to our Meeting. Within that Meeting we find a Quaker way of taking decisions and, at least in the main, avoiding disputes.

7 Leadership in Meeting

Introduction

According to the theory of Quaker theology, as we have said in Chapters 2 and 4, Quakers have neither ministers nor leaders. Their community is non-hierarchical. Theologically they see their Meetings, whether they be a full-scale Meeting for Worship or a business meeting of one of the committees of Meeting, as a search for the promptings of the spirit. In secular terms they practice consensus decision-making although their own literature consistently denies that what is being practised is in fact a search for a consensus because use of the word consensus is thought insufficient to encompass the spiritual aspect which Quakers seek and which is so important to Quakers.

When asked, large numbers of our interviewees from Meeting described the Quaker decision-making method as being a search for a consensus. The use of this term when answering a question put to them by another Quaker is significant. In most interviews that were undertaken for this study a considerable proportion of the interview time focused on looking at what exactly the interviewee thought was involved in Quaker decision-making. The question was not casually put nor lightly answered. Our interviewees were not trying to explain to an outsider what the method was, using terminology that an outsider might understand. Instead, whatever the theological accuracy of their language, they were using the word that made most sense to them and that they thought would best explain the process to another insider; consensus, 'a feeling that everybody is involved', was the kind of terminology most regularly used. This view was not universal. Some of our interviewees felt that what Quakers should be doing in any decision was, as Quaker theory and tradition would assert, to search for the will of God, but even amongst those who responded in this way, most seemed to feel that other members of Meeting did not agree with them and that what Meeting actually sought was consensus.

Notwithstanding the use of the language of consensus our Meeting sees itself as working in accord with the broad spirit of the theory of Quaker relationships and Quaker business method that we described in Chapter 4. Yet this ascription of an absence of hierarchy to Meeting and an insistence that Meeting works on the basis of a true and deep consensus seems to be at odds with some features of Meeting. In both our description of the theory of the relationships and the method in Meeting and in our initial description of Meeting itself there are a number of matters in both the formal constitution of Meeting and in its informal day-to-day life which, on first analysis, seem contrary to notions of absence of hierarchy or leadership and the search for consensus. It is these apparent contradictions which we address in this chapter. We will look at both the formal constitutional matters and then turn to the everyday life of Meeting.

Clerks and Convenors

Meeting has neither leader nor minister but it does have a Clerk. Committees in Meeting have no chairs but they do have Convenors. This inevitably brings the question to what extent in organisational terms do Clerks and Convenors simply take the place of leaders and chairs? The Clerk after all draws up the agenda for Preparative Meeting, takes Meeting through the business and draws up the Minute that concludes each item. Crossman, in his account of cabinet government, has noted the power inherent in being able to determine the agenda and write the minutes of a meeting (Crossman, 1970, pp. 55 and 63) *Quaker Faith and Practice* tells Clerks that 'meeting has given you a measure of authority which includes an expectation and an acceptance of leadership and firm guidance' (*Quaker Faith and Practice*, 1995, para. 3.13) Convenors commonly, though not universally, take on the same tasks for their Committees that the Clerk performs for Meeting. *Quaker Faith and Practice* tells Convenors that 'the term convenor is sometimes used as an alternative to *clerk*' and that in the case of committees 'the convenor is expected to perform the same functions as a clerk' (*Quaker Faith and Practice*, 1995, para. 3.21). Leadership is therefore something *Quaker Faith and Practice* expects from a Convenor. An argument that the official constitutional role of Clerk or Convenor involves the exercise of a measure of leadership should, however, not be put too strongly. *Quaker Faith and Practice*, in its section on the role of the Clerk, begins by reminding Clerks that they 'are the servants of the meeting' (*Quaker Faith and Practice*, 1995, para. 3.13). They are admonished to look to 'discern the meeting's united mind' (*Quaker Faith and Practice*, 1995, para. 3.13) and told that Meeting must accept a minute recording a decision as 'a deliberate act' in which Meeting must 'unite to accept it' (*Quaker Faith and Practice*, 1995, para. 3.14). Similar points could be made about *Quaker Faith and Practice's* view of the role of Convenors. Nevertheless one might ask how *Quaker Faith and Practice's* ascription of leadership to the role of Clerk and Convenor fits in with notions of consensus decision-making and absence of hierarchy.

All of our interviewees were asked about the role of Convenors. Only one, when asked, volunteered the view that the Convenor's task was that of a chair. Even that member immediately added that the Convenor had to be sensitive to those in a meeting and make sure that everybody was brought into the discussion. Another interviewee said that the job of being Clerk was 'impossible [because] they didn't have the authority of a chair'. The only other interviewee who compared the role of Convenor to an office outside Quaker circles described the job as being a secretary to the committee. A number described the role as being administrative in character. The Convenor's job was to see that the meeting started on time and make sure people received relevant papers. Some interviewees said that the Convenor's role was to make sure meetings ran in a Quakerly manner and others more specifically said that Convenors had to make sure everybody present at a meeting was involved in the discussions and decisions that were going on in the meeting.

Just as interviewees were asked about the role of Convenors so they were asked about the role of Clerks. Here interviewees talked in terms of the Clerk's need to be neutral, to be fair, to be 'a good listener'. The Clerk was not there, in the words of one interviewee, 'to impose himself or herself on Meeting' but to put things to Meeting 'in a clear fashion' and sum up Meeting's feeling. In the need to take Meeting through business there was, one interviewee thought, an element of being 'in charge' but the same interviewee also observed that the Clerk was not 'a ruler' and that that it was important for them to be familiar with the Quaker business method.

What members of Meeting think about the role of Clerk and Convenor may be different to their actual role in the life of Meeting. It is no more open to Quakers than it is to anyone else to argue that they understand the currents of their own lives simply because they are experiencing it (Nussbaum, 1997, p. 175). The internal point of view is not necessarily the correct point of view. Nonetheless the direction and strength of the response to our questions about the role of Clerks and Convenors cannot but be instructive. A number of those who were questioned had held these positions in Meeting (as has the participant author of this book). They were talking about their own experience as well as about their observations of others. Meeting clearly has internalised the Quaker theory that neither Clerks nor Convenors are, to any great extent, leaders of their Meeting of their committees.

The interviewees' description of the work of the Clerk and of Convenors matches the observations made by the participant author during the study. The Quaker method makes it difficult for either Convenors or Clerks to suborn the process and take on, in any strong sense, a leadership position.

Silences at the beginning and end of meetings and during points of difficulty during a meeting (though they are not always used in Meeting's committees) are a barrier to the normal forms of argumentative discourse and rhetoric that would be used to both cow opposition and create assent in meetings outside Quaker circles. Minutes written at the time of the meeting that have to receive the assent of that meeting are also a vehicle for insisting on the need for consensus (though in Chapter 8 we will see that this practice is not always followed in the work of Meeting's committees). There is, in any event, simply the Quaker culture which both means that attempts by an individual to dominate a meeting or a feeling that anyone has been left out of a decision at a meeting results in something which is 'not in right ordering'. Strong authoritarian leadership was doubtless not in the mind of those who drafted *Quaker Faith and Practice* when they suggested leadership was part of the role of a Clerk and a Convenor. In our Meeting's description of the work involved in both offices even weak notions of leadership are eschewed in favour of a discourse of service to the Meeting or to the Committee. Moreover, this description seems to fit the reality of practice. Practice between different committees varied depending on the personalities of those involved and the nature of the business of the committee. In some committees it was easy to see from our diary observations that the Convenor was attempting to steer the committee through the business on the agenda. In others it is difficult to identify who the Convenor was from our diary records. These latter observations do not necessarily betoken either a weak or ineffective Convenor. Some committees seemed not to need an active Convenor in order to transact their business.

The work of Convenors and Clerks in our Meeting (and the activities of others in this chapter) has to be seen in the context both of the wider Quaker history and culture that we have discussed in Part II of this book and in the context of the ongoing life of the community discussed in Chapter 6. In a community where there are close multiplex relationships with a culture which abhors authority the notion and practice of leadership takes on a different form to that commonly found in complex societies. In relation to Clerks and Convenors there are elements of power but the power is so slight as to rebut any notion of a hierarchy.

Overseers and Elders

As described in previous chapters the formal role of Overseers and Elders seems to ascribe to them a hierarchical function. Notwithstanding the protestations of *Quaker Faith and Practice*, to give Overseers responsibility for pastoral care within Meeting and to give Elders responsibility for the spiritual life of the Meeting seems both to give them power over other members in Meeting and, as a consequence, to make them more important than other members of Meeting. Nor can such suspicions be diverted to some extent by arguing that Overseers' responsibilities are simply pastoral. The policing function of social work has been extensively analysed.

In so far as Overseers in our Meeting are concerned the most telling argument against the suggestion that they have any dominance in any area is the fact that interviewees were largely unable to think of any task that Oversees were commonly performing. Since they have a comparatively small role they can do little to affect the power relationships within Meeting. In interviews, although most interviewed could describe the formal constitutional pastoral role of Overseers their picture of Overseers actual everyday work within Meeting was far from clear. One experienced member concluded that, with the introduction of Colour Groups into Meeting, they 'couldn't see to what extent Overseers were doing the traditional work of Overseers anymore'.

However, whilst Meeting is very ambivalent about the precise role of Overseers, Elders are clearly seen as an important body within Meeting. Their constitutional role as being responsible for the spiritual life of Meeting is seen as having real meaning. One interviewee said that Elders were there to make sure that Meeting was 'not just a social organisation'. It is precisely the reality of their role that creates some tension with the principles of absence of hierarchy and consensus that we have noted above. A number of interviewees noted that the Elder's function was 'to keep things on track'. A task of 'keeping things on track' suggests an authority from the Meeting to do so and one interviewee described the Elders' role as one of providing 'leadership'. Other members of Meeting would perhaps have more difficulty with the suggestion that Elders were there to provide leadership but it is significant that whereas in the case of Clerks and Convenors the role was seen in terms discerning the will in the meeting or in ensuring the involvement of everybody the Elders' role was seen as being much more proactive. The Clerk is seen as being responsible to Meeting, Convenors as being responsible to their Committees but the Elders are responsible for Meeting.

An illustrative example of the proactive role of Elders can be seen in relationship to their responsibility for Meeting for Worship. 'There is always the risk that someone will abuse the silence [in Meeting for Worship],' said one of our interviewees. Those who are not used to Quaker ways may seek to use Meeting for Worship as a venue for them to lecture members and others attending Meeting for Worship and even members of Meeting may lapse from Ministry into personal observations. Elders must seek to prevent both eventualities or, if they do occur, seek to prevent their re-occurrence. During the period of our study Elders had to do both things. Here there were clear examples of leadership and the use of authority. However, even though this is so, the degree of leadership and authority and the manner of its exercise has to be seen in the context of the whole life of Meeting. First, the number of such instances were very few. 'Eldering' a member of Meeting about their behaviour in Meeting for Worship would not be a matter for public debate or comment so we cannot be sure of the precise number of instances that occurred during our study. However, given the nature of our study, were it a regular matter we would have known about it. Our own sources of information led us to conclude that it rarely happened in our Meeting and conversations with Elders confirmed this. Secondly, in the infrequent instances where Eldering does take place its manner is rather different from cases of the imposition of authority outside Quaker circles. One of our interviewees reported an instance of an outsider, someone who was neither a Member nor an Attender, who attended Meeting for Worship and spoke in an inappropriate manner.

> Someone came in who had an axe to grind, [her contribution] was not focused and Elders sorted it out - they thanked her for her contribution and somehow managed to stop her ... it was done well, no jarring - people were becoming uncomfortable, but it preserved her dignity and was quite firm. They also spoke to her afterwards.

Elders on this occasion sought to preserve the spirit of the Meeting for Worship but at the same time they did so in a manner which did as little as possible to damage the feelings of the outsider (to have done so would have been as troubling to members of Meeting as was the unsuitable ministry) and they acted at a time when Meeting was united in wanting them to act.

Elders in our Meeting have also taken on a limited responsibility for organising contributions in Meeting for Worship by ensuring that extracts from *Quaker Faith and Practice* are read out during Meeting for Worship. One meeting of Elders that we observed discussed the legitimacy of doing this; spoken ministry is after all supposed to reflect the prompting of the Spirit rather than the result of any individual will. One Elder noted that they 'used to think it was awful to have something prescribed – not in the spirit of the Meeting - but since it hasn't been done, I've missed it'. Another Elder at the same meeting observed that they 'could ask someone to wait until they are inspired [to read out *Quaker Faith and Practice*] but they might not be inspired for two years'. Here there is a clear tension between the ostensible lack of hierarchy in Meeting and the need to ensure that Meeting and particularly new members of Meeting remember and reflect on Quaker traditions and beliefs. Whilst Elders do not force particular beliefs on members of Meeting they do ensure that beliefs and traditions are brought to the attention of members.

One interviewee said that to be suitable to be an Elder one needed 'some knowledge of what Quakerism is about and some sort of intellectual interest in Quakerism and religion'. Many suggested that Elders were responsible for seeing that Meeting worked in a Quakerly fashion. These views were consistently linked with the view already noted that Elders were responsible for the spiritual life of Meeting. This places a considerable burden on Elders. One Elder resigned as an Elder (though not as a member of Meeting) during the period of our study because they felt that they were in a 'spiritual cul-de-sac' and could not do the job properly. As we have noted Meeting is a place where a wide range of theological views are held. Quite what is 'Quakerly fashion' in Meeting is sometimes a matter for dispute.

The difficulty that Elders have in performing their leadership role was evident during our period of observations. This difficulty can be illustrated by one problem that Elders dealt with. A member of Meeting, a person who was plainly a weighty Friend, sent Elders a letter suggesting that members of Meeting should not, in Meeting for Worship, refer to the names of those who had previously ministered when they themselves ministered on the grounds that, first, 'ministry does not belong to an individual, it belongs to God' and, secondly, because such references 'exclude newcomers who may feel its a closed circle'. When Elders first discussed this the Convenor showed the meeting a draft minute which they had prepared which suggested that the practice of naming people who had previously ministered was acceptable because it helped people to get to know each other's names. Other Elders disagreed with this, some feeling that people did feel excluded because some people knew names that they did not. After some discussion it was agreed to hold the matter over to another meeting. At the next meeting of Elders discussion, although prolonged, was once more inconclusive. It was agreed that the Convenor would then talk to the author of the letter privately. Finally, through Preparative Meeting, the matter was put to all members of Meeting as something they should think about but with no binding rule being imposed. For Elders the problem with this issue was the unresolvable contradiction between the theological proposition that ministry comes from the Spirit, justifying the stance taken by the author of the letter, and the fact that Meeting wishes to engage everyone in its activities and feels, probably correctly, that rules about correct conduct inhibit that engagement.

The leadership role that Elders have is not entirely uncontroversial within Meeting. Whilst most members appear untroubled by the role of Elders, perhaps because they have not fully thought through the implications of the position, some members clearly find the idea problematic in what is a non-hierarchical body. During the period of our study one Elder resigned because they felt 'inhibited' by having the title Elder. Other Elders sympathised when they heard of the resignation though one Elder in an Elder's meeting said 'I think they have got Eldership wrong – they are talking about a separate ministry and that's not what we are about'. In fact there does seem to be an element of 'separate ministry', of leadership in the Elders' role, and few members of Meeting are untroubled when directly confronted with this fact.

Leadership is part of the Elder's role both in theory and, as we have seen, in the practice of Meeting. There is also the leadership that comes from being an Elder. Interviewees were asked which other members of Meeting they would look to for guidance. Some names came up fairly regularly. Most were or had been Elders. We would not argue that the fact of being an Elder means that other other members of Meeting then look at you in a different light, seeing you and your views as being worthy of greater respect by virtue of the fact that you are (or have been) an Elder. Instead, the matter is circular. Most Elders tend to have been in Meeting for some time, most Elders are Elders only for a period of six years, most people who have been in Meeting for some time have been Elders, most of those whose names came up as being members to look to for guidance had been in Meeting for some time. How likely is it that you would know that a person was someone to look for guidance unless that person had been in Meeting for sometime? Being, or having been, an Elder may add to the respect accorded to those with a lengthy knowledge of Quakerism and/or Meeting; being an Elder may also be a recognition of that lengthy knowledge.

Birthright Quakers and Weighty Friends

In looking at Elders we have seen that there are both aspects of constitutional leadership in their role and also the informal social leadership that comes from being someone to whom others will look for guidance. In talking with members of Meeting about its affairs in general and those whom they would look to for guidance in particular two phrases sometimes came up; 'birthright Quakers' and 'weighty Friends'.

As we noted in Chapter 2 the idea of a birthright Quaker, someone who is a Quaker by virtue of the fact that they were born into a Quaker family, ceased to have constitutional significance within the Society in 1959 (Dandelion, 1996, p. 12). Despite this the term is still in regular use in Meeting. Its survival testifies to its continuing significance. There are a number of birthright Quakers in meeting and some people were described as such when others mentioned them. A number of those we interviewed are birthright Quakers. Some described themselves as such when they were asked in the interview when they became a Quaker. Others who were birthright Quakers, perhaps in deference to modern usage, used some other formulation to describe their lifelong Quakerism.

The fact of being a birthright Quaker, if linked to a continuing commitment to Quakerism, brings with it the certainty of detailed knowledge of Quaker culture. Other members may gather that knowledge through reading and those who join when relatively young will gradually acquire it with age. Birthright Quakers, however, have that knowledge certified simply by their description. They are aware of this knowledge and when other members know what they are and know what it means they are also aware of the knowledge. Elders and overseers are *prima facie* in a position of authority in Meeting by virtue of the constitutional status of their office. In the social reality of Meeting this translates into real authority in the case of Elders but not in the instance of Overseers. In the case of birthright Quakers they appear to have authority by virtue of the cultural capital which is recognised by Meeting's continued use of the term.

It does not follow from the fact that the term birthright Quaker is still sometimes used in Meeting that birthright Quakers are disproportionately influential. First, any influence that they may have may not be disproportionate to their knowledge. An analogy with those members of Meeting who are lawyers may be helpful. Several members of Meeting are lawyers. It would be odd if their views on technical points of law relevant to Meeting were not looked at with some respect. Similarly, since birthright Quakers are almost necessarily knowledgeable about Quaker culture, it would be odd if Meeting did not use them as one of its sources of information about that which is in 'right ordering'. Secondly, being a birthright Quaker and being an active Quaker are not the same things. Some birthright Quakers are heavily involved in the life of Meeting. Some, for a variety of reasons, are not. Nonetheless it would seem for at least some members of Meeting the fact that a person is a birthright Quaker gives their views a weight they would not otherwise possess.

The idea that birthright Quakers possess a degree of influence by virtue of the fact that they are birthright Quakers would be contentious for at least some in Meeting although we would hold that it is in accord with our observations. However, the role that is played by 'weighty Friends' appears to be largely uncontentious. Speaking of his wider experience in Quaker circles outside of our Meeting one interviewee said that it was 'very easy for a lazy Meeting to allow weighty Friends to rule the roost'. The precise description of what a weighty Friend is as impossible as is the decision as to which members of Meeting are weighty Friends and which are not. A number of features coalesce to make a weighty Friend. Being born into a Quaker family is helpful as is being educated at a Quaker school. Long membership of Meeting assists as does involvement in the Quaker community outside Meeting and the Monthly Meeting of which it is a part. Publishing material about and in Quaker circles matters. Professional knowledge which is relevant to central Quaker concerns will help. As important as all these more or less tangible things, however, is the more intangible matter of the seriousness with which your views are taken and perhaps the seriousness with which they are held. A weighty Friend is, at the end of the day, someone who has thought about Quaker life for some time, and who is known to have thought about it, and has reached some, perhaps provisional, conclusions which are viewed by other members of Meeting as having substance. The essential difference between being a birthright Quaker and a weighty Friend is that in the first instance something which is objectively measurable, your parentage, is thought to reflect automatically on what you can bring to the life and work of Meeting whilst in the second instance an ascription of somebody as being a weighty Friend reflects what someone thinks about what that person has brought to the life and work of Meeting.

There seems little doubt that not all members are equal in Meeting. The word of weighty Friends weighs more heavily than those who are not. There is, in this sense, a hierarchy. Yet here again, as when dealing with questions of leadership earlier in this chapter the matter must be put into a careful context. The word of weighty Friends comes, at least in part, from their experience and knowledge. Meeting listens to them in part because they simply know more, in the same way that, on occasion, it will listen to its lawyers, its architects or social workers who, concerning a topic in issue, know more. The ease with which someone can become a Quaker perhaps gives more weight to the role of weighty Friends. No catechism need be learnt, no creed mastered and assented to. Despite this, *Quaker Faith and Practice* still suggests that Meeting should arrange to have passages from the Advices and Queries section of *Quaker Faith and Practice* read out in Meeting for Worship on a regular basis (*Quaker Faith and Practice*, 1995, para. 1.05). The traditions of Quaker culture are still seen as having a continuing place in its present life. Weighty Friends are one source of information about such traditions. This having been said, and the truth of it fully acknowledged, there is more to the role of weighty Friends than this. Weighty Friends do have some power simply because of who they are. Again this power has to be put into context. Weighty Friends have no constitutional position within Quaker culture (though the term is used widely and is not specific to our Meeting). The power they have is because of how they are treated not because of what, in formal terms, they can do.

Their efforts do not usurp the consensus. Rather, sometimes, the consensus will settle round them.

Informants have told us of other Meetings where one or more weighty Friends came to dominate Meeting. Such behaviour would not be in 'right ordering' but we have no doubt that it has occurred. We have no reason to think that any of the weighty Friends in our Meeting would wish to work in such a manner (nor, indeed, may weighty Friends in other Meetings be conscious of the effect that they have had). However, in any event, in our Meeting, its size makes it impossible for one member, weighty Friend or not, to dominate Meeting. Moreover, since weighty Friends in our Meeting come from different backgrounds within Quakerism, they not infrequently hold different views. Weighty Friends do not take decisions instead of Meeting, often they do not start in agreement as to what is the right decision that should be taken, but sometimes, not infrequently, their views are treated with a respect which is deeper than that accorded to others in Meeting.

Spoken Ministry in Meeting for Worship

To write about spoken ministry in Meeting for Worship, the oral contributions of members during a Meeting for Worship, in a chapter on leadership in Meeting may seem strange. Ministry is an expression of the theological nature of Meeting. It is concerned with Meeting's sense of the spiritual. (Collins provides an account of the ministry, including details of the spoken ministry, in one typical Meeting for Worship in his study of Dibdenshaw Meeting (Collins, 1994, pp. 197-180).) Ministry in Meeting for Worship is in many senses individual. In one of the Meetings for Worship that we observed one member ministered thus

> The Society of Friends is composed of individuals who all have an individual relationship with God - and the Society is not prescriptive - it accepts that we all come to God in our own way - and it seems to me that [that] is a fundamental strength of Friends.

In another Meeting for Worship a member said 'I have always been glad that Friends allow everyone to make their own spiritual journey.' The practice of spoken ministry in our Meeting reflects the Quaker belief in the priesthood of all believers discussed in Chapters 2 and 3.

Individual ministry may stem from previous ministry from other members and may lead on to still further ministry which then creates a feeling of collective depth which is greater than any of the individual acts of ministry, particularly in a 'gathered meeting', but each act of ministry comes from the individual. Moreover the ministry is not so much an attempt to persuade others present in Meeting for Worship as to the correctness of the member's views as a statement of things as the member of Meeting sees them. (Theologically, of course, ministry is usually seen as the result of 'the leading of the Spirit' (*Quaker Faith and Practice*, 1995, para. 2.55).) In this context ministry does not even have the leadership role that might be seen in a preacher's sermon. Nonetheless our observations of Meetings for Worship in our Meeting did indicate an element of leadership in ministry.

Most members of Meeting rarely speak in Meeting for Worship. Some never speak. This does not indicate that they either are, or feel they are, excluded or marginalised in Meeting. The silence in Meeting is as important or more important than any spoken ministry. The silence itself is ministry. ('We sit in silence so as not to trip over words' as *Quaker Faith and Practice* puts it (para. 2.69).) '[S]ilent worship is at the core of Quaker practice' (Dandelion, 1996, p. 15). Indeed an excessive number of contributions by a member of Meeting, or excessively long contributions or argumentative contributions could all lead to a member being 'eldered' (although this has rarely happened in practice in our Meeting). Silence remains the most distinctive feature of Meeting for Worship. In the Meetings we observed, silence predominated during Meeting for Worship.

Despite the overarching significance of silent worship spoken ministry does have a place in Meeting for Worship. During the time that we were observing Meetings for Worship most of the contributions that were made in Meeting for Worship came from a relatively small number of people. Most of the people who did contribute regularly were people who had been Quakers for some time. Other members did minister. Indeed, some ministry came from those who came to Meeting on the most irregular basis or even for a single occasion and who were not, in our terms, part of the Quaker community. The balance of ministry, however, was clear with a predominant amount of spoken ministry coming from no more than 10 to 20 people. Those people who spoke regularly tended to hold, or to have held, significant positions within Meeting's various committees and/or to have positions in national Quaker circles; some were birthright Quakers; some were weighty Friends.

Spoken ministry is important because of the power it has to influence the thinking of Members of Meeting. Even if those Ministering are not, in any ordinary sense, seeking to persuade others in the Meeting that their ministry is correct *Quaker Faith and Practice* nevertheless tells Quakers that if Meeting for Worship is to achieve its spiritual purpose this

can only be done if there is a willingness to be led by each of the ones ministering into a deeper level of what they were not only saying but what they were meaning to say, and perhaps even beyond into what something beneath us all was meaning to have said through what we were saying ...
(*Quaker Faith and Practice*, 1995, para. 2.70)

Quakers are thus enjoined to focus on ministry. As we have already seen in Chapter 6 they do not always do so. Members of Meeting in practice sometimes use Meeting for Worship as an opportunity for meditation or even, very occasionally, drift off to sleep. In such instances spoken ministry will be nothing more than a distraction. Nevertheless, sometimes spoken ministry will be the subject of Members' thoughts and, at those times, as *Quaker Faith and Practice* puts it, members of Meeting are 'led' by the Ministry and thus the person Ministering. One interviewee described themselves as 'probably being directed by ministry' during the Meeting for Worship. If spoken ministry is largely concentrated into a relatively small number of members of Meeting this 'directing' is similarly so concentrated.

As in previous parts of this chapter whilst this leadership role within Meeting is genuine its importance should not be over-estimated. Those who minister regularly are not a cohesive group representing any one tendency either in Quaker circles nationally or in our Meeting. Ministry comes from a number of different directions and to that extent Meeting is 'led' by ministry down a number of different and sometimes conflicting paths. Moreover, the small quantity of spoken ministry compared with silent Ministry reduces its effect. For non-Quakers this last observation will seem intuitively unlikely; in the comparative silence of Meeting for Worship that which is said would surely have a disproportionate influence. However, the matter needs to be analysed in the context of Quaker culture and the comments of our interviewees. The silence of Meeting is not a gap; it is, rather, the essence of Meeting. Moreover, Meeting in particular and Quaker culture in general is in many ways intensely individualistic. Spoken ministry is for some people 'a source of meditation' for members of Meeting, as one of our interviewees put it. However, as a source for meditation it is a beginning point for a member's worship, a starting point for their individual enquiry, not an end point where the member of Meeting reflects on the wisdom of what was said or the authority of the person who ministered.

Groups in Meeting and the Commune

One question all our interviewees asked was whether or not there were groups within Meeting. The question was asked because if there were groups it was also possible that power would centre on one or more of those groups. To a lesser or greater extent all of our interviewees thought that there were groups within Meeting but they regarded the way in which those groups arose and what they implied for Meeting in very different ways. Some saw groups as merely reflecting the different ages and interests within Meeting. Groups were seen as being functional in nature. One interviewee pointed out that the Friendly fringes were groups and several others pointed to groups such as those members who had small children or were of a similar age (around 60 was mentioned by a number of interviewees). 'These are groups but not cliques' as one interviewee put it. Other interviewees took a completely different stance. Thus one interviewee said, when asked if there were groups in Meeting, '[y]es, and it bothers me a lot ... I'm not for cliques' and another said

> Yes, definitely. And it's not a very helpful factor. People can feel in the 'in' group and feel excluded if not in ... there is a danger in the 'commune' ... if you are in that group you can get to know [things you wouldn't otherwise know].'

This interviewee spoke not from the disappointment of being an outsider but about a danger that they perceived from the existence of a group they saw themselves as belonging to. Another interviewee linked groups with that which we have discussed above under the heading of 'Birthright Quakers and Weighty Friends'.

> Yes [there are groups in Meeting]. I'm concerned about power - there is a lot of power in certain Friends - though they might be upset to see they had been cast in that way by outsiders. They are seen as people who have authority by longevity and because they are steeped in Quaker practice and [knowledge of] how things ought to be run and maybe give out signals that are intimidating ... It's much easier to criticize and difficult to make things different. Certain people carry a lot of roles and how can we spread that ou t...

One interviewee drew a distinction between our Meeting and another that they had previously attended saying, yes that there were groups in Meeting, including a group that was particularly interested with what went on at Preparative Meeting (another interviewee, in a similar vein, said that there was a group of people 'who got things done' and yet another referred to a 'good sorts/core group'), but that, unlike their previous Meeting, they could not see groups set up in opposition to each other. Another interviewee said that there were groups but that they 'weren't cliquey' but they immediately added that their view was perhaps held 'because I'm in the clique'. This interviewee went on to say 'there are people who are central [to Meeting] and on the whole have been here a long time'.

There was a common but not universal perception amongst our interviewees that there was a group of people within Meeting who were not just a set of individuals with power, ability or influence but were to some very loose degree linked together. Geographically that group was linked in a very loose fashion to living within 'the Quaker acre' though some people who were identified with it did not even live within the favoured postal code for Meeting and some people who lived within the Quaker acre were not seen as being in the group. The degree to which the group's existence was seen as being tangible was slight. No-one suggested that the group held meetings, was clear as to its membership or had any particular set of policy objectives or particular theological views. Rather it was that there was a group of members of Meetings set very slightly apart and, for some, very slightly above Meeting. The group was seen as being, in everyday terms, only lightly united. Indeed, the very existence of that group was opaque to some of our interviewees, including some who were said to belong to it. Several members who were interviewed who were identified as being in that central group either did not see groups as being of any importance in Meeting and did not see themselves as being a member of any particular group and we wholly accept that they genuinely have that perception.

The ethnographic diary that was completed during this study together with our other observations would support the view both that there are particular interest groups within Meeting and that there is a central core group. A greater quantity of spoken ministry in Meeting for Worship, the holding of offices both within Meeting and in wider Quaker circles, membership of discussion groups and the like within Meeting and comparatively high rates of attendance at Quaker events all coalesce in a relatively small number of members of Meeting. However, the core group can only be seen as being such in the context of a Quaker community which, both in theory and in reality, is largely non-hierarchical. The group's political power within Meeting is perceptible but equally its power is very slight. Moreover, the group lacks conscious cohesion, focus or direction.

The interest or sectional groups go beyond the semi-official Friendly fringes and include those whose members are linked together by age, family situation, employment and the geography of their homes. The existence of these interest or sectional groups is, in itself, not a contradiction of the principles of the search for consensus or the absence of hierarchy in Meeting. Meeting is relatively large. Interests of members are diverse.

Informal groupings of members are as much a way of creating intimacy in Meeting as are the various Meetings for Worship which are separate from or in addition to the Sunday 10.30 a.m. Meeting for Worship. Groups who meet socially do not necessarily, except in the very weakest of senses, affect the power relationships within Meeting. The central, core group, 'the Commune' mentioned by some interviewees is, of course, a different matter.

There is no evidence in our data from whatever source to support the contention that all members of Meeting have an equal say in its functioning. Even if we were to look at matters over a period of time, even if that time were to go beyond the length of this study, that finding would still remain true. It is true that members of Meeting have more or less say at different times depending on the matter in issue and the degree to which their external lives and their personal inclination lets them participate in Meeting. Nonetheless, taking all factors into account, some members have more say in Meeting and some have less. Meeting is in this sense both hierarchical, in that some members have more say than others, and also non-consensual. This finding is not unimportant (although equally not surprising to most). Yet it is equally important to note that this is not a finding that Meeting is in fact run, either by default or by the imposition of power, by a small central group of members.

An ethnocentric analysis of a community takes a feature of that community which is familiar to the observer and analyses that feature in the context of community from which the observer comes. The observation that there are groups in Meeting and that, in the eyes of many members of Meeting, there is a core group, may lead to the conclusion that this shows that, in practice, Meeting is structured and run in much the same way as any group or community in a society which is predominantly hierarchical in its form: Quaker theory, on this argument, gives way to the 'reality' of how human relationships are structured. To reach such a conclusion would be to misread the evidence above and to ignore the picture of Meeting seen in Chapter 6.

Those members who speak of groups within Meeting and those members who see 'dangers' in such groups are speaking in the context of their understanding of how Quaker Meetings should operate; they are suggesting that there is a slight lapse from perfection. Most are not, however, suggesting that the reality of Meeting differs little from the reality of meetings in most other non-Quaker communities. (Only one interviewee differed saying 'Quaker meetings in practice are not that different from outside meetings. Some people's voices get heard more than others - for example, weighty Friends'.) One part of the evidence for this general view is to be seen in the responses of interviewees to a series of questions about how Quakers take decisions and how that decision-making differs from decision-making by non-Quakers. Most interviewees emphasised the degree of difference. Some saw links between decisions taken in Quaker meetings and decisions taken by groups such as peace campaigners (whose members would, of course, contain a goodly proportion of Quakers) but, with the exception of the voice noted above, the general emphasis was on difference. What was seen as the manner of that difference varied from speaker to speaker and this will be analysed in Chapter 8. However, it is the perception of the fact of the difference that is important at this point. Notwithstanding the possible influence of a core group within Meeting decisions made by Meeting and its committees were still seen as being marked by a desire to involve everyone in Meeting. This is wholly at odds with any suggestion that Meeting is driven by a core group who are controlling it. Rather the suggestion seems to be that the power of the core group is as much the result of their willingness to work on behalf of Meeting and the degree to which Meeting turns to them for advice on Quaker culture.

Conclusion

From this chapter's examination of a number of different potential sources of power and authority in Meeting it is clear that Meeting does have a certain hierarchy within it. It exists in different ways. Some of the authority is short-lived, linked to particular offices, and acknowledged in Quaker literature. Other sources are more deep-rooted and come from the culture of our Meeting and the behaviour of its members. Malinowski's dictum that the life of a community lies both in what it say it does and in how it actually behaves needs to be remembered at this point. Members of Meeting largely subscribe to the theory of Quaker behaviour that we have outlined in Chapter 4. Most of them believe that that theory affects their lives. They judge themselves and other members of Meeting in the light of that theory and where they see people as failing (though none would use a word as harsh as 'failing' in relation to others) it is because they fail when measured against that standard. To some extent the personal relationships within Meeting do not reach the prescribed standard. Some people are not fully involved and some people have more influence. Measured against the standards of the non-Quaker world the degree of non-involvement and the degree of extra influence are relatively slight. Nevertheless, the ever-present standard of the theory of Quaker behaviour is also part of the picture of the life of Meeting.

8 Decision-Making, Dispute Avoidance and Dispute Resolution in Meeting

Introduction

Decisions are made in Meeting at three different levels. First, individuals make decisions, secondly, committees make decisions and thirdly, Preparative Meeting makes decisions. All decisions made by Quakers, including an individual's decisions, should be made in a Quakerly manner. Quakers are Quakers all the time. ('Bring the whole of your life under the ordering of the spirit of Christ' (*Quaker Faith and Practice*, 1995, para. 1.02.1).) However, in this chapter we will concentrate not on individual decisions but on the times when Quakers make decisions in and for groups. We have outlined the theory of the manner in which such decisions should be made in Chapter 4. When meeting in groups Quakers should search for the prompting of the Inner Light, not seeking to impose their views on others but, rather, listening to all that is said and seeking to include everyone present in the meeting in the decision. Here we will look at how far decision-making in Meeting matches the theory that we have sketched earlier. We will look first at the decisions that are made in committees and then at those that are made in Preparative Meeting. After this we will look at how Meeting deals with disputes when they occur.

Meeting's Committees

Business committees when they meet for business also meet for worship; committee meetings, said one interviewee, should be held in 'an atmosphere of worship'. However, in this chapter we are interested not in what should happen but in what does happen. How far does the experience of Meeting's committee meetings differ from the experience of decision-making elsewhere?

One interviewee said simply of Meeting's committee meetings, 'they feel nice – everyone is heard'. In many ways that rather naive observation captured the spirit of all our interviewees' descriptions of their experience of Meeting's committees. Only one interviewee saw the committee meetings of Meeting as being anything other than the lived experience of the theory of Quaker culture; even in that instance the interviewee's concerns about committee meetings emanated from measuring the meetings against a particularly high or pure standard of Quakerliness; their concern was not that meetings were not 'nice' but that in being 'nice' they were not truly Quakerly. Committee meetings, this interviewee said, should be about, 'seeking the will of God, not consensus'. In this person's view Meeting, in its committee meetings, was more concerned with finding out what members 'felt' than with searching for the will of God. Since they saw the Quaker business method as being, 'the one thing that is distinctive about us – the core of the Society now', this, for them, was a problem. Whilst the view of this interviewee was unique in seeing Meeting's committees as failing in general to adhere to the theory of the Quaker business method some other interviewees also saw the business method in terms of spiritual or religious values, 'the search for the will of God', 'spiritual insight', 'waiting on God' and so forth, rather than a search for a consensus amongst Meeting's members and some of these interviewees saw Meeting's committees as sometimes failing to work at this level. However, this group did not see the problem as being that great; it was an occasional lapse from grace rather than a permanent departure from the right path.

What, then, is it that made Committee meetings in Meeting 'nice'? Here there was a striking uniformity in answers both as between each interviewee and as compared with most aspects of the theory of the Quaker business method. The idea that meetings were non-confrontational, that you spoke not to impress but to say something that you thought was a new contribution to discussion, that everyone was always involved, and that, as one interviewee put it, things were said 'in a calm measured way' were ideas that constantly came up in the interviews. Decisions were made with little if any stress in the atmosphere of the meeting even though the matter being discussed might be of great concern to some or all of the members present. Interviewees who reported this were both those of many years' membership of Meeting (who might be presumed to be comfortable with what went on because of becoming habituated to it) and those who were very new both to our individual Meeting and to Quakers as a faith community. Equally striking was the commonalty in the institutional features of the method that interviewees thought were important in a committee meeting. Voting was seen as inherently confrontational and divisive; its absence in committee meetings was therefore seen as a positive matter. A period of silence at the beginning and end of meeting, as well as 'during any sticky points', was seen as a mechanism for achieving the calm and serious atmosphere that was needed. A period of silence, observed one interviewee, enabled a committee to be 'well-centred' before it began its work. Others made similar comments. 'Contributions,' said another 'should come out of the silence and go into it'. A final institutional feature that was seen as being important was the fact that minutes of the meeting were framed and agreed to at the time of the committee meeting. These features which interviewees saw as being present in Meeting's life closely conform to the theory of Quaker decision-making that we have explored in Chapter 4.

The high measure of agreement about what were the important institutional mechanisms which ensured that the Quaker business method was adhered to is impressive because in fact these institutional features were not present in all the committee meetings that we observed. In Preparative Meeting matters such as the period of silence before the meeting and the practice of writing the minutes at the time of the meeting were usually scrupulously observed. However our field observations showed that practice in committees varied depending on the committee and the convenor. Some committees stuck to the institutional practices with much the same rigour as Preparative Meeting but in others meetings which, for example, did not begin with a silence were not uncommon. Some interviewees were clearly aware of this gap between what they thought ought to happen in meetings and what did sometimes happen. One interviewee, for example, said that they 'felt cheated' when there was no silence at the beginning of a committee meeting. However, even most of these interviewees may have been unaware of how regularly meetings departed from what were commonly held up as the desirable institutional practices of Quaker decision-taking. (One interviewee did say that the idea that Meeting's committees used the Quaker business method was 'a bit of a charade'.) Despite this, we do not feel that our observations of actual committee meetings held without silences and with minutes sometimes being prepared after the meeting represent the 'reality' of Meeting's world whilst the interviewee's comments about what happened and the theory of the Quaker business method should be regarded as mere rhetoric. On the contrary, the vigour and regularity with which interviewees put forward their views about what should happen in committee meetings testifies to the strength with which those views are held and the centrality that they have in Meeting's culture. The norm may be departed from but it remains the norm. Moreover we would not wish to over-emphasise the discrepancy between practice and theory. As we have said, some committees regularly followed all or most institutional practices and some institutional practices were always adhered to in every committee meeting; for example, no committee ever took a decision by voting during our period of observation nor did we ever hear of committees deciding matters by voting during the entire period of our study. Equally, whilst some people made more contributions than others to discussions in meetings we did not observe any meeting where one person stayed completely silent throughout the meeting. Meetings were always inclusive, at least in formal terms, even when some of those being included plainly had no grasp of the matter under discussion.

In what the meetings were trying to achieve interviewees were divided. Some saw it as in some sense being a search for the promptings of the Spirit, sometimes seen more specifically in terms of the will of God; others, the majority, saw it as a search for consensus. Thus, whilst some saw the purpose of the meeting as being to reach agreement others saw it as being a search for a correct decision which had, in various different senses, been pre-ordained. This point of difference is, of course, important for members of Meeting. It is reflective of some of the fundamental theological divisions that there are in Meeting. Their difference is however, in a sense, as much about the manner of the method as about the result. Both groups are united in thinking that if the Quaker method is followed properly all members will feel involved in and accepting of any decision.

It is necessary to emphasise our interviewees' perceptions of the exact nature of what Meeting's committees were seen to be searching for when they made decisions. A decision can, in literal terms, be consensual if it fits with the fleeting whim of all those making the decision at the moment when it is made. In instances of decisions made in this manner some who assented to the decision at the time that it was made may come to regret and resent that decision very soon after it has been made. Such decisions are consensual but do not touch the heart of those that make them. This is not what interviewees saw as being what Meeting's committees sought to achieve or indeed what, in the main, they did achieve. Many interviews spoke about the length of time that it took to reach decisions in committees. Decisions came only after full deliberation. One interviewee made the point that outside Quaker circles 'groups make decisions and just wait for the fall-out, whereas Quakers anticipate fall-out and find a way of addressing it'. The decision is intended to be permanent, to be fully worked out and to work for all members of Meeting whether that was because it was seen as the will of God or because it represented a deeply-rooted consensus view. State law is sometimes talked about as a dispute avoidance mechanism; legally binding contracts can, for example, be seen in this way. However, even when law takes this form it often functions only as a very rough and ready form of dispute avoidance; the contract allows for some but not all eventualities because it is too time-consuming, too difficult or simply too economically inefficient to attempt to predict all possible future developments. Quaker decision-taking involves a much more intensive attempt to reach the 'correct' decision which will still be correct even in the light of future developments. This is not to say that this attempt is always successful but, even when it is unsuccessful, the dominant concern in Quaker decision-taking is different to that which is predominant in decision-taking outside Meeting.

The nature of different individual committees sometimes had an effect on the way in which their meetings ran. Meetings of House Committee, which is responsible for matters such as the maintenance and repair of the Meeting House, rarely involved discussion of any matter which courted deeply rooted controversy. Matters did not usually touch the hearts of committee members and frequently involved the consideration of technical issues where the views of outside experts had been sought. Whilst things were taken seriously and the inclusive nature of Quaker decision-taking was manifest some of the institutional features of the Quaker business method were either absent or dealt with very swiftly. Thus, for example, meetings did not always begin with a period of silence or, if there was one, it was very short. Similarly, whilst a note of a decision was taken at the time that it had been made the minute was frequently written up after the meeting; the decision itself was seen as being important but the precise wording of the minute was seen as having little impact on the nature of the decision. Meetings of Elders had, however, a different flavour. Because of the nature the role of Elders meetings regularly involved discussion of aspects of Quaker principle and policy. As we have seen in Chapter 7 Elders arguably have something of a leadership role and plainly have a responsibility for the spiritual life of Meeting. Here much more careful attention was paid to the writing of minutes with minutes being written and rewritten during the meeting in order to catch the precise tenor of any decision taken. When Elders met there was almost always a silence before the meeting and the notion of a committee meeting also being a meeting for worship became much more manifest. However, the difference between meetings of different types of committees should not be exaggerated particularly when one comes to compare the atmosphere, even with committees like House Committee, with that to be found in committee meetings in the larger world outside Meeting. Our diary notes for both meetings of House Committee and meetings of Elders were alike in the sense that they showed that meetings took the form of prolonged conversations rather than protracted debates. Both these meetings and other meetings which we observed completely lacked the regular atmosphere of confrontation which is typical of committee meetings in non-Quaker settings.

It would be wrong to suggest that interviewees did not see disadvantages and imperfections in the way in which Meeting's committees made decisions. Many interviewees mentioned the fact that decisions took a long time to make. 'It takes ages to get through a business agenda,' said one interviewee, '[it's] very loose - decision-making is very slow', the same interviewee went on. Our diary observations of meetings confirmed the sometimes glacial speed with which meetings progressed and, indeed, on occasion regressed. Not only did meetings take a long time but, if it was to be impossible to reach a consensus or discern the will of God at a meeting, matters might be left over to a later meeting, delaying the decision still further. The making of minutes further added to the time taken by the procedure. Minutes presented to meetings did not receive the almost automatic approval usually found in meetings outside Quaker circles. Members often took the drafting of minutes very seriously. Draft minutes were changed and in some cases wholly rewritten in order to properly and fully express the sense of that which had been agreed. Minutes drafted in this way were truly, as *Quaker Faith and Practice* suggests they should be, 'a deliberate act'.

In part the fact that decision-making was a lengthy business was seen as being inherent in the method and, indeed, as being desirable. One of our interviewees said that one of the important tasks for a convenor was 'to slow down a committee meeting'. Time allowed a deeper consensus to develop. However, some interviewees thought that sometimes there were other reasons for the lengthy duration of meetings. '[A] lack of structure means people can get out of control – convenors tend not to "chair" meetings.' Whatever their length not all meetings reached a decision that everyone saw as being the will of God or one that was consensual. 'There must be occasions when some people disagree with a decision but are prepared to accept it – [it] shouldn't happen but it does.' It is, however, clear that our interviewees saw very few decisions as falling within this category.

Preparative Meeting

Committees in Meeting take decisions of varying importance. Different committees are, in themselves, of varying importance. Each committee is necessary or it would not be there. Each committee is a burden to Meeting creating a constant need to staff it. However, Nominations Committee for example, which plays the greatest part in deciding who serves on committees, makes decisions of a different order, to take another example, to Catering Committee. In the end however, whatever their status, most committees are subservient to Preparative Meeting. (Both the group of Elders and the group of Overseers are technically a part of Monthly Meeting and responsible to that Meeting.) 'Preparative Meeting is there because things have to be decided,' as one interviewee put it. 'We need a decision-making body.' Preparative Meeting is that sovereign body in Meeting and the way in which its decisions are taken in practice therefore has a special significance for this study.

Many interviewees noted that attendance at Preparative Meeting was an 'obligation'. Membership of Meeting meant that one should go to

Preparative Meeting. At the same time these same interviewees noted that they did not always go to Preparative Meeting. Like attendance at Sunday Meeting for Worship the numbers attending Preparative Meeting varied during the period of our study. However the average figure was approximately 20 to 25 members. In comparison to the number of members in Meeting (200) this figure is small. It remains low even when compared with the number of Members of Meeting (130) which excludes Attenders who have no absolute right (or obligation) to attend Preparative Meeting and is still fairly low when compared to the average numbers attending the Sunday Meeting for Worship (60 to 80) which often precedes Preparative Meeting. The number of members attending Preparative Meeting was, said one interviewee, 'pathetic'. Our observations suggested that much the same group of members attended each Preparative Meeting whilst some members rarely if ever went. This impression was also one which came out of the interviews. One interviewee commented 'Preparative Meeting has to be there but it doesn't really impinge upon me'. (This interviewee 'didn't really know' what the function of Preparative Meeting was.) Another interviewee, a Member of many years standing who had experience of involvement in both Meeting's committees and Quaker committees at national level, said that they had never been to Preparative Meeting and did not know what its purpose was.

The contrast between what was, for most people, the acknowledged purpose of Preparative Meeting and the rate of participation in it is, of course, striking. One might argue from it that it suggests either that members of Meeting do not participate very fully in Meeting or that Preparative Meeting is important to Meeting only in a formal sense under the constituent rules of Meeting. If the first suggestion is true then this study loses a very considerable part of its potential value. If members of Meeting participate only shallowly in Meeting then the possibility of calling Meeting a community and ascribing to it a particular view of the world is put in doubt. For communities to exist there must be continuous interaction amongst their members. We do not believe this first suggestion to be a complete or even a significant explanation for low attendance rates at Preparative Meeting. Some members of Meeting are of course only peripherally involved. In most communities some people live on the borders. However the picture we have painted in Chapter 6 is of a vibrant, active and healthy community and this we think is an accurate reaction to our various sources of information. If it is true that Preparative Meeting is important to Meeting only in a formal sense then the way in which decisions are made in Preparative Meeting is of less consequence than we have previously argued in this chapter. If the Meeting is of purely formal significance then it has little to offer when we look at how decisions are actually made in the everyday life of Meeting. However, once again, we do not think that this suggestion explains in any significant way the low attendance rates at Preparative Meeting. The kind of decisions made on a regular and frequent basis during the period of our study belie any such argument.

In practice in our Meeting Preparative Meeting makes both decisions which have a direct effect on the lives of members of Meeting and decisions which effect the relationship between Meeting and the wider outside world including the wider outside Quaker world. Thus, for example, during our period of study Preparative Meeting decided that Meeting should send a representative to the Chaplaincy of a near-by university. This decision, which is seemingly inconsequential to a non-Quaker, involved a difficulty of principle for some members of Meeting. The Chaplaincy in the university concerned is a Christian institution. It is established as a Local Ecumenical Partnership funded primarily by the Church of England. Other non-Christian faiths are, at least in formal constitutional terms, not involved in the Chaplaincy on an equal basis. These faiths have representatives in the Chaplaincy but the representatives cannot be termed 'chaplains'. They are not entitled to sit on the Chaplaincy Council and therefore have no direct say in the running of the Chaplaincy. For all members of Meeting, and particularly for those members who are not Christocentric, this situation was problematic. Very early in *Quaker Faith and Practice* members of Meeting are asked

> Do you work gladly with other religious groups in the pursuit of common goals? While remaining faithful to Quaker insights, try to enter imaginatively into the life and witness of other communities of faith, creating together the bonds of friendship.
> (*Quaker Faith and Practice*, 1995, para 1.02)

As we saw in Chapter 6 some members of Meeting hold dual membership of Meeting and another church or associate their Quaker faith with other faiths in their description of themselves ('I am a Zen Quaker'). The Chaplaincy's apparent assertion of the exclusivity and superiority of Christianity was thus troubling to members of Meeting. After prolonged discussion the decision to join the Chaplaincy only went through because one member of Meeting stressed that the Chaplaincy was in practice inter-faith and another member said that they had talked to the Church of England chaplain in the Chaplaincy whom they found in fact to be very ecumenical. Decisions such as this relate to the theological centre of Meeting and are not consistent with an argument that Preparative Meeting has only formal significance in its decision-making. Other kinds of decisions made by

Preparative Meeting were much more mundane but had important practical consequences for members of Meeting. Thus, for example, during the period of our observations Meeting made a series of decisions relating to the fabric of the Meeting House and the car park adjacent to it. These had both an immediate and continuing impact on, amongst others, members of Meeting who use the Meeting House and its car park on a regular basis. Preparative Meeting is thus not just ostensibly the sovereign body in Meeting; it also has that role in reality.

The reason for low attendance at preparative Meeting lies in two directions. First, as a number of interviewees who were relatively frequent attenders noted, Preparative Meetings do tend to be relatively long. Meetings of two to three hours are not uncommon. Attendance is onerous. If meetings are held after Sunday Meeting for Worship, as they sometimes are, then a considerable part of the day is taken up (a problem particularly for those who have non-Quaker spouses or partners or who have young children). If Preparative Meeting is held in the evening on Sunday, again as it sometimes is, this may clash with other activities or, if the Meeting is held on a Wednesday, members of Meeting may feel too tired to attend because of their day's work. Finally some members of Meeting 'indulge' themselves, as one interviewee put it when talking about their own attitude, by treating Meeting as a place for worship without wishing to involve themselves in its central organisation. (This last observation might be taken to cast doubt on whether Meeting is truly a community suggesting that, contrary to the picture painted by Chapter 6, it is instead merely a place where some people meet for worship. We should therefore note that whilst we found that some members of Meeting never attended Preparative Meeting we were unable to trace any member who merely used Meeting as a place of worship. Every member played some part in either Meeting's committees or took some part in some of Meeting's social activities. There were some people who attended Meeting for Worship on an *ad hoc* basis but these were neither Attenders nor Members and were not included in our analysis of Meeting's community.)

In his analysis of Quakers Dandelion writes of the Quaker double-culture, a liberal culture where the question of which beliefs are acceptable is concerned and a conservative culture where the question of organisational practices is at issue (Dandelion, 1996, p. 131). One of our interviewees, who was not familiar with Dandelion's work, unconsciously put forward the same view, putting the matter thus,

> [t]here are so many new people in the Society [now] with new ways of looking at life – but I am not sure there should be new ways of doing business ...

This double culture is evident in our Meeting's holding of Preparative Meeting for here the institutional features of the Quaker business method are most greatly developed with periods of silence and minute writing being punctiliously observed whilst the decisions themselves reflect the theological diversity of Meeting. However, on the basis of our observations we would argue that Dandelion's 'double-culture' is much more true of Preparative Meeting than it is in committee meetings where, as we have noted above, the degree to which the business method was adhered to was much more variable. As in committee meetings many items discussed in Preparative Meeting resulted in long conversations about the appropriate course of action and here, perhaps because of the greater size of the group as compared with the average committee, the conversation was even longer than in committees and, sometimes, much more diffuse. However, the pattern of inclusiveness, the general absence of an atmosphere of confrontation and the search for the promptings of the spirit or consensus were just as apparent in Preparative Meeting as they were in committee meetings.

Quaker Decision-Taking, Quaker Dispute Avoidance and Quaker Dispute Resolution

In theory if Meeting takes its decisions in accordance with the Quaker business method disputes cannot occur. This point is worth emphasising. Quaker decision-taking is also Quaker dispute avoidance since one cannot dispute a decision which one has freely and fully consented to or which one accepts was made according to the promptings of the spirit. In practice during our period of observations there were disputes within Meeting. As we have already noted at various points in this book whilst the Quaker business method was generally adhered to there were, in a variety of ways, departures from it in practice. One interviewee directly ascribed disputes in Meeting not to any general phenomena but to a failure to adhere to the Quaker business method. '[I]f the method/rules/pattern are not right it leads to so many difficulties.' Departures from the method did not always lead to disputes but on occasion a dispute did arise. Disputes noted by our interviewees during the period of our observation related to matters of theological principle, practical issues relating to the Meeting House and more general personal relations between individual members; some were regarded as trivial but others were seen as being substantial. Equally, some interviewees noted the existence of substantial disputes over what they regarded as trivial issues. However, before we discuss the way in which our Meeting deals with disputes we think it is important to stress the atypical nature of disputes.

When we first contemplated this study we saw it as being a study of Quaker dispute resolution procedures. Our early observations soon showed that there would have been comparatively little material upon which to ground this book if we had continued to adopt this approach and that to focus our study on dispute resolution procedures would be to misrepresent the nature of Meeting. Our observations have shown that Quakers in our Meeting are not normally or even frequently in dispute with each other and that they enjoy a measure of calm and order in their community which is unusual (although not unknown) in circles outside the Quaker faith community.

Whilst members of our Meeting seemed generally happy about the way in which decisions were taken, seeing it as being both Quakerly and effective (although time-consuming), they were generally unhappy with Meeting's ability to resolve disputes. The degree to which they were unhappy varied. Some felt that efforts at dispute resolution were 'variable' but others were more critical feeling that it was done 'badly' or that Meeting was 'absolutely abysmal' in this area of activity. When asked about Meeting's ability to deal with disputes a number of our interviewees argued that Meeting tended to pretend that they did not happen. In other circles, disputes are given a much more prominent position in the social life of the group. Felstiner, Abel and Sarat have identified a process of naming, blaming and claiming in dispute settlement (Felstiner, Abel and Sarat, 1980, p. 631).

> An individual perceives himself as suffering some injurious experience, identifies this as originating in a legal wrong, blames someone for this and institutes a claim against him or her, setting in train a process that will put matters to rights.
> (Palmer and Roberts, 1998, p. 7)

All the stages of this process seemed largely absent in Meeting. Meeting sought not to individualise a dispute and not to allocate responsibility for individual error to particular people. Many interviewees suggested in various ways that modern Quakers had an overwhelming urge to be 'kind and nice' which resulted in difficulties in first accepting the fact of the dispute and secondly in addressing ways of resolving the dispute. One interviewee went so far as to note a lack of 'honesty' in dealing with people because of this urge to be 'nice'. Although Meeting sought to avoid individualising a dispute, the feelings of those individuals involved in a dispute were of great importance to Meeting. When discussing how Meeting should deal with disputes one interviewee said dispute resolution should include meeting the person who had been 'hurt' and another talked about the 'upset and distress' inherent in a dispute. This personalising of disputes and this attempt to address the feelings of those involved in a dispute was characteristic of many replies although interviewees often seemed unconvinced that Meeting was good at easing the feeling of being 'hurt'. One interviewee stressed the importance of making each person in a dispute still feel 'valuable'. Here the importance of continuing to include those involved in a dispute in Meeting came out and another interviewee who regarded Meeting's ability to be able to deal with disputes as being 'absolutely abysmal' directly ascribed Meeting's way of dealing with disputes as being a 'fear that if you push to hard, [Meeting] would split'.

In this instance the general tenor of our interviewees' observations about this issue matched our field observations. Disputes when they arose tended to be protracted and in many cases were never really resolved; instead they finally 'faded away' (in the words of one interviewee) as the issue inherent in the dispute became less important with the passage of time. In so far as they were dealt with disputes often led to a retaking of the decision which was at the heart of the dispute; a retaking which did not necessarily involve a change in the decision but instead was an attempt to reconsider whether or not the Spirit really was leading in the particular direction already taken; a form of judicial review rather than an appeal.

Quakers do have a number of formal dispute resolution procedures. Elders and Overseers are given the primary responsibility for resolving disputes (*Quaker Faith and Practice*, 1995, para. 10.21) but it is also recommended that Monthly Meetings

> appoint a group of experienced and knowledgeable Friends who would be available to give general assistance in the amicable settlement of disputes.
> (*Quaker Faith and Practice*, 1995, para. 4.21)

Furthermore *Quaker Faith and Practice* suggests that

> [t]echniques of problem-solving, mediation, counselling or meetings for clearness may be appropriate in particular instances where disputants wish to mitigate the consequences of confrontation.
> (*Quaker Faith and Practice*, 1995, para. 4.21)

Meetings for Clearness have a number of different purposes within Meeting other than that of dispute resolution. Some Meetings hold them where a couple in Meeting propose to marry. Some Meetings hold them so that a particular concern of a member of Meeting can be looked at (*Quaker Faith and Practice*, 1995, para. 12.23). In essence any such Meeting for Clearness is a meeting where those participating in the meeting focus on a particular issue which is of concern to some or all members of Meeting. In the case of a meeting held because of a concern of a member of a Meeting the issue to be considered will be that concern whilst in the case of a couple marrying the issue for consideration will be their relationship with each other and with other people. In the context of dispute resolution a Meeting for Clearness might be held where there are

> [i]nterpersonal differences that sour relationships, or a meeting may have identified a particularly fraught area of divergence of opinion or belief in its membership. Any of these and similar situations, if they are faced openly and with love, may be tested in an atmosphere of worship. So those concerned may find a way forward.
> (*Quaker Faith and Practice*, 1995, para. 12.23)

Here the issue for the Meeting for Clearness is either the relationship which is 'sour' or the area of divergence which is 'fraught'. The 'clearness' that Meetings for Clearness seek is an awareness of 'possible options and ways forward' (*Quaker Faith and Practice*, 1995, para. 12.24). What a Meeting for Clearness seeks is not something that is different from that which is sought in a normal Quaker meeting. Rather a Meeting for Clearness attempts to heighten the institutional practices which characterise the normal Quaker business method so as to ensure, to an even greater degree than is usual, that elements of confrontation are removed from the meeting. In order to facilitate the search for clearness *Quaker Faith and Practice* suggests that whilst such a meeting can be a private matter Elders and Overseers should normally be involved and

> [f]our or five trusted Friends ... should be invited to participate. Their main qualification will be that they are likely to be able to contribute constructively in the process of discernment.
> (*Quaker Faith and Practice*, 1995, para. 12.24)

When asked about dispute and disagreements in Meeting only one interviewee mentioned the possibility of a Meeting for Clearness (noting that they were not used in practice in our Meeting). None of the interviewees specifically mentioned Elders and Overseers in connection with dispute resolution although, when asked what the function of Elders was, some interviewees described their general leadership role which might be taken to include an implicit reference to a role in dispute resolution. This silence on the part of our interviewees is matched by our observations of Meeting. No Meeting for Clearness was held during the period of our study and it was clear that Meeting had used them on only the most infrequent of occasions during its past. Our own observations of Elders show little evidence of them specifically taking on a role in dispute resolution. Where disputes did arise and where those outside the immediate dispute did become involved some of those were active were Elders. Others involved in attempts at dispute resolution, however, were frequently not Elders and the reason for involvement in attempts at dispute resolution seemed more to do with proximity to the dispute, proximity being measured in a variety of social and geographical ways, than to the fact of holding any particular office or being on any individual committee.

If members of Meeting see Meeting as being poor in the matter of dispute resolution it might at first sight seem odd that Meeting makes so little use of the formal mechanisms of dispute resolution that exist within Quaker structures. Of course one might argue that it is the fact that Meeting fails to use these mechanisms that explains its failure to be successful in dealing with disputes. However, we think that the explanation for the perception of being poor at dealing with disputes, and sometimes the reality of being poor at dealing with disputes, whilst simultaneously refusing to use formal mechanisms of dispute resolution lies in a different direction. The culture of Meeting tends to generalise the responsibility for dealing with dispute resolution rather than particularise it in one individual or group of people. It was Meeting as a whole that was seen as being bad at dispute resolution by most interviewees rather than individual members of Meeting; it was a collective responsibility not an individual one. This attitude is much more clearly compatible with Meeting's generally inclusive culture and with its general absence of any high degree of division of labour than the formal structures laid down in *Quaker Faith and Practice* which tend to allocate responsibility to particular people. In this respect the practice of our Meeting could be said to be more Quakerly than *Quaker Faith and Practice*. However, the fact of this generalised responsibility taken together with an unwillingness, on the part of members of Meeting, to cause offence or pain or to do anything which might make a person feel less a part of Meeting resulted in a failure to attend to the dispute with sufficient vigour. As a consequence of this there was the observable tendency for disputes to drag on until the issue was no longer of relevance or was gradually solved by slow incremental changes by the parties involved. Thus, to a degree, the failure of dispute resolution in Meeting sprang from the same source that led to the successful use of the Quaker business method in Meeting in making decisions.

Meeting's failure to resolve disputes does not generate great problems for Meeting because disputes are, when compared with most non-Quaker communities, comparatively few in number. Disputes, being so unusual, do not damage the general atmosphere of Meeting. They may, however, be of great concern to individual members of Meeting and because they are not resolved with any great speed they do on occasion cause long-term damage to the relationship between the member and Meeting. In some instances this can result in the withdrawal of the member from Meeting so that they can go to some other Quaker Meeting or so that they can take up exclusive membership of some other faith community. In other instances the damage results in the member living on the fringes of the community of Meeting, rarely if ever participating in its activities. The size of Meeting and the fact that many people have been members for a long time testifies to how infrequently the former occurs. The vibrancy of Meeting that we noted in Chapter 6 shows how few in number are the latter. Nonetheless disputes and failures in dispute resolution do occur in Meeting and members do suffer because of this fact.

9 Law, Warfare and the Quaker Way of Life

Introduction

In his short editorial introduction to a collection of essays on legal anthropology Bohannan wrote '[t]here are basically two forms of conflict resolution; administered rules and fighting. Law and warfare' (Bohannan, 1967, p. xiii). Bohannan's analysis is intended to apply to all types of societies whether they be simple or complex; conflicts, according to him, can either be resolved by the destructive method of physical violence or by the more socially constructive mechanism of reasoned argument on the basis of accepted norms of behaviour. Bohannan's introductory essay is pregnant with implications, most of which remain unexplored in its short compass. If law and warfare are the two forms of conflict resolution then, no matter how complex the society becomes, this always remains so; warfare always lurks behind law as an alternative method of dealing with disputes if law fails. And warfare can be at a local level. Sectarian conflict, gang fights and even individuals acts of violence within a complex society can all be seen as examples of the continuing possibility of warfare as an alternative means of dispute resolution (Patrick, 1973; Thompson, 1967). However, Bohannan's analysis can be seen not only as dividing law and warfare as means of conflict resolution but also as uniting them. Implicit within Bohannan's division is the notion that 'law is warfare carried on by other means'. Law and warfare are twin souls and the universe of conflict resolution is their joint dominion. Law for Bohannan's purpose encompasses of course a much broader notion of law than just state law in complex societies; it is, for him, 'custom ... restated in order to make it amenable to the activities of the legal institutions' (Bohannan, 1967b, p. 47). The collection from which this quotation is taken from includes essays on dispute resolution in supermarkets and Albanian blood feuds; one essay is about law, the other about warfare (Maccullum, 1967; Hasluck, 1967). Law, in this wide sense, is not an alternative to warfare; it is *the* alternative to warfare, but law and warfare carry within themselves very similar genes.

Whilst Bohannan's notion that law and warfare are closely linked is an insight unique to him the idea that law and violence are some way intertwined is one which has been widespread within legal theory. Cover, for example, writes that

> [l]egal interpretation takes place in a field of pain and death ... A judge articulates her understanding of a text, and as a result, somebody loses his freedom, his property, his children, even his life.
> (Cover, 1986, p. 1601)

Law, on this analysis, is warfare but warfare in a form where the violence is sublimated so as to improve the chances of continuing social cohesion. According to Cotterrell 'law is experienced as a matter of power' (Cotterrell, 1975, p. 17) and that power is 'an experience of having the ability to coerce' (Cotterrell, 1975, p. 4). Hart identifies one of the key questions for jurisprudence as being how 'law and legal obligation differ from, and how they are related to, orders backed by threats' (Hart, 1994, p. 7). Looking more widely, Western jurisprudence was long dominated by the notion that the presence of a sanction was integral to the concept of law and distinguished law from custom. Seen in this way law becomes itself only when it takes on this dim form of an aspect of war. Even in the sophisticated and complex theory of Kelsen 'a legal order'

> command[s] a certain behavior by just attaching a disadvantage to the opposite behavior, for example, deprivation of life, health, freedom, honor, material goods, that is, by punishment in the broadest sense of the word.
> (Kelsen, 1970, p. 25)

More subtly than the connection between law and violence, almost all legal theory concentrates on law as a mechanism for resolving matters when things go wrong; a mechanism for **introducing,** and usually imposing, order when things have fallen apart. Even in Collier's *Zinancantan*, where, following on Barkun, law is 'a system of manipulable symbols' (Barkun, 1968, p. 92) and symbols are manipulated not just by those who judge the law but also those who use the law (Collier, 1973, p. 3), law can be imposed on an unwilling litigant (Collier, 1973, p. 1004). As important as the fact that law has been seen as something to be imposed in times of trouble is the fact that modern legal theory has been predicated on the premise that within societies things are constantly about to fall apart. Bohannan notes '[c]onflict is useful. In fact, society is impossible without conflict' (Bohannan, 1967, p. xii). Implicit in the work of most legal theorists are the ideas that conflict within communities is unavoidable and endemic and that law is the way of dealing with that conflict. Thus Barkun writes that '[c]onflict is so much a part of every society that it is difficult to imagine living in its absence' (Barkun, 1968, p. 36) and that 'a world without conflict would neither need nor have a legal system' (Barkun, 1968, p. 36).

Such ideas go beyond the work of legal theorists concerned with the nature of law and its relationship to social structures. They also underlie both doctrinal and non-doctrinal accounts of the behaviour of legal systems. Doctrinal accounts of legal rules in the common law world concentrate on discussion of cases. They are about who won and who lost; once again they are about the violence of law. Doctrinal discussion in text books and monographs could primarily be discussion of the ideal standards of behaviour that are laid down in the law. In doctrine the statute and even more the principle are as much a matter of law as is the individual case and arguably are more important (Goff, 1983). In practice however in doctrinal accounts of law the focus is on analysing what happens when those ideal standards are ignored. Individual litigants, individual winners and losers, are constantly brought to the fore. The focus is on the violence of law that lies in the continual victories and defeats that constitute the individual cases that are studied. Non-doctrinal, socio-legal accounts of law, for all their many differences with doctrinal accounts, follow a similar pattern. Typically, the object of research is the court or that which leads up to the court; the dispute or that which leads up to the dispute. These ideas stretch from research projects into teaching, dominating the pedagogic agenda of the law curriculum. Law is about what happens when things go wrong and about how things are once more wrested onto the right course. Moreover these views even feed back into and are reflective of views about the practice of law. Women are thought by some practitioners to be inherently incapable of being good lawyers because they are not aggressive enough (Spencer and Podmore, 1987; Sommerlad, 1998).

Central to all of the above is not an argument that law is only ever seen as violence or that law is only ever theorised in terms of social breakdown. Cover, for example, notes that '[t]he judges deal pain and death' but then immediately observes that '[t]hat is not all that they do. Perhaps that is not what they usually do' (Cover, 1986, p. 1609). Rather, the argument above is that, whilst other aspects of law are sometimes acknowledged by both theorists and others, it is mainly the violence and use of law in cases of breakdown which receives attention. Thus, for example, Llewellyn and Hoebel acknowledged that law was the 'intended and largely effective regulation' of social behaviour (Llewellyn and Hoebel, 1941, p. 20). However, they chose to analyse it in terms of 'trouble cases', 'instances of hitch, dispute, grievance, trouble' (Llewellyn and Hoebel, 1941, p. 21); a method which was likely to show little about how law worked when it was being a mechanism for the 'largely effective regulation' of social behaviour. Similarly Cover chooses to focus his essay on what, in his words, judges do not 'usually do'. Although common in academic analyses of law this focus of attention on the violence of law, on its similarity to warfare, and on its role in cases of failure is not universal. De Sousa Santos for example, in his Pasargada study, acknowledges that law is about dispute avoidance as well as being about dispute settlement (de Sousa Santos, 1977, p. 10). He discusses both aspects in his analysis of the work of the Residents Association (de Sousa Santos, 1977, pp. 38-89). Even in this study, however, more space is given to law as dispute settlement than to law as dispute avoidance.

To follow this traditional approach, focusing on law in relation to violence, discord and breakdown, would be to distort the subject of our study. Quaker law is not a form of law as violence. Quakers, as we have noted in previous chapters, both in our Meeting and more widely do have disputes. Conflict is sometimes part of the Quaker way of life. It is not, however, normal nor is it normally seen as being natural and inevitable. Only one of our interviewees expressed the view that conflict was 'natural' even within Meeting and that interviewee implicitly accepted the atypical nature of their views by being critical of Meeting for not taking the view that conflict was natural.   Another interviewee observed that anger can sometimes be fruitful but again saw their view as being atypical for Meeting. Meeting in this respect largely conforms to the stereotype of Quakers that is to be found in the popular media. (*Quaker Faith and Practice* observes that 'tension [in Meeting] is not only inescapable, however much hidden, but when brought into the open is a positive good' (para. 10.25) but tension, particularly tension in Quakerly terms, is a long way from conflict.) Conflict is not seen in Quaker culture as being a mechanism by which societies advance their understanding of themselves or the external world. It is thus unsurprising that Quaker law in one important sense is about avoiding the possibility of conflict. It is also about ensuring the inclusion of all members of Meeting in Meeting. Quaker law is about avoiding violence not just in the direct physical sense but also in the equally important psychic sense. Violence can be seen in the physical sanction of imprisonment or the wresting of property from someone through a fine or an order for damages. However, there is also an act of violence in practices like shaming, ostracism or ridicule. The degree of violence inherent in such practices can increase or decrease according to the nature of the cultural setting. Even before Malinowski's more famous exploration of the notion of shaming (Malinowski, 1926, pp. 55 and 118; Malinowski, 1929, p. 16) Hartland had noted the existence of

> a very real and serious sanction ... ridicule and contempt. In a small and intimate society ridicule is a very potent weapon ... It is insupportable [for the

subject of it] in a society where everyone knows everyone else, and where, beyond the provision of the day's needs, all thoughts and all conversations are fixed upon one's immediate companions and one's relations with them...
(Hartland, 1924, p. 161)

However, notwithstanding the particular potency of shaming and ridicule in small-scale societies, even in a complex society with the most highly developed form of organic solidarity, reflecting a large degree of individual differentiation (Durkheim, 1933, p. 131) there is also some degree of violence, some degree of deliberate harming, in such practices (Friedman, 1975, pp. 101-104). In its drive to avoid violence in all its forms, no matter how subtle, Quaker law, reflecting both Quaker culture in general and the culture of our Meeting in particular, is something different from either Bohannan's law or Bohannan's war. It is also something different from the kind of law that has been focused on in the previous kinds of discussions of law noted above.

Quaker Law

Quakers do have their own law but it has dominion over a different kind of social world to that normally imagined by legal theorists or those concerned with the analysis of complex legal systems. The comparatively calm nature of that world is a manifestation of this difference but this tranquillity does not go to its essence. Although our Meeting is in a modern cosmopolitan city, and although the members of our Meeting are on superficial acquaintanceship fully and wholly integrated into the social life of that city, they also have what, in another context, has been described as 'the neighbourhood norms and customs of a pre-modern world' (Cotterrell, 1975, p. 309). As we have shown in previous chapters the Meeting is much more, in Gluckman's terms, a 'multiplex' society, where relationships among members of Meeting 'serve many interests' than it is either complex or simple (Gluckman, 1955, p. 19). Individual members of Meeting are as much, and in many cases more, part of the society of their Meeting than they are part of the society of the city around them. The inter-relationship of members of Meeting is not the myriad meetings of many individuals, each meeting operating on just one level with just one connection, that is typical of the modern world. We have noted that Meeting is not just a faith community; that members meet not just for worship but for a large number of social, political, cultural and educational reasons as well. Whilst it certainly is a faith community that shared faith leads to contact for a large number of different social and cultural purposes. Quaker law matches this social reality of Meeting.

Members of Meeting live without the law of their city and the state within which that city is found: 'without the law' in the sense that they do not accept state law's idea of its unlimited jurisdiction or authority, 'without the law' in the sense that they do not accept that state law has anything of great value to say to them about matters that they regard as being of central significance in their lives and 'without the law' in the sense that they look to a quite different legal code than to state law for guidance about the conduct of their lives. Of course members of our Meeting honour their contracts, refrain from murder or assault and do not defame others as, in each instance, the law of their state requires of them. But they would do these things anyway and they do them because they would do them anyway and not because of the commands of the law of the state. Members of our Meeting obey the traffic laws of the state, at least largely, but they do that because the laws seem sensible, at least largely, and because the laws do not controvert any Quaker principle and not simply because of the authority of state law. This is not to say that members of Meeting do not have engagement with state law or that they lead a life wholly detached from state law and its requirements. In fact they are engaged with state law, some in a very direct sense. Two members of our Meeting are practising lawyers; several hold office as a Magistrate. Other members of Meeting deal with state legal rules on a daily basis in the course of their employment. Meeting has appointed one of its members as a registering officer, an office set out in one of the state's statutes, the Marriage Act 1949, so that marriages conducted in Meeting will be recognised by the state. Part of the registering officers function involves administrative duties relating to the registration of marriages laid out in state law and meaningful only to state law and not to the Quaker community. But in all instances the manner of members of Meeting's engagement with state law differs radically from the engagement which state law expects. State law is something that members of our Meeting take account of, its injunctions are of consequence to them, but the degree of that consequence is limited. State law may be of consequence is matters of detail and in things which are mundane. Members will transfer title of their house by conveyance according to state law when they sell their house even when they sell it to other members of Meeting. However, for members of Meeting Quaker law supersedes state law where there is any conflict between the two. For many members of Meeting such conflict is unlikely to occur. Their choice of employment and their social position does not put them into conflict with state law. Thus for most members of Meeting this allegiance to Quaker law even when it conflicts with state law though real is rhetorical. However, the fact that Quaker law is, in some aspects at least, rhetorical should not be taken as signifying that Quaker law is merely something of trifling symbolic significance. Rhetoric need not be mere rhetoric (Campbell, 1986). Thus it is perhaps more important to note that it is in Quaker law not state law that members of Meeting find their values reflected and reinforced and Quaker law that they turn to when they come to consider their behaviour. What, then, is Quaker law?

Quaker law is not a matter of particular prescriptions. As we have noted in previous chapters neither the mores of our Meeting nor the wider Quaker culture says very much about the precise details of how a Quaker should conduct their life (Dandelion, 1996, pp. 175-179). Quaker law is not even a matter of general principles of behaviour. This is not to say there are not such general principles; there are and these principles of behaviour are articulated and debated in Meeting. Simplicity, for example, is often seen as a virtue by members of Meeting as is a lack of excess in living. It is one of the testimonies discussed in Chapter 3. But these are not laws because these principles impose no precise obligations on members of Meeting. The debate is on-going and never reaches any settled conclusion about what is or what is not 'Quakerly'. What counts as simplicity, what counts as excess, is for individual members of Meeting to determine and not every member of Meeting would use the term in their thinking about their lives. Members will consider what other members would think about their more major purchases and may ponder for example, as did one of our interviewees, whether their car is too ostentatious but the decision, if any, is one for them. So too with other Quaker principles.

Quaker law lies at a deeper and more penetrating level than that of general principles of social behaviour. Quaker law lies in the obligation of continual and all-embracing inclusion in the community that each member of Meeting accepts with regard to all other members of Meeting and with regard to themselves. Quaker law, where law is understood as mutually binding obligations which are known and accepted within the community, lies in their business method. Members are part of Meeting, their lives are part of Meeting's life and this must be so for all members of Meeting. It is vital in this analysis to note that this is regarded as a mutually binding obligation and that it is relatively precise in its nature. It is not a vague commitment to community that might typify many social relationships within modernity. For Meeting it is important that all members of Meeting feel valued and included and it is the responsibility of all members of Meeting to see that this happens. In saying this we are not suggesting that Meeting is in any sense akin to a commune. Equally, Meeting is a long way from the Israeli kibbutzim (Spiro, 1975). Members live separately in families or alone and even those most intimately involved in Meeting's spiritual and social life also have a social life outside Meeting. But in being members of Meeting members accept a set of obligations about how they behave towards others, and particularly how they behave towards other members of Meeting, which are expressed not in rules but in the values that are internalised by members and that are inherent in the aspirations of the business method.

For Barkun a jural community exists where 'one or more key procedural norms - how things are to be done - sets the jural community apart' (Barkun, 1968, p. 76). The Quaker business method, as applied in our Meeting, identifies the Meeting as just such a jural community. Quaker law is not the decisions that are taken by Preparative Meeting or, under the authority of Preparative Meeting, the decisions taken by the various committees and office holders within Meeting using the Quaker business method. These decisions do say what Meeting will do. They bind members of Meeting. Nevertheless, whilst these decisions are an expression of Quaker law but they are not the law itself. Quaker law lies in the way in which each member of Meeting has willed each decision of Meeting. (Here we are seeing the business method as being the reaching of a genuine, full-blooded consensus decision. In Quaker theological theory, and in the view of some members of our Meeting, as we have noted in previous chapters such an analysis would be incorrect; the method is instead about an effort to reach the promptings of the Spirit. We would simply note that a universal knowledge of, and an assent to, the promptings of the Spirit amongst members of Meeting would have the same result in terms of our analysis of Quaker law as would the search for full consensus.) Quaker law is more about dispute avoidance than it is about dispute resolution. 'Board meetings at work', said one of our interviewees

> are very different [from Quaker decision-taking] – [Board meetings at work take decisions and] just wait for the fall-out whereas Quakers anticipate the fall-out and find a way of addressing it.

Quaker law seeks to avoid disputes by making sure that each corporate decision by Meeting is at one and the same time the personal and individual decision of each member. Disputes are impossible because no member of Meeting can dispute with what they themselves have decided should be done. If, on the other hand, there is no decision of Meeting then no member of Meeting is bound to follow any particular course of action nor are they under any obligation. Bax has argued that even for anarchists, who reject completely the imposition of authority by any person over any other person for any means whatsoever, a contract is an acceptable form of law-making because there is no imposition of authority in a contract, it is no more than a person's decision about what to do with their own lives, a decision which they themselves in an act of 'juridification' put at a higher level than the ordinary moments of life (a contract in this sense being a wholly personalised agreement willingly assented to by all parties rather than the standard terms imposed under the typical contract found in modern complex communities) (Bax, 1980, p. 170). The Quaker business method takes the same form as Bax's contract but, as in the case of Bax's contract, the all-important point is that no part of Meeting's decision, no part of the contract, should be the result of anything other than complete and unconditional assent.

This difference between the Quaker form of law and forms of law found in other communities is easy to underestimate. Law in any community sometimes forms a background to the way in which people reach decisions about what they will do and plays some part in their planning for the future. The image of 'bargaining in the shadow of the law' is commonly used in academic literature (for example, Burman and Rudolph, 1990, p. 253). Thus a succession of studies on the business community's use of contract law have shown that such law plays some part in at least some business people's planning of their future relationships (Macaulay, 1963; Beale and Dugdale, 1975; Vincent-Jones, 1989). Equally, however, such studies have shown that law plays much less of a part in the planning of relationships than might be supposed; that law has only a 'marginal role' (Vincent-Jones, 1994, p. 230). In some instances a state legal rule may have as its sole purpose the planning by individuals of their futures in the event of certain contingent events. Thus, for example, in South Africa '[t]he purpose of the antenuptial [marriage] contract is to exclude all, or some of, the common law or statutory purposes of marriage' (Cronjé, 1990, p. 281). However, even in these kind of instances, although the role of law is, at least in formal terms, far from marginal in people's planning of their futures the decisions made are frequently, indeed usually, either imposed on one party by another or are only half thought out or both. Thus, for example, in the case of South African antenuptial agreements 97 per cent are concluded on the basis of a standard form (Cronjé, 1990, p. 293). Such use of law does not resemble the use of contract described by Bax. A standard form does not represent deep personal introspection and full assent by all parties. Rather, by its very nature it is either coercive on one or more of the parties or does not involve the full articulation of the wishes of one or more of the parties; these wishes sometimes being as opaque to the parties themselves as they are to others. Law in these kind of forms is a world away, a social world away, from the form of law found within the Quaker community.

The difference in the role law plays in its community in the Quaker setting as compared with its setting in other communities extends to the connection between the law, taken as a whole, and its community. Writing about the rule of law in the eighteenth century Thompson observes:

> [i]f the law is evidently partial and unjust, then it will mask nothing, legitimize nothing, contribute nothing to any class's hegemony. The essential precondition for the effectiveness of law, in its function as ideology, is that it shall display an independence from gross manipulation and shall seem to be just.
> (Thompson, 1975, p. 263)

Thompson's concern here is to rebut the notion that there is no connection between the law and its community and, in particular, the argument that the law is merely their to enhance class domination; rather, he argues, law is bonded into society and, to some extent, serves all of society. However in this argument the phrase 'seem to be just' is as important as the phrase 'an independence from gross manipulation'; appearance not reality are what is required. On the existence of the rule of law in eighteenth-century England Thompson reaches

> not a simple conclusion (law=power) but a complex and contradictory one. On the one hand, it is true that the law did mediate existent class relations to the advantage of the rulers ... On the other hand, the law mediated these class relations through legal forms, which imposed, again and again, inhibitions upon the actions of rulers.
> (Thompson, 1975, p. 264)

For most theorists, not just for Thompson, the relationship between law and its community is 'a complex and contradictory one'. Law's role in creating a community is limited even though vital. Cotterrell, for example, comments that

> [i]f law cannot create commitment it cannot create solidarity or community. But it can aim to create the conditions that symbolize a moral commitment of the community in its care for its members as individuals.
> (Cotterrell, 1975, p. 269)

Without wishing to deny the general truth of either Thompson or Cotterrell's observations we would argue that it is precisely in their lack of applicability to the Quaker situation that the difference in the nature of Quaker law is highlighted. The relationship between Quaker law and the Quaker community is not 'complex and contradictory', it is simple and straightforward. Quaker law does not 'create conditions that symbolize a moral commitment of the community', it is an expression of that commitment. There is no caveat in the relationship between Quaker law and its community either when seen through the lens of Quaker theory or when examined in the ethnography of our Meeting. Quaker law and the commitment in and to the community are one.

'Legal concepts are the concepts within a community that define community structure' (Barkun, 1968, p. 92). The business method defines Meeting's structure in the sense of defining the relationship between members of Meeting and Meeting and thus defining the structure between one member of Meeting and another. Where a member of Meeting has not willed a decision of Meeting, where they have not truly assented, as sometimes happens in practice, either the member of Meeting feels themselves estopped from raising that lack of volition on their part because the failing is their own, a failure to participate in the community, or Quaker law has in fact failed and then a new decision must be made that is in keeping with the law. Not all such failures are brought to the attention of Meeting and not all 'failures' are seen as failures by others. What is agreement (or what are the promptings of the Spirit) is not always immediately apparent or is more apparent to some than it is to others. Quaker law like any system of law is subject to interpretation and argument even if the argument is gentle and hardly perceptible. Within the articulation of the law some phrases, tropes and arguments have rhetorical and symbolic significance. An argument articulated in the Quaker language whose existence we noted in Chapter 5 will have more impact on many members of Meeting than an argument articulated in terms of more ordinary discourse even though the rational and logical content of both arguments are the same. The phrases, tropes and arguments of the Quaker language persuade; they persuade in a way which is more than the sum of their rational content; they are the rhetoric of Quaker law. But the phrases, tropes and arguments are not Quaker law. Quaker law is what gives the rhetoric its rhetorical significance. Malinowski said that in the Trobriand Islands law lay in reciprocity, in the interlinking exchange of goods and services that underwrote the society (Malinowski, 1926, pp. 47 and 67). Quaker law lies in the very fact of nature of the intimate interlinking of the community that is Meeting.

One objection to the analysis of 'law' above is that it fails to distinguish Quaker law from Quaker custom. It might be said that there is nothing in the above that separates out and raises up Quaker law from the life of the community as a whole. It might be argued that we have identified no specific legal institutions; that we have not delineated either legal rules or even legal symbols; that we have ignored those actors in Quaker life which either in Quaker theory or in actual practice have disciplinary power such as Elders or weighty Friends; that we have shown only what is at best a bureaucratic procedure. However, what makes the business method law, what separates it out from other aspects of Quaker life, is precisely its obligatory character. In a community where little is prescribed (even if what individuals do often has much in common with what other individual members of Meeting do) the method is one of the few obligatory points (Dandelion, 1996, p. 109). We acknowledge that our strong account of the position of the business method does not accord with the views of all members of our Meeting. 'It's not so very different [to methods of taking decisions outside Quaker circles]' said one interviewee and we know a number of members of Meeting who would agree with them. But that view does not accord with our observations or with the view of the vast majority of those members of Meeting who we interviewed nor is it in accord with previous analyses of other Meetings or of Quaker culture in general (Dandelion, 1996; Sheeran, 1985). Equally we acknowledge that at times the method is not used when it should be used. Such failures are sometimes failures in part and sometimes failures in whole. Business meetings may not open with a silence, for example, or an entire committee meeting may be conducted in the same manner that would normally occur outside Meeting. Quaker law sometimes fails. Law in all communities sometimes fails. The fact of failure does not negate its existence. On the contrary the occasional failure of Quaker law only serves to highlight both what it is and its power to order the Quaker community.

Quaker Law and Alternative Dispute Resolution

Much writing on the merits of Alternative Dispute Resolution has been devoted to extolling its superior value in terms of consumer satisfaction. Thus Roberts has noted at the heart of many arguments about the merits of mediation in the settling of family disputes is

> a simple and attractive idea: that in many instances of family conflict it is desirable for the parties themselves to arrive at some kind of agreed solution, instead of presenting a matter to a judge for his decision.
> (Roberts, 1983, p. 537)

This picture of the potential merits of Alternative Dispute Resolution, that this is something that involves the parties to a dispute themselves arriving at a settlement, is one which arises not just in the personal and intimate world of family disputes and not just in the specific context of notions of meditation. It is also found in other, wider arguments about the merits of Alternative Dispute Resolution.

On first appearances our discussion of Quaker law would seem to be a discussion of the kind of system which advocates of this form of Alternative

Dispute Resolution aspire to. Our analysis has provided the empirical evidence of the viability of a system of law which depends wholly on the full engagement in decisions that lies at the heart of consumer satisfaction arguments about Alternative Dispute Resolution. Using secular terms the Quaker business method is precisely about arriving at an 'agreed solution' of a very deep and lasting variety. Moreover, although our analysis is only an analysis of a few years in the life of Meeting, the fact that Meeting has existed in much the same form and with much the same Quaker law for many decades before our study adds weight to the argument that our study provides evidence that Alternative Dispute Resolution can not only be an aspiration but a reality, even in a complex community dominated by individualistic and competitive values. Equally, the fact that Meeting is large and in some senses diverse also seems to make it a good illustrative example of the kind of system which Alternative Dispute Resolution exponents advocate. We, however, would argue that such a response to the Quaker example would be too simplistic and perhaps too optimistic.

It is important to note that Quaker law is not in the first instance a form of dispute resolution. To a much greater extent than is the case in other forms of law, whether they be state law or non-state law, Quaker law is about dispute avoidance. To the extent that Quaker law is about dispute resolution it is largely about a retaking or a reconsideration of decisions which have resulted in conflict rather than a separate way of resolving conflict. Quaker law reflects a type of relationship between individuals that exists before any dispute arises, a type of relationship that members of Meeting (at least usually) continue to aspire to when disputes arise and a type of relationship towards which the settlement of any dispute is directed. It is a type of relationship that, in its multiplex nature, is unusual in modern society. General discussion of dispute resolution is usually a discussion of situations in which one or more of these elements found in Meeting is missing.   General discussion of dispute resolution is frequently about breakdowns in relationships which are relatively distant and which focus on single issue connections between the parties concerned. The disputes are employer/employee disputes, disputes about a failure in contractual relations and so on and so forth. Neighbour and neighbourhood disputes involve something closer to the situation in a Quaker Meeting but for most people in modern society neither their neighbourhood nor even their neighbours evoke the same attraction and interest that Quakers have in their Meeting. Even where the relationship in dispute is in the intimate setting of the family there is frequently no desire on the part of all parties to return to that intimacy; the dispute is about how the consequences of ending the intimacy are determined. Indeed, even in the family setting it is legitimate to query how often the full individual involvement has been part of the setting prior to the dispute.   On average how deeply engaged in their relationships are people in modern times? In such a context one might well argue that the results of our study caution against the possibility of success for Alternative Dispute Resolution in terms of the arguments for consumer satisfaction noted above rather than provide evidence in its favour.

In the context of similar arguments in America, where some authors have called for a return within the legal system to a notion of reconciliation rather than confrontation in dispute settlement, an argument that they have rooted in part in the values and experiences of some religious communities, Fiss has responded that

> [f]rom the perspective of an insular religious community, distinguished by its cohesiveness and the devotion of its members to a set of shared values, there may be reason to doubt the claim of those who turn to the courts that reconciliation is not possible. There may even be reason to force the claimant to try those mechanisms that might restore the relationship, for what is at stake is not just a claim of right, but the totality of relationships known as community.   But once we stop thinking about the Anabaptists and start thinking about Chicago, once we stop thinking about the ancient Hebrews and Christians and turn to modern America, we can see that there is no reason to engage such assumptions.
> (Fiss, 1985, p. 1671)

We would draw similar conclusions. The Quaker way involves a prior acceptance of the value of taking account of everyone's concerns, a genuine desire to engage everybody in the community at a very deep level, a feeling that one's own superficial and immediate demands may not be as important as the overall feeling of the community and a willingness to search for that overall feeling over, if necessary, a protracted period of time. Quaker culture is integral to Quaker law.

When our interviewees were asked whether the Quaker method of taking decisions could be used by people outside the Quaker community their response was frequently somewhat ambivalent. Several noted examples of decision-making akin to the Quaker method that they were aware of and one person suggested that people used the method 'all the time without knowing what it is'. Others said more generally that they thought that non-Quakers could learn to take decisions in the Quaker manner, in our terms to live according to Quaker law, if they were trained to do so. These responses would seem to belie the conclusions that we have drawn above. However, on closer examination the responses of our interviewees were not so positive as at first appeared and their responses sustain the thesis that we have put forward. Although forms of decision-making akin to the Quaker way were seen by our interviewees outside Quaker circles our interviewees thought that in outside groups it was done less well than in Quaker circles. Indeed, one interviewee described an attempt to use something akin to the Quaker silence in their place of business to quieten down acrimonious meetings as being 'a total shambles'. In explaining why outside groups were only partially successful when they adopted forms of decision-making akin to the Quaker method another interviewee said that it was flawed because the groups concerned 'did not know Quaker procedures and did not have a good set of procedures'. Here there was a desire in the group to reach the goal of Quaker decision-making, inclusion of all those in the group making the decision, but a failure to appreciate the importance of the institutional features of that decision-making which we noted in Chapter 8. Training in decision-making was seen as being possible but interviewees doubted whether people would wish to train. Equally a number of interviewees queried whether people would be willing to take the time that was necessary to come to decisions in a Quakerly manner. Others noted that outside Meeting you could not presume the shared culture that was present in Meeting and which underpinned the use of the Quaker business method. 'You can make assumptions about Quakers even if you don't know them', said one interviewee. Our interviewees had no desire to assert a monopoly of ability with regard to decision-making because any such assertion of superiority would in itself have been seen as un-Quakerly. 'Quakers have no monopoly over the right attitudes', said one interviewee. Nevertheless, their overall view was that other people would not have the necessary commitment to make decisions in a way which could be said to be fully and wholly in accord with the Quaker manner. Any argument about Alternative Dispute Resolution is, in the end, a suggestion about introducing something into the parties lives after they have already reached a position of conflict. Some arguments for Alternative Dispute Resolution and some forms of Alternative Dispute Resolution involve a period during which the parties are tutored in the philosophy of the particular type of Alternative Dispute Resolution that is to be used (Pavlich, 1996, p. 48) but this tutoring, even if successful, produces something which is very different from the on-going organic life of a Quaker Meeting. The psychology and philosophy of the individual who has learnt that for the purposes of this dispute in question it would be better if the parties could reach an accommodation amongst themselves is very different from the psychology and philosophy of the Quaker member of Meeting.

The results of our study can be taken to suggest that exponents of some forms of Alternative Dispute Resolution both demand too little in what they ask of people and direct their attention to the wrong moments in people's lives. Exponents of Alternative Dispute Resolution, as much as more traditional lawyers and legal analysts, implicitly accept the necessity of conflict and the necessity of resolving that conflict. Alternative Dispute Resolution is almost invariably as much another form of warfare as is state law. (Alternative Dispute Resolution would, of course, for many be a form of law and in some instances a form of state law.) As such Alternative Dispute Resolution like law involves the acceptance of the inevitability of violence. Even in the purest form of mediation which comes closest to the Quaker way, where there is an essentially pacific way of settling the dispute with the full engagement of the parties in reaching a solution which accommodates all their needs, that dispute settlement comes after the violence of the dispute. '[P]arties ... arriv[ing] at some kind of agreed solution' (Roberts, 1983, p.537) is very like the Quaker manner but if this is what exponents of this form of Alternative Dispute Resolution want then the results of our study would suggest that their energies are misdirected. What is needed is not a focus on how to resolve disputes but, rather, a focus on how to take decisions. Violence in a dispute is inevitable if a life is based on violence. The attempt in this form of Alternative Dispute Resolution to ignore the reality of that everyday violence may be misconceived and may explain its comparative failure thus far.

Quaker Law and Legal Pluralism

If our study is gloomy when viewed in the context of arguments about the viability of Alternative Dispute Resolution it is more optimistic when looked at in the context of arguments about legal pluralism. Although a number of authors have previously written about the existence of pluralistic legal systems within complex legal systems these non-state legal systems have either seemed to be of extremely limited jurisdiction and impact (Maccullum, 1967) or to have arisen only because of the extremely marginal nature of the community in which the law has arisen. Often the legal system has been associated with a community which is materially poor and dispossessed or ignored by the main forces within the complex community within which it is found (de Sousa Santos, 1977; Burman and Schar, 1990). In important cultural senses Quakers are marginal within contemporary British society. Their mores are far from the mores of mainstream British communities. However, they are neither materially poor nor can it be said that their position and needs are wholly ignored by British society. Even within the British state legal system an acknowledgement of the special position of Quakers can be traced back through the centuries with special exemptions from the normal legal structure being granted and legal accommodations to the Quaker way of life being made. Two and a half centuries ago Lord Hardwicke's Act of 1753, for example, exempted Quakers along with Jews from new statutory provisions which sought to prevent clandestine marriages. Such attempts to accommodate Quakers continue to the present day with, for example, the special position of the Quaker marriages in state law which we have already alluded to in this chapter. Previous studies of plural legal systems in complex societies largely seem to show that such systems arise in resistance because of the degree to which the community concerned has been oppressed. In the case of our study the legal system arises because the state legal system, despite its attempt to accommodate Quakers, cannot meet the needs of Quakers. The Quaker community is in resistance to state mores but it is not oppressed; it is simply in opposition. Quaker law goes beyond the ambitions of state law. In one classic example of legal pluralism, De Sousa Santos's study of Pasargada, state law, Brazilian law, seeks to prevent the purchase and sale of the houses that form Pasargada whilst Pasargada law, the law of a favela, permits and facilitates these transactions (de Sousa Santos, 1977, p. 52). State law, however, does not seek to prevent what Quaker law facilitates. It simply does not wish to trespass in the arenas in which Quaker law operates. Quaker law like Pasargada law meets the needs of the community where state law does not but there usually is no conflict between the rules of state law and decisions taken according to Quaker law. Here pluralistic legal systems enriches the life of an individual community without heightening tension between that community and the wider complex society within which it is found. Quaker law signals the possibility of communities creating their own legal systems without recourse to the state in a situation which does not place them in constant on-going conflict with the state.

Social theorists from Durkheim to Giddens may have over-estimated the atomised nature of modern life (Durkheim, 1933, ch. 5; Giddens, 1990). Giddens, for example, observes that

> [a] person walks the streets of a city and encounters perhaps thousands of people in the course of a day, people she or he has never met before - 'strangers' in the modern sense of the term.
> (Giddens, 1990, p. 143)

That this condition of continually meeting thousands of strangers and meeting virtually no-one else is the condition for many is clear. Perhaps even more important for the reception of the idea (which, of course, has a long and respectable intellectual lineage) is the fact that this will be true for most academics who read the books of Giddens and others who argue this position. Yet during the period that we have been writing up this study we have spent time in, amongst other places, a small Ohio town in the United States where we were informed inhabitants rarely locked their houses and where the crime rate was virtually nil and in a small hamlet in France where the situation was much the same. In both the stranger, to differing degrees, is rare; multiplex relations rather than complex interactions are much more the norm. Such settings are very different from the streets in Giddens' city. The city may be the paradigm for modernity but empirically it is not the place, even in modern states, where everybody lives their lives. Even in the city things can be different. 'It is not different, really, here in the city. Just like back in the village, we live our lives together as one' says the central character in Mda's South African novel *Ways of Dying* (Mda, 1997, p. 12). Small communities where individual relations occur on a multiplicity of levels and where individual interaction on a variety of levels is an everyday matter continue to thrive in modern complex societies. They may not be the norm but they certainly exist. In such communities for most people constantly meeting strangers to the degree instanced by Giddens, and the social consequences of such a life amongst strangers, is not the paradigmatic experience. Giddens to some extent recognises this in his work but argues that

> [e]ven ... the smallest neighbourhood store ... probably obtains its goods from all over the world. The local community is not a saturated environment of familiar, taken-for-granted meanings, but in some large part a locally-situated expression of distanciated relations. And everyone living in the different locations of modern societies is aware of this. Whatever security individuals experience as the result of the familiarity of place rests as much upon stable forms of disembedded relations as upon the particularities of location. If this is more obvious when one shops at the local supermarket than at the corner grocery, the difference is not a fundamental one.
> (Giddens, 1990, p. 109)

It is true that all communities are now at best only semi-autonomous, invaded by the world around them (Moore, 1978). We find the same goods in shops throughout the world, we see the same television programmes and we are constantly exposed to the wider world wherever we are. As Giddens argues the remotest location in part derives its identity from features and artefacts, and relations created and implied by those features and artefacts, which are in origin far removed from it. But the difference between the local supermarket and the corner grocery can, despite this, be a fundamental one. First, the existence of semi-autonomous social fields which 'can generate rules and coerce or induce compliance to them' (Moore, 1978, p. 57) suggests that modernity may in its most immediate sense for the individual be experienced differently in different settings. Secondly, if the fact that in modernity people usually meet each other as strangers is as important as Giddens and others before him have argued then the fact that in some communities strangers are infrequently seen must be equally important. Equally, the fact that in some communities people meet some people as strangers but also regularly meet a significant number of people drawn from outside their families as 'not-strangers' must also be important. In a society where one knows others as 'strangers' the creation of, and the experience of, trust and security for individual takes on a particular form (Giddens, 1990, ch. III). Trust and security are different however, even in complex societies, in communities where either the majority are 'not-strangers' or where individuals alternate between passing thousands of strangers on the street and engaging with a community of non-familial 'not-strangers'. One interviewee described Meeting as feeling 'like coming home'. 'Home' is not modernity. You do not meet thousands of strangers in what you feel is your home.

Our study shows that communities partially separated from modernity can and do exist in large cities. It is in these communities that forms of law suited to the needs of the individual community can arise. Because of the way in which it arises such law can be tailored much more precisely to the needs of that community. In a complex society comprised of strangers state law can exist as violence. In English law we can sue our neighbour and hope for damages precisely because we do not sue our neighbour. Even if we sue the person next door in suing them we dispense with them as neighbours. They become simply the people next door. The prevailing conditions of modern life make both this action and this form of law possible. It is arguable that in order to preserve our psychological health as individuals we may need to interact with some other people on a more intimate level than that of the stranger; '[f]or most people identity derives from the private sphere' (Bocock, 1976, p. 33). However, we do not need any particular person to be anything to us other than a stranger. Accidents of biology, employment or geography do not necessarily lead to intimacy. We select from our biological family, those who we meet in employment, those we meet socially and so forth those with whom we wish to be intimate. We can continue to interact with other individuals on the necessary levels of single exchanges of goods and services even though they are strangers and even though we have successfully sued them. We may not choose to do so as the literature on the use of contract law by the business community discussed above shows. However, it is our choice as to whether we choose to deal with them as strangers or not; our choice as to whether or not we sue. Indeed one can go beyond the argument that in such a society law can exist as violence and suggest that in such a society law must exist as a form of violence. Very little can be presumed about the connection that individuals have or wish to have. Law must be imposed and no presumption of relationship made. In communities like our Meeting however modernity remains at bay and law can be expressive of not just the aspiration to but the reality of community; can be expressive not of the fear of conflict, discord and dissolution but the reality of continuing connection.

Our study shows an alternative way of dealing with law. It is precisely that; it is an alternative way of dealing with law; it is not necessarily a better way of dealing with law. Atomised life is not necessarily less attractive as a way of life than the community that we have observed in Meeting. Solitude may be the only reality and the community that Meeting thinks that it has may, on closer examination, be nothing more than a comforting myth (Sartre, 1973, p. 28). Intimacy and privacy are antonyms; to the extent that one exists the other is limited. Community and connection carry with them obligations which may be more onerous than the burdens of solitude. Individual choice, the simple pleasure of following one's own path, can conflict with the needs of a community. This is not, of course, to suggest that our Meeting keeps a rigorous control over the lives of its members. Everything that we have described suggests the reverse. Nonetheless there is a necessary lessening of individuality in any community.   Between atomised life and Meeting there is a choice to be made. And with that choice goes a choice as to form of law. Atomised life leads to atomised law: Quaker life leads to Quaker law. Our study suggests everyone can choose between the two. However, our study also suggests that the choice has to be made. One cannot live under both forms of law nor can one choose one kind of community and another kind of law; community and law are a package deal.

Bibliography

Abel, R. (1982), *The Politics of Informal Justice*, Academic Press, New York.

Akhtar, S. (1989), *Be Careful with Muhammad! The Salman Rushdie Affair*, Bellew Publishing, London.

Allen, R. (1995), *Yours in Friendship*, Quaker Home Service, London.

Arnold, M. (1960), *Culture and Anarchy*, Cambridge University Press, Cambridge.

Arthurs, H. (1985), *'Without the Law': Administrative Justice and Legal Pluralism in Nineteenth-Century England*, University of Toronto Press, Toronto.

Bailey, S. (1993), *Peace is a Process*, Quaker Home Service, London.

Bailey, S. and Gunn, M. (1996), *Smith and Bailey on the Modern English Legal System*, Sweet and Maxwell, London.

Barley, N. (1983), *The Innocent Anthropologist*, Penguin Books, Harmondsworth.

Barlow, F.R. (1982), *Woodbrooke 1953-1978*, William Sessions Ltd, York.

Barkun, M. (1968), *Law without Sanction*, Yale University Press, New Haven.

Basham, R. (1978), *Urban Anthropology: The Cross-Cultural Study of Complex Societies*, Mayfield Publishing Company, Palo Alto, California.

Bax, C. (1980), 'Kropotkin on Law', in T. Holterman and H. van Maarseveen (eds.) *Law in Anarchism*, Erasmus University, Rotterdam.

Beale, H and Dugdale, T. (1975), 'Contracts Between Businessmen: Planning and the Use of Contractual Remedies', 2 *British Journal of Law and Society* p. 45.

Bocock, R. (1976), *Freud and Modern Society*, Thomas Nelson and Sons, Walton-on-Thames.

Bohannan, P. (1957), *Justice and Judgement Among the Tiv*, Oxford University Press, London.

Bohannan, P. (1967a), 'Introduction', in P. Bohannan (ed.) *Law and Warfare*, University of Texas Press, Austin, Texas.

Bohannan, P. (1967b), 'The Differing Realms of Law', in P. Bohannan (ed.) *Law and Warfare*, University of Texas Press, Austin, Texas.

Boulton, D. and Boulton, A. (1998), *In Fox's Footsteps*, Dales Historical Monographs, Dent.

Bradney, A. (1992), 'Ivory Towers or Satanic Mills: choices for university law schools', 17 *Studies in Higher Education*, 5.

Bradney, A. (1993), *Religions, Rights and Laws*, Leicester University Press, Leicester.

Bradney, A and Cownie F. (1996), 'Working on the Chain Gang?', II, 2 *Contemporary Issues in Law* p. 15.

Bradney, A. (1998), 'Law as a Parasitic Discipline', 25 *Journal of Law and Society* p. 71.

Bradney, A. (1999), 'Children of a Newer God: The English Courts, Custody Disputes and NRMs', in S. Plamer and C. Hardman (eds.) *Children in New Religions*, Rutgers University Press, New Brunswick.

Braithwaite, C. (1995), *Conscientious Objection to Compulsions Under the Law*, William Sessions Ltd, York.

Brandes, S. (1992) 'Sex Roles and Anthropological Research in Rural Andalusia' in J de Pina-Cabral and J. Campbell (eds.) *Europe Observed*, Macmillan, London.

Brierley, P. and Wraight, H. (1997), *UK Christian Handbook 1996/7 Edition*, Christian Research, London.

Brimelow, E. (1989), *In and Out the Silence*, Quaker Home Service, London.

Brown, H. and Marriott, A. (1993), *ADR: Principles and Practice*, Sweet and Maxwell, London.

Burgess, R. (1984), *In the Field*, George Allen and Unwin, London.

Burman, S. and Rudolph, D. (1990), 'Repression by Mediation: Mediation and Divorce in South Africa', 107 *South African Law Journal* p. 251.

Burman, S. and Schar, W. (1990), 'Creating People's Justice: Street Committees and People's Courts in a South African City', 24 *Law and Society Review* p. 693.

Cairns, A. (1994), *Of One Heart Diverse Mind*, Quaker Home Service, London.

Campbell, T. (1986), 'Introduction: Realizing Human Rights' in T. Compbell, D. Goldberg, S. McLean and T. Mullen *Human Rights: From Rhetoric to Reality*, Basil Blackwell, Oxford.

Chambers, G. and Harwood-Richardson, S. (1991), *Solicitors in England and Wales: Practice, Organisation and Perceptions: Second Report: The Private Practice Firm*, The Law Society, London.

Clifford, J. (1988), T*he Predicament of Culture*, Harvard University Press, Cambridge, Massachusetts.

Collier, J. (1973), *Law and Social Change in Zinancantan*, Stanford University Press, Stanford.

Collier, R. (1998), '"Nutty Professors", "men in Suits" and "New Entrepeneurs": Corporality, Subjectivity and Change in the Law School and Legal Practice', 7 *Social and Legal Studies* 27.

Collins, P. (1994), *The Sense of the Meeting: An Anthropology of Vernacular Quakerism*, PhD Thesis, University of Manchester.

Comaroff, J. and Roberts, S. (1981), *Rules and Processes*, University of Chicago Press, Chicago.

Cotterrell, R. (1995), *Law's Community: Legal Theory in Sociological Perspective*, Clarendon Press, Oxford.

Cotterrell, R. (1977), 'Durkheim on Legal Development', *4 British Journal of Law and Society*, p. 241.

Cover, R. (1986), 'Violence and the Word', 95 *Yale Law Journal* p. 1601.

Cownie, F. and Bradney, A. (1996), *English Legal System in Context*, Butterworths, London.

Cronjé, D. (1990), *The South African Law Of Persons And Family Law*, Butterworths, Durban.

Crossman, R. (1970), *Inside View: Three Lectures on Prime Ministerial Government*, Jonathan Cape, London.

Dale, J. (1996), *Beyond the Spirit of the Age*, Quaker Home Service, London.

Dandelion, P. (1996), *A Sociological Analysis of the Theology of Quakers*, Edwin Mellen Press, Lampeter.

Decisions, Decisions; A Quaker View of the Process, (1998), Compiled by Members of the Committee on Truth and Integrity in Public Affairs of the Religious Society of Friends (Quakers), London.

Denley, J. and Roylance, G. (1994), *Holding up a Mirror to the Religious Society of Friends*, Janette Denley, Selly Oak, Birmingham.

Dignan, J. 1(983), 'A Right Not to Render unto Caesar: Conscientious Objection for the Taxpayer', 34 *Northern Ireland Legal Quarterly* p. 20.

Doi, A, (1984), *Shariah: The Islamic Law*, Ta Ha Publishers, London.

Doncaster, L.H. (1958), *Quaker Organisation and Business Meetings*, Friends Home Service Committee, London.

Douglass, W. (1992), 'Anthropological Methodology in the European Context', in J. de Pina-Cabral and J. Campbell (eds.) *Europe Observed*, Macmillan, London.

Dummett, A. (1986), 'Race, Culture and Moral Education', 15 *Journal of Moral Education* p. 10.

Durkheim, E. (1933), *The Division of Labour in Society*, Free Press, Glencoe, Illinois.

Edwards, J. (1994), *The Flight of the Bumblebee*, Bumblebee Booklets, Youlgrave, Derbyshire.

E.S.R.C. (1994), *Review of Socio-Legal Studies: Appendix VII*, E.S.R.C., London.

Evans-Pritchard, (1940), *The Nuer*, Clarendon Press, Oxford.

Felstiner, W., Abel, R. and Sarta, A. (1980) 'The Emergence and Transformation of Disputes: Naming, Blaming, Claiming ...' 15 *Law and Society Review* p. 631.

Ferber, M. and Loeb, J. (1997), *Academic Couples: Problems and Promises*, University of Illinois Press, Urbana.

Fiss, O. (1985), 'Out of Eden', 94 *Yale Law Journal* p. 1669.

Flood, J. (1983), *Barristers' Clerks*, Manchester University Press, Manchester.

Foulds, E. V. (1960), *The Story of Quakerism* (2nd edn), Bannisdale Press, London.

Foulds, E.V. (1975), *George Fox and the Valiant Sixty*, Friends General Conference, Philadelphia.

Freeman, D. (1983), *Margaret Mead and Samoa*, Harvard University Press, Cambridge, Massachusetts.

HM Judge Nigel Fricker and Walker J. (1994), 'Alternative Dispute Resolution – State Responsibility or Second Best?' 13 *Civil Justice Quarterly* 29.

Friedman, L. (1975), *The Legal System: A Social Science Perspective*, Russell Sage Foundation, New York.

Friedman, L. (1977), *Law and Society: An Introduction*, Prentice-Hall Inc., Englewood Cliffs, New Jersey.

Gardiner, A.G. (no date), *The Life of George Cadbury*, Cassell, London.

Giddens, A. (1990), *The Consequences of Modernity*, Polity Press, London.

Gillman, H. (1988), *A Light that is Shining*, Quaker Home Service, London.

Gold, R. (1957), 'Roles in Sociological Field Observations', 36 *Social Forces* p. 217.

Goff, Lord, (1983), 'The Search for Principle', LXIX *Proceedings of the British Academy* p. 169.

Gorman, G. (1978), *The Society of Friends*, Religious and Moral Education Press, Exeter.

Gluckman, M. (1955), *The Judicial Process Among the Barotse in Northern Rhodesia*, Manchester University Press, Manchester.

Gluckman, M. (1969), 'Concepts in the Comparative Study of Tribal Law' in L. Nader (ed.) *Law in Culture and Society*, Aldine Publishing Co., Chicago.

Halliday, R. (1991), *Mind the Oneness: the Foundation of Good Quaker Business Method*, Quaker Home Service, London.

Hammersley, M. and Atkinson, P. (1995) *Ethnography: Principles in Practice*, Routledge, London.

Hampson, D. (1982), 'Feminists and Quakers', 24 *The Friends' Quarterly* p. 123.

Hart, H. (1994), *The Concept of Law*, Oxford University Press, Oxford.

Hartland, S. (1924), *Primitive Law*, Methuen and Co., London.

Hasluck, M. (1967), 'The Albanian Blood Feud', in P. Bohannan (ed.) *Law and Warfare*, University of Texas Press, Austin, Texas.

Heathfield, M. (1994) *Being Together: Our Coporate Life in the Religious Society of Friends QHS*, London.

Heron, A. (1992), *Caring, Conviction, Commitment: Dilemmas of Quaker Membership Today*, Quaker Home Service, London.

Heron, A. (1995), *Quakers in Britain*, Curlew Press, Kelso.

Hetherington, R. (1993), *Universalism and Spirituality*, Pendle Hill Pamphlet 309, Pendle Hill Publications, Wallingford, PA.

Hewlett, A. (1996) 'Points of View', 15 November 1996 *The Friend* p. 10.

Heydecker, J. (1986), 'Nomination or Affirmation?', 24 *The Friends' Quarterly* p. 35.

Hill, C. (1965), *Intellectual Origins of the English Revolution*, Oxford University Press, Oxford.

Hill, C. (1975) *The World Turned Upside Down*, Penguin Books, Harmondsworth.

Holdaway, S. (1983), *Inside the British Police*, Basil Blackwell, Oxford.

Holdsworth, W. (1922), *A History of English Law: Volume I* Methuen, London.

Holdsworth, W. (1924), *A History of English Law: Volume VI* Methuen, London.

Hoskins, G. (1993), 'The Ethnographer's Magic', in G. Hoskins (ed.) *Obervers Observed*, University of Wisconsin Press, Madison, Wisconsin.

Housman, A.E. (1961), 'Introductory Lecture', in *A.E. Housman Selected Prose*, Cambridge University Press, London.

Hubbard, G. (1974), *Quaker by Convincement*, Penguin Books, Harmondsworth.

Irvine, Lord (1998), Press Statement 27, July 1998, LCD Home Page.

Kaberry, P. (1960), 'Malinowski's Contribution to Field-Work Methods', in R. Firth (ed.) *Man and Culture*, Routledge and Kegan Paul, London.

Kelsen, H. (1970), *The Pure Theory of Law*, University of California Press, Berkeley.

Kloos, P. (1996), 'The Production of Ethnographic Knowledge: A Dialetical Process' in J. van Bremen et al. (eds.) *Horizons of Understanding: An Anthology of Theoretical Anthropology in Europe*, Research School, CNWS, Leiden.

Knott, K. (1986), *Religion and Identity, and the Study of Ethnic Minority Religions in Britain*, University of Leeds Community Religions Project, Leeds.

Kropotkin, P. (1970), 'Law and Authority', in R. Baldwin (ed.) *Kropotkin's Revolutionary Pamphlets*, Dover Publications, New York, p. 195.

Kuper, A. (1996), *Anthropology and Anthropologists*, Routledge, London.

Leggatt, M. (1988), *Shakespeare's Political Drama*, Routledge, London.

Leonard, A. (ed) (1995), *Yours in Friendship*, Quaker Home Service, London.

Levi-Strauss, C. (1967), *The Scope of Anthropology*, Jonathan Cape, London.

Lewis, I. (1976), *Social Anthropology in Perspective*, Penguin Books, Harmondsworth.

Lewis, J. and Melton, J. Gordon (eds.) (1994), *Sex, Slander and Salvation*, Centre for Academic Publications, Stanford.

Llewellyn K. and Hoebel E. (1941), *The Cheyenne Way*, Oklahoma Press, Norman, Oklahoma.

Lofting, H. (1922), *The Story of Doctor Doolittle*, Jonathan Cape, London.

Lord Chancellor's Department (1996a), Press Statement, 3 January 1996, LCD Home Page.

Lord Chancellor's Department (1996b), Press Statement 15 March 1996, LCD Home Page.

Loukes, H. (1970), *The Discovery of Quakerism*, Friends Home Service Committee, London.

Lowry, K. (1993) 'Evaluation of Community-Justice Programs', in S. Engle Merry and N. Milner (eds.) *The Possibility of Popular Justice: A Case Study of Community Mediation in the United States*, University of Michigan Press, Ann Arbor.

Lubbock, Sir John (1875), *The Origin of Civilisation and the Primitive Condition of Man*, Longmans, Green and Co., London.

Macaulay, S. (1963), 'Non-contractual Relations in Business', 28 *American Sociological Review* p. 45.

Maccullum, S. (1967), 'Dispute Settlement in an American Supermarket', in P. Bohannan (ed.) *Law and Warfare*, University of Texas Press, Austin, Texas.

Mackay, Lord (1994) *The Administration of Justice*, Stevens and Sons/Sweet and Maxwell, London.

Mackay, Lord, (1996a), Press Statement, 28 March 1996, LCD Home Page.

Mackay, Lord (1996b), Speech at All Souls College, 14 June 1996, LCD Home Page.

Malinowski, B. (1926), *Crime and Custom in Savage Society*, Kegan, Paul, Trench, Trubner and Co., London.

Malinowski, B. (1935a), *Coral Gardens and their Magic: Volume 1*, George Allen and Unwin, London.

Malinowski, B. (1935b), *Coral Gardens and their Magic: Volume 2*, George Allen and Unwin, London.

Malinowski, B. (1953), *Argonauts of the Western Pacific*, E.P. Dutton & Co., New York.

Malinowski, B. (1967), *A Diary in the Strict Sense of the Word*, Routledge and Kegan Paul, London.

Mangin, W. (1974), 'Latin American Squatter Settlements: A Problem and a Solution', in D. Heath (ed.) *Contemporary Cultures and Societies in Latin America*, Random House, New York.

Marshall, P. (1992), *Demanding the Impossible*, Harper Collins, London.

Mda, Z. (1997), *Ways of Dying*, Oxford University Press, Cape Town.

Merry, S. (1990), *Getting Justice and Getting Even*, University of Chicago Press, Chicago.

Moore, S. (1978), *Law as Process*, Routledge and Kegan Paul, London.

Morris, W. (1977), 'News from Nowhere', in W. Morris *Three Works*, Lawrence and Wishart, London.

Muetzelfeldt, M. (1989), 'Fieldwork at Home', in J. Perry (ed.) *Doing Fieldwork*, Deakin University Press, Geelong, Victoria.

Nussbaum, M. (1997), *Cultivating Humanity*, Harvard University Press, Cambridge, Massachusetts.

Palmer, M. and Roberts, S. (1998), *Dipsute Processes: ADR And the Primary Forms of Decision Taking*, Butterworths, London.

Patrick, J. (1973), *A Glasgow Gang Observed*, Eyre Methuen, London.

Pavlich, G. (1996), *Justice Fragmented*, Routledge, London.

Pitt-Rivers, J. (1992), 'The Personal Factors in Field-Work', in J. de Pina-Cabral and J. Campbell (eds.) *Europe Observed*, Macmillan, London.

Pluss, C. (1995), *A Sociological Analysis of the Modern Quaker Movement*, DPhil Thesis, Lincoln College, Oxford.

Pollard, F.E., Pollard, B.E. and Pollard, R.S.W. (1949), *Democracy and the Quaker Method*, Bannisdale Press, London.

Punch, M. (1993), 'Observations and the Police: The Research Experience', in M. Hammersley (ed.) *Social Research: Philosophy, Politics and Practice*, Sage, London.

Punshon, J. (1986), *A Portrait in Grey*, Quaker Home Service, London.

Quaker Faith and Practice (1995), *Quaker Faith and Practice: The book of Christian discipline of the Yearly Meeting of the Religious Society of Friends (Quakers) in Britain*, The Yearly Meeting of the Religious Society of Friends (Quakers), London.

Raistrick, A. (1968), *Quakers in Science and Industry*, David and Charles, Newton Abbot.

Redfern, K. (1993a), *A Handbook for Clerks*, Quaker Home Service, London.

Redfern, K. (1993b), *What Are Our Monthly Meetings Doing?*, Quaker Home Service, London.

Richardson, N. (1999), 'Britain Yearly Meeting's Membership of Ecumenical Bodies', *Quaker Forum*, Part 2, p. 23.

Roberts, S. (1979), *Order and Dispute: An Introduction to Legal Anthroplogy*, Martin Robertson, Oxford.

Roberts, S. (1983), 'Mediation in Family Disputes', 46 *Modern Law Review* p. 537.

Rose, J. (1994), *Prison Pioneer; the Story of Elizabeth Fry*, Quaker Tapestry Booklets, Kendal.

Roseneil, S. (1993), 'Greenham Revisited' in D. Hobbs and T. May (eds.) *Interpreting the Field*, Clarendon Press, Oxford.

Sartre, J. (1973), *Existentialism and Humanism*, Eyre Methuen, London.

Sharman, C.W. (1991), *George Fox and the Quakers*, Quaker Home Service and Quakers United Press, London.

Sheeran, M. (1983), *Beyond Majority Rule*, Regis College, Denver.

S.L.S.A. Research Directory (1999), Butterworths, London.

Snyder, F. (1981), 'Anthropology, Dispute Processes and Law: A Critical Introduction', 8 *British Journal of Law and Society* p. 141.

Social Trends 1996 (1996), H.M.S.O., London.

Sommerlad, H. (1998), *Gender, choice and Commitment*, Ashgate, Aldershot.

de Sousa Santos, B. (1977), 'The Law of the Oppressed: The Construction and Reproduction of Legality in Pasargada', 12 *Law and Society Review* p. 5.

de Sousa Santos, B. (1981), 'Doing Research in Rio's Squatter Settlements', in R. Luckham (ed.) *Law and Social Enquiry: Case Studies in Research*, Scandanivian Institute of African Studies, Uppsala.

Spiro, M. (1975), *Kibbutz: Venture in Utopia*, Harvard University Press, Cambridge, Massachusetts.

Spradley, J. (1980), *Participant Observation*, Holt, Rinehart and Winston, New York.

Spradley, J. (1988), *You Owe Yourself a Drunk: An Ethnography of Urban Nomads*, University Press of America, Lanham.

Stationery Office (1998), *Modernising Justice*, (1998), Cm. 4155.

Steiner, G. (1970), *Poem into Poem*, Penguin Books, Harmondsworth.

Tamanaha, B. (1993), 'The Folly of the "Social scientific" Concept of Legal Pluralism', 20 *Journal of Law and Society* p. 192.

The Friend, 11 October 1996, pp. 23-24.

Thompson, E. (1975), *Whigs and Hunters*, Allen Lane, London.

Thompson, E. (1988),*Writing by Candlelight*, Merlin Press, London.

Thompson, H. (1967), *Hell's Angels*, Penguin Books, Harmondsworth.

Torstein, E. (1978), 'The Mediator, the Judge and the Administrator in Conflict-Resolution', in S. Goldman and A. Sarat (eds), *American Court Systems: Readings in Judicial Process and Behavior*, W. Freeman and Co., San Francisco, p. 31.

Travers, M. (1993), 'Putting Sociology Back into the Sociology of Law', 20 *Journal of Law and Society* p. 438.

Twining, W. (1973), *Karl Llewellyn and the Realist Movement*, Weidenfeld and Nicolson, London.

van Maanen, J. (1995), 'An End to Innocence: The Ethnography of Ethnographies', in J. van Maanen (ed.) *Representation in Ethnography*, Sage, London.

Vincent-Jones, P. (1989), 'Contracts and Business Transactions: A Socio-Legal Analysis', 16 *Journal of Law and Society* p. 166.

Vincent-Jones, P. (1994), 'The Limits of Near-contractual Governance: Local Authority Internal Trading', 21 *Journal of Law and Society* p. 214.

Walvin, J. (1997), *The Quakers: Money and Morals*, John Murray, London.

Weller, L. (1974), *Sociology in Israel*, Greenwood Press, London.

White, R. (1999), *The English Legal System in Action*, Oxford University Press, Oxford.

Whitney, J. (1937), *Elizabeth Fry: Quaker Heroine*, Harrap and Co., London.

Whyte, W. (1984), *Learning from the Field*, Sage, London.

Wilson, G. (1987), 'English Legal Scholarship', 50 *Modern Law Review* p. 818.

Windsor, D.B. (1980), *The Quaker Enterprise: Friends in Business*, Muller, London.

Winstanley, G. (1973), *The Law of Freedom and Other Writings*, Penguin Books, Harmondsworth.

Woolf, Lord (1995), *Access to Justice*, Woolf Inquiry Team, London.

Yngvesson, B. (1993), 'Local People, Local Problems, and Neighbourhood Justice: The Discourse of "Community" in San Francisco Community Boards' in S. Engle Merry and N. Milner (eds.) *The Possibility of Popular Justice: A Case Study of Community Mediation in the United States*, University of Michigan Press, Ann Arbor.